WALKING IN HIS WAY

Aligning with the God of the Universe

WALKING IN HIS WAY
Aligning with the God of the Universe

First edition: December, 2021

Editor: Dan Worley
Consultant: Darda Burkhart
Cover design and photos: Dan Worley
Layout: Dan Worley

ISBN
978-1-887400-65-7 (paperback)
978-1-887400-66-4 (kindle)

Earthen Vessel Productions
www.earthen.com

CONTENTS

To John and Thomas

WALKING IN HIS WAY

1

WALKING WITH THE MOST HIGH GOD

It was pitch black. You'd expect that from being deep inside a geological formation named "Dark Cave." The ground was slippery and full of humps and dips and there were no guard-rails or safety lights. It felt damp, hence the slick rocky floor underfoot. I could smell bat guano. I could hear the echoes of the voices of my fellow tourists bouncing off the walls of the cavern. Their voices were small—swallowed up in the huge empty space that I could not see. Our guide was leading the way. I decoded his broken English to mean, "Watch out for that big hole. Some English tourists fell in and we could not get them out." I don't know if he was making it up for local color or to get us to behave, but you can be sure we were stick-ing as close to him as possible. Here in Malaysia, there were no safety laws. If you fell in, oh well. You were warned. It's up to you to follow your guide.

We were in one of the Batu Caves—a vast hollow space in the earth where bats clustered and brave Malaysians guided interested tourists through a place that had to be felt rath-er than seen. Though it was more than fifty years ago, I re-member two things—how scary it was to try to walk on that treacherous floor, and how completely black it was. It wasn't my idea of fun, but Dave, my classmate on the university ship, had talked me into joining a group of adventurous be-ings and now I was slipping and sliding as I hurried to keep up with the intrepids who were obviously enjoying it more than I. Dave, who always seemed prepared for anything, had brought a flashlight—not a wimpy personal three-incher, but a big, industrial-strength one with D cell batteries. To our surprise, in that vast darkness its beam was as feeble as a pen light. It was almost no good at all. But the torch our guide carried was powerful in the darkness, its yellow-orange flames surprisingly bright and its coverage wide as it revealed the looming walls and their curving, glistening sides.

Thinking back on that walk through the Dark Cave, the image that is still emblazoned in my mind is that torch, clearly visible wherever it went, brighter and more eagerly sought because of, not in spite of, the blackness everywhere else. I was twenty years old, and by then I had already been losing my night and peripheral vision for years, but I could easily see the torch. It was surprisingly effective in making visible things I didn't know were there, revealing beauties I couldn't have otherwise seen.

I'm certain you can see the application. The manmade light was no help at all in a place so deep in the earth, but Jesus is the Light and He will lead the way, a pillar of cloud by day, a pillar of fire by night. He was the torch that passed with the smoking oven through the halves of the slain animals, confirming the covenant with His people God alone was committed to keep. Surely we need this guidance more than ever for the days are getting darker faster and the paths that once seemed so clear and predictable are no longer there. More and more we need to trust our God and follow Him in faith. In the Batu Cave, vigilantly keeping our eyes on the torchlight, we followed closely and did not stray.

That brings an interesting Scripture to mind. God says, "But now, all you who light fires and provide yourselves with flaming torches, go, walk in the light of your fires and of the torches you have set ablaze. This is what you shall receive from my hand: You will lie down in torment." (Isaiah 50:11 NIV)

To me, it means we can't possibly know what's really there, and trying to see it on our own, figure it out, decide what to do with what we've reasoned is reality, ignoring God and going our own way—well, He says if we insist on doing what's right in our own sight, He'll let us. We're hearing so many experts who are emphatic and even bombastic in their pronouncements on the current crisis, whichever one they're talking about. When I asked God about it, He said, "Nobody knows."

Everyone is projecting based on their own reasoning. And human beings tend to focus on one aspect of the problem, direct all their efforts into solving that problem, implementing their solution without knowing what it will engender. A well-documented example is from the 1940s and '50s. Back then, when a baby was a certain number of weeks premature, it was put in a sealed incubator into which pure oxygen was pumped. This was to insure the lungs would function. They didn't know pure oxygen would cause other aberrations including problems with the retina of the baby's eyes. In the years before a doctor figured out the problem, 10,000 babies suffered severe damage to their eyes. Many went totally blind, among them, Michael Hingson and Stevie Wonder. The oxygen therapy worked for the lungs, but parents wouldn't necessarily notice that their child couldn't see until years later. By then, doctors wouldn't necessarily associate it with the treatment for the premature baby. Nobody chose to test the procedure before administering it. Many years later, one lone doctor figured out how pure oxygen caused retinal aberrations and the carnage stopped, but 10,000 children and their families were seriously affected in the meantime. The body is complex and intricate. You can't look at just one thing, and you can't anticipate what will result from a treatment in the future. Nobody knows. Nobody.

WALKING BY FAITH, NOT BY SIGHT

I love this elaboration on the word "faith" from the Amplified Bible. It says faith is the leaning of your entire personality on God in absolute confidence and trust in His power, wisdom, and goodness. It isn't a nebulous abstraction, it's solid security based on a relationship. It's so secure and real and true that you can rest your whole weight upon His character and intentions toward you. That includes times when there is no light at all, times you have to walk in total darkness, by faith and not by sight.

I'd been dealing with that myself for decades of increasing insecurity. Finally I decided to get help from a sentient being with good eyes who would be dedicated to watching out for me and keeping me safe. But learning to be a guide dog team is harder than you'd think. I had to learn to follow my guide dog Hedy. It wasn't intuitive. Because I still had residual sight, I could discern obstacles in certain lights, so I didn't pay much attention to her as she threaded me through crowded streets during daylight hours. In fact, sometimes I overrode her, a dangerous thing to do because I really couldn't see as well as I thought. However, at night I was totally blind. It was then I had to rely on Hedy and trust her completely. The Lord reminded me that was when I most loved and appreciated her. I had to let go of my opinions and guesses and my ideas of what had to happen. It was a necessary surrender, a crucial releasing to Hedy the responsibility for a safe and successful arrival.

There's no way I can express the elation and overwhelming love for Hedy that flooded my heart whenever we did a night route. The Lord said, "It's that way with Me. The darker it is, the more you have to trust Me to lead you safely where you need to go. That's when you are most willing to let Me lead and that's when your love for Me blossoms."

Love grows when trust increases. I found that with Hedy. The darker it was, the more I had to depend on her. The more I depended on her, the more I trusted and appreciated her. In this context, you can see how dark times can actually grow your relationship with the Lord faster and deeper than at any other time, and in that regard, those hard times become a very special blessing.

This book is about walking in God's way. I assume you're reading it because you already want to, but perhaps you want more clarity in what that means. In my forty-five years of following Jesus, I've had plenty of time to be contaminated with apostasy, watered-down truth, and the incorporation of the values of the world, the flesh, and the devil. I've needed a lot of course correction. And God, being totally good, loving, and righteous, has made sure I received the guidance I need to keep traveling through my life in the best alignment possible.

Scripture says, "How can two walk together unless they agree?" (Amos 3:3) We need to be sure we're in agreement with God on what matters most to Him. How can we know? The Bible has a lot to say about it, and I'll be bringing up certain significant areas later in this book, but you can do a quick checkup by reading what Jesus says to the seven churches in Revelation 2 and 3. He tells the Ephesian church they're doing good work, but they've left their first love. I want to start from there, because you can't love unreservedly unless you trust. Trust is a big deal to God. In fact, when Scripture says "believe in God," the word "believe" is not an acknowledgement that He's real, it's "trust." You can substitute "trust" almost every place you see "believe."

To love unreservedly, you need to be able to trust. How do we grow in our trust, in our faith in God? Romans says faith continues to come by hearing and hearing by the Word of God. But just what are we reading here? The Bible is thousands of years old—66 books written by more than 40 authors. It's been reproduced, scrutinized, questioned, and disputed to the point that even we who are serious in our commitment to Jesus have our reservations about the historicity of some biblical accounts, the reliability of certain passages, and wonder if it's truly, fully, completely trustworthy to guide us in our present lives and in the days to come.

You can trust God, and He doesn't expect you to do so in blind faith. He's left ample evidence that what He is telling you is true. One of the ways is the Bible. I'll be showing you some mind-boggling proofs it's absolutely true and supernaturally given, but first I want to share some of my favorite evidence: biblical archaeology. It grounds our faith in the historicity of everything the Bible says about places, individuals, civilizations, events, landmarks, lifestyles, and cities. They are all there, even the things skeptics emphatically declared were not, and have never been. As archaeologists continue to dig into the past, there is increasing evidence that what the Bible says is reliable, trustworthy, accurate, and true. And it's full of living words whose light will supernaturally guide you through whatever darkness lies ahead.

2

WALKING IN THE PAST

Is the Bible nothing more than myths and legends? When I was growing up, that's what I thought. I'd heard a few stories—Noah's ark, David and Goliath, the parting of the Red Sea. When I was in college, I took comparative religions and was told humans made up religions in order to explain things they didn't understand and to make themselves feel better about death. I read the *Epic of Gilgamesh* with its flood story, the *Bhagvad-Gita*, and creation stories involving the backs of turtles... I don't remember the details well.

I have only one clear memory. I was in grad school at UC Davis, attending a lecture by Houston Smith, who wrote *The Religions of Man*, my favorite book from my comparative religions class. Standing before a packed auditorium Smith produced a large chart on which all the world's great religions were represented, along with the lists of similarities in their principles and stories. His conclusion, which totally thrilled my heart, was there were so many of the same things said about God that he could state, with caution, that God probably does exist.

When I was in Asia, I went to temples and museums and looked upon blue deities and golden ones with many arms, Ganesha, the elephant god with his huge, round belly, and Chinese gods that had bulging eyes and cruel, hideous faces. There wasn't anything remotely realistic or recognizable like what is described in the Bible.

I remember very little about the places and beings written in the scriptures of other religions, but I know, recorded in our Bible, there are places, dates, names of rulers and people groups, kingdoms, rivers, bodies of water, mountains, constellations, structures, battles, specific trees (25 kinds) and many animals (some described in detail including ecological niches and personality traits). Nevertheless, ever since the Age of Enlightenment many people have been elevating reason above revelation, and the material world over its Creator. Especially in intellectual circles, there was a concerted effort to prove the Holy Book nothing more than ancient stories.

About 150 years ago, as archaeology began to develop as a scientific discipline, scoffers who doubted the Bible became even more confident that none of it happened. There was no evidence. Since religions developed from human beings trying to make sense out of what they see around them, then there are no absolutes, no divine moral laws, and no accountability to anyone after this life is over. You can see why they would want to discredit the Bible. If there never was a Torah (the first five books of the Bible), God did not create anything, the Patriarchs never existed, there never were a people called the Israelites who were slaves in Egypt, then left it in a great exodus, crossing the Red Sea, and establishing themselves in a land called Canaan. Furthermore, there never was a Mount Sinai. No surprise there. What better place to prove never existed than the mountain where God gave the Ten Commandments? Some seem particularly focused on discrediting the Judeo-Christian faiths. I suppose I shouldn't be surprised that so much effort and so much press has been dedicated to discounting the Bible through any means possible, including the historical record that lies buried in the earth.

However, the longer time goes on, and the more intelligently archaeologists select their sites, the more evidence turns up to verify the historicity of the Bible. To me, this is one of the most fun ways God shows the truth of what He wrote.

In Unearthing the Bible, 101 Archaeological Discoveries that Bring the Bible to Life, Professor of archaeology at Biola

University, Titus Kennedy, offers proof that the Israelites were who God said they were. Because a lot of the attack is focused on the history of the Hebrew people, I want to mention two finds, one from their days of slavery, the other from their establishment in Canaan. Archaeologists have found an Egyptian papyrus dated 1700 B.C., which includes biblical Hebrew names in the list of household servants. The other find is the Menepta Stele. A stele (pronounced STEE-lee or STELL-uh) is a wooden or stone slab, usually taller than wide, used as a monument with carved or painted writing. Menepta was a pharaoh of Egypt in the late 13th Century B.C., about the time of Judges and when Israel was settling the land.

Kennedy said, "The Menepta Stele is the first time we see the name Israel outside the Bible. It's written in such a way that we know it's a group of people. It's not a location. It's not a personal name. It's the most prominent group of people in Canaan, so we know they've established themselves there."

We now have proof of Hebrew settlements at both ends of the Exodus account. What about between? There were those who said Moses never existed. He was just another myth. Though lots of people had dug around Mount Sinai, nobody had ever found anything—no pottery, no tools, no campsites, no altars, no artifacts of what the Bible says should have been there. Of course, the mountain they were claiming is the one of the burning bush didn't fit any of the biblical descriptions, but a 4th century Byzantine empress confirmed her belief in the authenticity of the site by constructing a church there (St. Catherine's). Since the Empress Helena declared it the sacred mountain, and since she was Constantine's mom, it stuck. Except it's on the Sinai Peninsula in Egypt, and the Bible clearly says repeatedly they left Egypt before they got to the mountain.

In the 1980s, Bob Cornucke, an FBI trained crime scene investigator, and an adventurer named Larry Williams, went in search of the real Mount Sinai. Using the Bible text for directions, they located Jabal Lawz in Saudi Arabia, the ancient land of Midian, where YHWH ("Yahweh" or "Jehovah" if you add vowels for pronunciation) I AM from the burning bush said Moses would bring the people back to worship Him. Moses was in Midian at the time, tending his father-in-law's flocks, so it makes more sense for the real Mount Sinai to be there, not on the Sinai Peninsula. What they found was quite a lot of convincing evidence, but they were arrested and their film confiscated so they had no way to prove what they had seen.

Four years later, Jim and Penny Caldwell and their two children found the same mountain and, over a period of eight years, were able to go back fourteen times, bringing back photos and videos that confirmed what Bob and Larry had seen in their explorations.

What did they find? A lot. I'll tell you a few of my favorites.

They found a huge stone altar thirty feet by thirty feet, with bovine figures carved into its base. The etched images were exactly like Egyptian bulls, long horns and all. There were sheep and goats in the land of Midian, but no cattle. Also, the images looked like Apis, one of the gods of Egypt. What do you think? Could it be the altar of the golden calf?

The explorers found almond trees (as in Aaron's rod that budded) and acacia trees. The frame of the tabernacle required long, straight boards. Items such as the altar of incense and the ark of the covenant were also made of that wood. Archaeologists have recently found on the coast of the Red Sea a ship breaker's yard where new ships would have been built and old ships dismantled to recycle the lumber. Egyptians used acacia wood for building ships because it is hard, durable, and resistant to insects and decay. My guess is that seasoned and prepared lumber might have been among the spoils the Egyptians generously gave the departing children of Israel. Or God could have provided everything from the existing acacia grove there at Mount Sinai.

When I look at the exact requirements for the construction of the tabernacle, its furnishings, the oils and incense, gemstones, precious metals, curtains and coverings and the garments for the priests, I wonder how they could manage to find such specific and unusual materials, let alone have enough of them to complete such an elaborate project, yet Exodus says they had everything God required, and so much of it that Moses had to tell them not to bring any more. It reminds me what Calvary Chapel pastor Chuck Smith always said, "Where God guides, God provides." That's a good thing to remember when you feel you're out in a deserted place wondering how you're going to accomplish the impossible task God has set before you.

One striking feature of the reddish-brown granite mountain range was the top of its highest peak. It was black and shiny, as if the rocks had melted. When the explorers broke some rocks, they found reddish-brown granite on the inside and black melted rock on the outside. A geologist confirmed the outside was metamorphic rock. That means when God descended as a blazing furnace, it was really hot up there.

But most spectacular is the split rock. I pictured something a few feet high shape like a boulder. Oh, no! This is a monolith, towering forty feet high and utterly stunning. It looks like a work of art. The crack runs the entire length from crown to base, the separation clearly visible even at a distance. And at its base, granite rock worn smooth from millions of gallons of water rushing down into a basin big enough to keep a couple of million people and their animals watered in a land known for its lack of rainfall. What I love about this evidence is that God obviously prepared everything ahead of time.

KING DAVID

In the 1980s and early '90s, most historians and archae-ologist were leaning toward the view that King David never really existed. They claimed he was a legend like King Arthur because they had no inscription from around his time that mentioned him by name. Then, in 1993, while digging at the site of Tel Dan in Northern Israel, archaeologists unearthed a broken piece of a stele, and part of it mentioned the House of David in context to the dynasties of Israelite kings.

Why is this important? Because if there was no David, there was no David and Goliath. There was no temple in-spired and supplied for his son Solomon to build. If there was no David, all the battles and accounts of narrow escapes are just interesting fiction, and all those psalms that were writ-ten about such things as God's deliverance from his enemies are also fantasy, myth, legend. Psalm 22, the prophetic song Jesus quoted from the cross must have been somebody's cre-ative poetry. You can see why David is so important. Most of all, if there was no David, there can be no Messianic line, no King forever on the throne of David that Yahweh promised the man after His own heart—the son of David Who is also his Lord (Ps 110), the Lion of Judah who will reign during the thousand years with a rod of iron and then forever after, King of kings and Lord of lords.

But there *was* a King David, and he was who the Bible says he was. We have archaeological proof and some empirical evidence that what is reported in the Bible happened just as Scripture says.

Sergio and Rhoda are a young couple who travel the Holy Land sharing their explorations in YouTube videos. One of their episodes was in the valley of Elah where David met Go-liath in single combat. I Samuel 17 says the army of Israel-ites were arrayed on one side and the Philistine army was on the other with the valley between. It is a spectacular vista in real life. The valley is wide and long and the mountains are high. The couple decided to test the biblical account. First they found the brook, which was dry at that time of year, but would run with water in other seasons. The stream bed was full of smooth stones. They took some and, using a home-made slingshot, tested the accuracy of David's chosen weapon. Though neither Sergio nor Rhoda had ever used a slingshot, they found it could hurl a smooth stone with surprising force and accuracy. Then they tested to see whether Goliath, shouting taunts at the army of Saul, could have been heard by those on the mountains. With Rhoda positioned on the Israelite side, Sergio went farther and farther into the valley till he was quite far away, and wherever he went, every word he shouted of Goliath's challenge could be clearly heard and understood. I found that to be delightful verification of the truth of the account of the stripling lad going up against armored, nine-foot tall Goliath.

It was astonishing to see the landscape and the stream bed full of smooth stones and the way sound carried from the floor of the valley to the mountain sides where the soldiers listened nervously as Goliath insulted their God. But here's something you miss if you're satisfied with familiarity with the plot. It's in the chapter before David encounters Goliath. It's the incident where the prophet Samuel anoints David king of Israel. I Samuel 16:13 says Samuel anointed David "and from that day the Spirit of the Lord came upon David from that day forward." (NKJV)

Why is this important? Because it wasn't only that David trusted God and was zealous for His honor. God had given him an anointing, always evidence of empowerment to carry out his ordained purpose. These days people pick their own paths, careers, professions. Too many decide to be pastors without having been called by the Most High for that sacred and difficult work. Some jobs can be accomplished with training and determination, but God's work cannot be fully realized without abiding in Him in alignment with His values, and the humility that responds to His voice and calling alone. Power does not flow unless you're plugged into the Source, firmly connected and creating no resistance.

JERICHO

According to Titus Kennedy one of the most controversial digs was Jericho. People tried to say the conquest wasn't historical. In the 1950s, a British archaeologist concluded it was around 1550 B.C. when the walls fell, too early for the Joshua account to be true. I encountered this view when I attended a church in a sophisticated college town with my friend Cathy, who wanted me to see the artwork in the building. The pastor began her message by saying archaeology has shown that, by the time Joshua and his army claimed to have entered the Promised Land, all the big and powerful cities were already in ruins. She said the Israelites fabricated the accounts of their conquests to make them feel better about being a small, insignificant group living in a powerful and hostile culture. What troubles me most about this is the congregation accepted it without question, unaware of the violence she was doing to their understanding of the Bible, its historical accuracy, or its truths. She went on to adjust the message of the biblical text to show how you have to find your own narrative when living in a difficult culture and make up your own history in order to survive. Sounds a bit like Existentialism to me: There is no God to confer value on you, so you have to create your significance and meaning for yourself. By the way, it turns out the British archaeologist was digging in the wrong part of the city, but it's not clear whether the news of her mistake was ever published in any public media.

But back to Jericho. God told them the city was devoted to destruction. That meant it was to be burned and nothing taken from it except, as the Scripture says, "all the silver, and gold, and vessels of brass and iron, are consecrated unto the

Lord: they shall come into the treasury of the Lord." (Joshua 6:18) The Bible says Jericho was a walled city, shut up tight for fear of the Israelites. According to archaeologist J.B. Garstang, the gate tower was an imposing edifice 54 ft x 24 ft, remarkably well built of gray brick. Its ruins still stand 16 feet high. Formidable, to be sure. When Joshua contemplated those walls in the moonlight, he must have been wondering how they would ever be able to get past them. God had a plan Joshua could not have thought up himself—one that required supernatural intervention. The Angel of the LORD, Captain of the Hosts of God, Jesus in a pre-incarnation appearance, said He would fight for them. Joshua was thinking of the mechanics—like the disciple Philip trying to figure out how to buy enough bread to feed all those thousands of people. Often we face towering obstacles, thick walls and things shut up tight, but God has ways. And if He tells us to go straight up before us and take the city, He will open the way.

The ruins show the walls fell outward, which is significant when you think of the physics, and also that Joshua had instructed his army, "Every man run up straight before him." (Joshua 6:5) They were able to use the fallen bricks as a ramp they could run up, each one straight before him. In his several excavations of Jericho, Garstang reported finding well-supported houses built on the walls. The Bible says Rahab's house was built into the wall. Kennedy said it was a common practice at that time because of the lack of space within the city walls. Furthermore, Garstang found the city had been thoroughly burned but not plundered. They discovered stores of grain, burned but untouched. And all the gold, silver, bronze and iron was missing. Then the city was abandoned for a long time. Kennedy said, "All of this fits exactly with the story we see in Joshua." But what about the dates? All this is for naught if it happened before the Israelites arrived in Canaan. Kennedy said, "We can say from at least two lines of evidence from specific types of pottery and also the Egyptian royal scarab seals, that it happened around 1400 B.C., which is around the time Joshua and the Israelites would have attacked Jericho."

Here are a few more proofs of the historicity of the Bible:
- There are Babylonian documents telling of conquering Israel and carrying off the captives.
- People said Daniel made Belshazzar up and therefore Daniel wasn't a reliable book. Then archaeologists found a cylinder from Belshazzar's father saying he put his firstborn son in charge.
- Basically all the locations mentioned in the New testament have been found.
- Many of the people mentioned in the New Testament have been attested in Roman inscription, including whoever Paul ran into that was in some political position, such as Erastus in Corinth, Sergius Paulus from Cyprus, Gallio in Corinth.
- Caiaphas, the High Priest who was involved in Jesus' trial was a very prominent and powerful person. The Jewish historian Josephus mentions him. In about 1990, they found the tomb of the Caiaphas family and inside they found an elaborate estuary or burial box. It has his name on it. Inside are the bones of a sixty-nine year-old man. It's in Jerusalem. It's from the first century.

HEZEKIAH

Sennacherib was an Assyrian king who ruled in the late 8th and 7th centuries B.C., around the time of Hezekiah, when the Assyrian empire was probably the most powerful kingdom in the ancient Near East. He went down to attack Judah so he would have more control over his kingdom. He launched this attack, defeated the city of Lachish, then went to Jerusalem and besieged it. Sennacherib's messengers harassed the people on the wall in their own language, telling them their impending doom in detail to demoralize and terrify them. Then Sennacherib sent a very nasty letter in which he thoroughly demeaned the God of Israel, even using His sacred name, YHWH, declaring His impotence to protect His people. Hezekiah read the letter, went to the house of the Lord, and spread it out before Him.

The first thing Hezekiah said was Who God was to him, recounting His deeds, and acknowledging His Being, particularly His place as Creator. Then he prayed, "Yes, Sennacherib destroyed a lot of impressive nations, burning their gods, but those gods weren't real; they were nothing but wood and stone, and You, O LORD, created all the nations." Then Hezekiah said, "Look what he's saying about You! He says the gods of the other kingdoms couldn't save them and You aren't going to do any better!" I especially like the last line of the prayer where Hezekiah says, "save us out of his hand, that all the kingdoms of the earth may know that You are YHWH God, You only." (2 Kings 19:14-19) Not long after, the Angel of the LORD destroyed 185,000 of Sennacherib's army and Sennacherib went back to Nineveh.

HEZEKIAH'S TUNNEL

One reason the siege wasn't successful is Hezekiah had the rivers that supplied waters for the city re-routed so it ran through a tunnel and not out where Sennacherib's troops could get water to help sustain them. (2 Chronicles 32) It worked.

Some say the tunnel was already there. Some say Hezekiah wouldn't have had time to have it dug. Some say he only widened it. Those that say he didn't have time to do either are probably basing it on the fact it had to be dug quite a long way through solid rock, an engineering feat, especially in the ancient days. A flurry of issues about time comes up in my mind when I read the objections that say Hezekiah wouldn't have had time. The most obvious one is the God-factor. If God inspired it, He would have enabled it.

There are many physical improbabilities cited in the Bible, one being Nehemiah's rebuilding of the wall. With a trowel in one hand and a sword in the other, with hecklers and enemies causing political objections bringing about enforced halts in the rebuilding of the wall, they still got it done in fifty-two days. And there are two incidences of God sovereignly altering the position of the sun—one in Joshua's long day (Josh. 10:8-15), and when the shadow on the sundial went backwards ten degrees (2 Kings. 20:8-11). These accounts are among those that caused the Charles Templeton character in the movie Billy, the Young Years to declare what so many have said to discount the Bible's truth.

Templeton: "Do you really believe God made the sun stand still in the sky? Do you honestly believe that the Earth stopped revolving? Where is the hard science to back these stories up? And if the Bible is not true in each and every case, then doesn't that cast doubt on all of it?"

Billy: "Charles, it's the Word of God."

Templeton: "But what if it's wrong, Billy? Nothing more than feeble stories written by men like you and me attempting to answer the great questions of life, and it's wrong. Then what about the rest?"

Actually, Chuck Missler shows God didn't have to violate any natural laws to hold the sun in the sky an extra full day without flinging everyone off into outer space, but the physics is beyond me. I'll just add that Missler said a number of ancient cultures changed their calendars after that.

About ten years after the siege of Jerusalem, Sennacherib collected all his campaigns, memorializing them in prisms, which are made of clay with Assyrian wedge-shaped cuneiform writing on them. Kennedy reports, "He sends them around the empire. On them he records the Assyrian version of these events and, of course, he has the campaign against the kingdom of Judah. He mentions it by name and he mentions King Hezekiah by name. He says he defeated forty-six strong cities of the Judeans and that he went up to Jerusalem, he besieged it, and Hezekiah was like a bird in a cage. Then he talks about the tribute Hezekiah gave him and it even matches the biblical narrative in the amount of gold that is given. And then the narrative just stops. He doesn't say that he took Jerusalem and, of course, he doesn't mention that his army was partially destroyed, or that any of his officers were killed. That's it. That is the way these ancient kings would render their losses or defeats or even their draws. They would either try to make it sound like they won or they would just leave the information out. But the Sennacherib prism has all of these parallels to the biblical account."

HEZEKIAH'S TUNNEL, PART 2

Going back to the controversy about whether Hezekiah built the tunnel. Some didn't want to give him any credit at all, even though the Bible specifically speaks of it. Fast forward to the early 1880s. An adopted boy is playing hooky from school and somehow slides down this tunnel and there, about twenty feet from the end, is some ancient writing chiseled into the rock. In ancient Hebrew it describes the stone cutters, two groups tunneling towards each other, striking their pick axes hard against the rocks in order to locate each other. This is part of the translation of the inscription:

And on the day of the breaking through, the excavators struck, each to meet the other, pickaxe against pickaxe; and there flowed the water from the spring to the pool over (a space of) one thousand and two hundred cubits. And... of a cubit was the height of the rock above the heads of the excavators.

From this description, you can see there was no tunnel in existence before this one. Two groups of workmen were digging towards each other through the rock. They weren't widening a pre-existing tunnel or they would have known where the other group was. They called it "the breaking through," which also indicates no tunnel was there before. And then they describe the water flowing. It does not say they were sloshing through a steadily flowing river as they went along widening the walls. Again, that means there was no tunnel there before. And the date of the inscription? Kennedy said, "Because of the analysis of the way it was written and the style of the letters, scholars were able to date it to the time of Hezekiah." I love how God decimates cool, educated logic based on human reason alone. Miracles happened, and this is one more solid example to rest your faith upon.

EVIDENCE-BASED FAITH

We Christians need to know there's evidence, there are artifacts, steles and prisms and cylinders, and papyruses and ancient buildings and inscriptions and melted rocks. Our faith is not mindless belief in fictions made up by people who wanted to create a history for themselves to make them feel better about being small and insignificant in a hostile culture. Our faith is evidence-based, and history is one of the ways we can be grounded in its reality. So, to recount Templeton's objection in the reverse, if these unlikely and sometimes supernatural events have been archaeologically verified in such precise detail and accuracy of placement in history, shouldn't we be able to trust that the rest is also true?

The discoveries in this chapter are only a scant few of the overwhelming evidences for the veracity and historicity of the Bible, but I am most moved by what Bob Cornuke and Larry Williams said about their time retracing the exodus journey.

Larry Williams declares, "God had people walk among us here. Moses was real. Religion isn't just some story that somebody wrote. This stuff really did take place."

Bob Cornuke says, "I realized that the Bible isn't just a compilation of good stories. It's historical fact—that the words printed on the pages of Scripture are God's Words actually breathed upon its pages." Cornuke concluded, "I've always been told by a secular world that the Bible is myth and legends, allegories, ancient stories, fun, tells us a good moral message. Doesn't really apply to history. But when I stood on the scorched rocks and looked at the valley below, and saw all the things that the Bible talks about existing there, that flame that was a small little flicker in my heart became a burning flame. To this day, it still burns in my heart."

FOLLOWING THE MESSIAH

A few more things I want to share, things I've seen in a video series called "Following the Messiah," which takes you all the places Jesus was, from birth to ascension. Jeremy Dehut and Barry Britnell host this series that brings the landscape of Messiah's time on Earth into vivid reality. It's astonishing to follow in the footsteps where Jesus walked, many of which are still there. Here are the ones that moved me most.

A First Century road still exists in Jerusalem. It was built by King Herod, and is still in pretty good shape except for holes—not potholes. They were big. Why? Because in 70 A.D., when Herod's temple was set on fire, the gold melted and ran into the cracks where the blocks were fitted together. To get it, the soldiers tore the entire building apart, pushing the huge stones off the temple mount. Some of those stones rolled down the hill and hit the road causing holes big enough to swallow a car. Piles of those stones still remain, their precisely cut blocks attesting to Herod's demanding standards of construction and Jesus' prophecy that not one stone of the temple would remain on another.

This one is surprising. I had heard about it before, but I wasn't sure of its veracity. Recently, it has been confirmed by three different sources, including the one I saw on the episode on Bethlehem. In the hills near Bethlehem are caves into which shepherds retreated with their flocks when the weather was bad. Carved into the rocky interiors are mangers for their sheep. It is very likely that Mary and Joseph, unable to find lodging, found refuge in a cave and laid their newborn baby in a manger cut in stone. So much for the little wooden mangers packed with straw that we see on Christmas cards. Thirty-three years later, Jesus would be laid in a tomb cut into stone, the end of His life echoing its beginning, symbolizing the purpose for His incarnation start to finish. It humbles me to know the Word of God, the Creator of everything, came to Earth specifically to die for us—that we might live. In view of such love, can you trust your precious life each step of the way to Him?

One more thing. Scripture says after Jesus was baptized, the Spirit led Him into the wilderness to be tempted by the devil. What do you picture when you think of "wilderness"? I envisioned flat, dry, pale baked earth, so I was surprised to see rugged cliffs and steep, inhospitable reddish rock faces. It was craggy and rough and thoroughly desolate. When Barry and Jeremy were there, it was 100 degrees and it didn't look like there was any shade. Jesus was in the wilderness of Judea forty days and nights unprotected from the desiccating heat and the freezing nights, alone except for wild animals, eating and drinking nothing. I'm sure Jesus prayed but I have the feeling that, for crucial reasons, Father God let Him face the Accuser alone.

Imagining Jesus in that desolate, forbidding landscape, I wonder if He ever got a break. Was He harassed every minute of those forty days and nights? Did the devil come in waves of attacks? Or did Satan leave Him to the effects of starvation, dehydration, and the extremes of physical suffering till the last days when Jesus was at the limit of what a human being can survive?

We know Satan came when Jesus was weakest from hunger, tempting Him to meet His needs by taking matters into His own hands. But I think, for Jesus, it was never about that. It went beyond the realities of 960 grueling hours of personal sufferings. Hebrews says the Author and Finisher of our faith, for the glory set before Him endured the cross, despising the shame. His eyes were on the goal—on the defeat of death, on the redemption of what was lost, on the restoration of what He had made for Himself. It wasn't like some monumental pass/fail cosmic exam to prove He could resist whatever temptations the devil threw at Him. He was Author and Finisher, the One Who started it and the One Who completes it. For the glory set before Him He endured the cross. For the glory set before Him, He endured the wilderness of Judea. For the much bigger purpose than what was happening directly to Him, He endured. He persevered. He did it for us. He did it for love.

This morning I thought about the huge piles of stone blocks from Herod's magnificent temple, not one stone remaining on top of another. Not one! It reminds me that Jesus said every word of His prophecies would come true. Every one. That includes what He told us is yet to come. We have been given this life in this crucial time with it's unprecedented trials and uncertainties. In the desolate wilderness, we know from His Word there is more at stake than we can see or comprehend. We also know the One Who loves us most is coming for us, to take us Home to be with him forever, whether in death or in the catching away as He calls our name to meet Him in the air. That's a fact. This is not all there is.

The other thing I realized is we face times of unremitting heat, nights so black and freezing cold we cannot warm ourselves or find comfort in whatever we can wrap around ourselves. In the dark every sound is magnified—from the howling wind to the snicker of wild beasts skulking in invisible realms. Accusations will come, temptations to meet our overwhelming, legitimate, crying needs by taking matters into our own hands in ways outside the will of God. How can we make it through intact, trusting Abba, our Heavenly Father, keeping always in mind the Big Picture?

Lord, may each of us know we have a higher call than the brief span of years in a physical human life on Earth. May we know You designed us for a purpose that will change the world around us—that people will be affected by the light we bear and the words we share. May we remember always that there is much more going on than we can see, and we were placed in history for such a time as this. We have destiny planned from before the beginning of time. Then, we will be able to trust You in whatever comes because It will no longer be all about ourselves. We are part of Your Great Adventure and You have promised to walk with us every step of the way.

3

WALKING GROUNDED

As you therefore have received Christ Jesus the Lord, so walk in Him, rooted and built up in Him and established in the faith, as you have been taught, abounding in it with thanksgiving. (Col 2:6, 7 NKJV)

It was late. I was tired. Somewhere ahead in the distant cluster of lights was my destination—a clean room reserved for me after a long drive across unfamiliar territory. I would have been worried as I sped along in the dark, except the screen showed the road ahead and I knew the navigator's voice would give me plenty of warning when I had to take an off ramp and make my way through the city. Turn-by-turn guidance is a thing of beauty when you haven't a clue where you're going. So I followed the directions off the highway and down into the streets, past the brightly lit gas stations and row of hotels. I was a little uneasy as I obeyed the voice that took me into a residential area and past some industrial buildings, wondering if my hotel was located away from the others. Sometimes they are, but my navigator had always gotten me to my destination, so I decided to trust the programming and kept following the directions, though everything that looked hospitable was now far behind and the land became less and less inhabited. Finally I saw something ahead, pulled into the parking lot, and stopped with my headlights on the sign on the chain-link fence. In large letters it said, "City Landfill."

Really? How could something designed to get me safely to my destination actually take me to the garbage dump? Faulty programing? Interference? Weak signals leading to lost contact and confused connections? In this life we are always going to find ourselves traveling in unfamiliar lands. How can we get safely to our rightful destination with accurate turn-by-turn guidance? At this point in history, when it's late and dark and unfamiliar, we need that certainty more than ever. And we have it. Or, rather, we have Him.

Faulty programming, disconnections, interruptions, and weak and incoherent signals cannot only lead us away from our intended destination, they can get us dead-ended at the garbage dump.

In these chapters, I'll share with you some of the ways we and our families can be confused and led far from our place of security in Jesus—the dwelling place He has provided for us, not only when this life is over, but now, as we live on Earth during these momentous times. On His last night on Earth, Jesus told His disciples, "Let not your heart be troubled; you believe in God, believe also in Me. In My Father's house are many mansions; if it were not so, I would have told you. I go to prepare a place for you. And if (since) I go and prepare a place for you, I will come again and receive you to Myself; that where I am, there you may be also. And where I go you know, and the way you know."

Thomas said to Him, "Lord, we do not know where You are going, and how can we know the way?"

Jesus said to him, "I am the way, the truth, and the life. No one comes to the Father except through Me." (John 14:1-6 NKJV)

How shall we know the Way? His name is Jesus, and He has given us His Word. Through it, we have revelation of the entire purpose of God for us from the Beginning, before there was anything, to the intended End we could not ever otherwise know except for direct, divine revelation. It's a supernatural life we've been given—one so far beyond what we can imagine—and the possibilities, opportunities, potential, scope, and adventure are on a scale that is astonishing for us to see, much less participate in. So here we go, with the first thing you have to know: your Navigator can be trusted.

I have always heard that, in order to grow as a Christian, I had to read the Bible. So I did, plus commentaries and study aids and footnotes, but I was always afraid to put my weight on it because I'd also heard there were mistranslations and ways it had been altered to create a different truth from the one God intended us to have. One day my friend Dan sent me an email with the words, "This will blow your mind." It was "Beyond Coincidence," a YouTube video by well-respected Bible scholar and Information Scientist Chuck Missler. Part 1 is on the origins of the universe. Part 2 is an in-depth investigation into the divine origin of the Bible as wholly God-breathed. It changed my life. As Christians, we need to know what God says to us, and what He means by it. And now that I am confident it's what He really wants us to know, and have proof of His divine authorship, I can stand on solid, holy ground. And so can you. In this chapter I'm offering you some samples of the kinds of delights that await you as you discover the reliability of this precious gift from our Savior God.

I'm hoping the proofs in this chapter will release in you what they did for me—replacing all doubts and fears with joy and freedom to embrace the whole counsel of God, which He went to great lengths to protect and preserve in its entirety for us, His beloved heirs. It's our inheritance, you know. His Last Will and Testament, our light, our sword, our way to know the truth that makes us free, the guarantee of guidance on paths that will lead us to productive, fruitful, fulfilling lives. Especially in times of turbulence and emergency, we and our families absolutely must know the Bible can be trusted. And, guess what? We can! In this chapter are indisputable proofs. Too good to be true? Read on!

HEPTADIC STRUCTURE

This is the first of the mind-blowing things I learned from Chuck Missler, an exercise in creating a genealogy. Here are the specific requirements:

- Create a genealogy in which the number of words is divisible by seven with no remainder.
- Now count the number of letters you used. They also must be divisible by seven.
- The number of vowels must be divisible by seven.
- The number of consonants must be divisible by seven.
- The number of words that begin with a vowel must be divisible by seven
- The number of words that begin with a consonant must be divisible by seven.
- The number of words that occur only once must be divisible by seven.
- The number of words that occur in more than one form must be divisible by seven.
- The number of words that occur in only one form must be divisible by seven.
- The number of nouns must be divisible by seven.
- Only seven words won't be nouns.
- The number of names must be divisible by seven.
- Only seven other kinds of nouns should be permitted.
- The number of male names must be divisible by seven.
- The number of generations must be divisible by seven.

Have you guessed what this is? It's rules that are operating in the genealogy of Jesus Christ in the first eleven verses of the Gospel of Matthew. Chuck Missler says they meet all those rules. It's called heptadic structure. That means it's constructed on the number seven.

Missler said he found thirty-four such rules. In order to put this in perspective, he calculated what it would take to generate a genealogy that met those thirty-four rules. Using a million super computers that could do 400,000,000 of these genealogies per second, how long do you think it would take? More than 4,000,000 years.

We can go through the rest of this Gospel and find it obeys dozens of these seven-fold challenges. Almost every characteristic that you measure turns out to be a number that's an exact multiple of seven, and both Testaments in their original languages maintain this heptadic structure. As you investigate the text, you'll find it has properties that cannot be simulated. It certainly couldn't be done by random chance. What kind of super-mind could do such a thing? The One Who created everything. Only God has that mental power. When I see this, I just go, "Wow!" It's a supernatural Book He gave us, and this, and other proofs you're going to read about, are verifiable ways He made sure we'd know He, Himself, wrote it just so we'd know for sure it's from Him.

The one who discovered this astonishing supernatural structure is Dr. Ivan Panin, born in Russia, immigrated to the United States, then graduated with a PhD from Harvard in 1882. Somewhere along the way, he found Christ. As seems to be often the case, Jesus, the Word Himself, honored Panin's zeal for the Bible by revealing to him its heptadic structure. It was 1890, long before computers. As for the genealogy rules we just went through above, Panin actually found a total of seventy-five. He committed the rest of his life, fifty years, generating over 43,000 pages of discoveries. Missler says, "Very dry reading, but staggering in their implications. Among other things, there are all kinds of properties of the Torah (the first five books of the Bible) that depend on the precise letters that you're using, which tells you that not only did God give Moses the Torah, He gave it to Moses letter by letter. You pull one letter out of that and some of those properties start to dissipate."

I don't know if this does anything for you. For me, it was a game-changer. I had read those footnotes that said "Earlier manuscripts do not contain this verse." Does that mean God didn't really mean for us to have it then? The one that troubled me the most was at the end of the Gospel of Mark, the verse that starts, "These signs will follow..."But guess what? It fits that same heptadic structure! Here, verified at last, is the verse I loved.

And these signs will follow those who believe: In My name they will cast out demons; they will speak with new tongues; they will take up serpents; and if they drink anything deadly, it will by no means hurt them; they will lay hands on the sick, and they will recover. (Mark 16:17-18 NKJV)

Divine authorship is the only way you can get such intricate design. This is one of the most convincing proofs that the Bible is God's Word. However, even if that passage were not stunningly verified by its glorious divine structure, Jesus did all those things in His time, and told us we would too, and more. So let us not be daunted by thinking if a manuscript doesn't contain the passage, then its contents are nullified. I feel stupid to admit I thought that, but there it is.

This structure based on sevens is mind-boggling, but so what? Does it help you pay your rent or get along with a cranky boss or mend shattered relationships within your family clan? Repeatedly we hear everything in the Bible is significant. It all means something and will apply to us in that it is also a supernatural book—a living Word to us, not merely print on a page.

What do we gain from knowing the Bible is written with such outrageous complexity that no human minds could have written it so precisely over a period of so many years? That same Mind is interested in each one of us individually. He carefully designed each one of us, set us in specific families in a specific time in history to bring about something of His purposes that could not be done better by anyone other than ourselves. The incredible precision of that letter-by-letter dictation of the revelation of God to us gives us a glimpse of the kind of Superior Intellect that can also design the mysteries of quantum physics, organize the properties of time, energy, matter, gravity, light, sound, beauty, consciousness, and life itself—and expressions created in every possible form from quarks to galaxies. That same Mind knows every hair on every head of every human being, along with the thoughts and intents of every heart. And not a sparrow falls without His knowing—or caring. When I asked the Lord the significance of the heptadic structure to us, He said that same superb Mind is concerned about each one of our concerns, no matter how big, no matter how small. And He is not only interested in working out the details of His Plan of the redemption of all He created, He wants to work every aspect of our little lives together for our good because, above all else, He truly, deeply, overwhelmingly loves each of us, a precious creation, treasured and cherished as uniquely one-of-a-kind.

ACCURACY

One of the biggest criticisms of the Bible has to do with its transmission to us over time. They cite human error as well as human agenda. Considering the ancient origins of the Bible, the lack of technology, and the logistics involved in copying manuscripts that were long and had a lot of words, they figured there had to be errors and they probably got worse as time went on. Like playing the telephone game. The first person whispers something into the ear of the next person in line, and on and on until the last person, who speaks what they heard Then everyone laughs because it isn't even remotely close to what it started out to be. Have you heard that criticism of the Bible? Well, here's some facts about the process involved in copying the Holy Scriptures in the ancient times.

In the old days, there were no printing presses. Thousands of years ago, everything had to be copied by hand. When the

Scriptures talk about books, they're referring to scrolls. Books with pages were not invented until 2 B.C., and were extremely rare. The ancient Hebrews beat a reed called papyrus into strips that were assembled into sheets that were flat on one side and rough on the other. Their books were long rolls of papyrus with text written in columns in ink on the smooth side. The exception to this was title deeds. There are a lot of words in the Torah (Genesis to Deuteronomy) and the rest of the Old Testament, and each copy had to be done by hand. No spell-check. How can we be sure the text is accurate?

Hebrew is not your average language with an alphabet of letters that have no significance in themselves. When God created this living language, He imbued it with surprising richness. Each Hebrew letter has a name, a symbol, a numerical value, a picture, a sound, a meaning, even a musical note. When scribes copied sacred scrolls, they counted up the numerical value of all the letters in the row, both vertically and horizontally. If one number didn't match the original, they burned the copy. That's why the Dead Sea Scrolls are so accurate.

THE GOD-BREATHED BOOK

Now for my favorite methods of verifying the divine authorship of this holy book:

1. Heptadic Structure: It means "seven." We already talked about the divisible by sevens in genealogies and other aspects of the text, but there are many other patterns. To the Greek mind, prophecy is prediction and fulfillment. To the Hebrew mind, it is revealed in patterns. All through the Bible you'll find sevens. There are lists of sevens, from the days of creation to the articles of furniture in the tabernacle. There are seven compound names of God, seven redemptive gifts (Romans 12), seven last words of Christ on the cross, seven miracles in the book of John, etc. As you've probably guessed, there are lots more lists of seven, but that's enough for now.

2. Equidistant Letter Sequences (ELS): I'm sure you've heard of hidden Bible codes. The most popularized ones are pretty bogus, but there are real ones everywhere in the original texts, and rabbis have known about them for centuries. It's rather simple, actually. You look for the first letter in a word, then count seven letters or multiples of seven to find the next letter. Without computers, the ancient Hebrew scholars found hundreds of these hidden messages. Here are some of my favorites.

A. Esther: Some scholars think the Book of Esther doesn't belong in the Bible because it doesn't mention God. But it does. By using Equidistant Letter Sequences, you can find YHWH several times, spelled both forwards and backwards, depending on the context of the meaning of the text.

B. Ever wonder why, in the midst of the gripping story of Joseph in the Book of Genesis, you suddenly have a detailed account of the sordid business with Tamar tricking Judah, her dishonorable father-in-law, into sleeping with her? Using ELS, you can find within the text at forty-nine letter intervals, the names Boaz, Ruth, Obed, Jesse, and David—Messiah's family line through Tamar's son Perez in the tribe that descended from Judah. The names are encrypted in Genesis 38, all in chronological order. Statistically the probability of that happening by accident is less than one in 70,000,000. Omit one letter and it falls apart. It's unlikely some Hebrew scribes would have deliberately added the Messianic line into the Torah, so it shows me its Divine Author wanted us to know He wasn't letting anything thwart His Plan of Redemption and the fulfillment of His prophecies and promises to bring Messiah through the tribe of Judah.

The other day I was reading the genealogy of Jesus in Matthew and came across the name of Boaz. Remember the story in the Book of Ruth? Boaz was a near-kinsman and qualified to redeem Naomi's lost land and marry Ruth, but there was a nearer kinsman than Boaz that had the first right of refusal, so to speak.

So Boaz, an honorable man, met with the man before the elders of the city and offered Naomi's land redemption to him. The man said sure. Then Boaz added that, by the law, he would also have to take Ruth as his wife, whereupon the man said, "no thank you," gave Boaz his shoe to signify his rejection of the option, and Boaz happily took Ruth as his wife.

Ever wonder why the man was so hasty to refuse? Because everyone knew the prophecies of the coming Messiah, and everyone wanted Him to come through their family line, so they were very careful not to let their bloodline be tainted, not allowing any contamination from lesser human beings.

Okay, so here's Messiah's genealogy and there's Boaz and Ruth. You know who Boaz's mom was? Rahab! So now you have this Gentile woman from Jericho giving birth to Boaz, who marries another Gentile woman, and one of their descendants is David, and then there's Solomon, whose mom was Bathsheba, who used to be the wife of Uriah. Oops. That wasn't a pretty picture. But moving right along, one of Solomon's descendants is Hezekiah, a really good king, whose son is Manasseh, a really bad king, in fact, one of the worst. It's instructive to note that Manasseh was conceived after God granted Hezekiah another fifteen years. Sometimes it's better to go with the will of God even if you're not quite ready to die.

You know what struck me about this list of the ancestors of Jesus Christ, Who would be the sinless sacrificial lamb for all sins for all time? His genealogy has Tamar, who slept with her father-in-law; Rahab, a prostitute from a people group so defiled they all had to be destroyed; Ruth, from the race of the hated Moabites; Bathsheba, whom David took in a very inappropriate way, then tried to hide it by murdering her husband; and an extremely wicked king. What does that tell us about how God feels about us? We're all included in Messiah's line. He identifies with and accepts us, tainted bloodlines, checkered pasts, hated races, willful choices and all. And it shows me how very powerfully God can redeem and make holy even humanity's weakest and most defiled.

C. This one completely blows me away. In twelve verses of the end of Isaiah 52 and the start of Isaiah 53, you can find the names of all the disciples (except Judas), Caiphas, three Marys, and the name "John" connected to the name "Mary" because Jesus left His mother in the hands of the beloved disciple.

3. Prophecies: Prophecies in Daniel about kingdoms rising and falling are so accurate scholars thought that part of the book had to have been added on after the fact. However, there are no "lost years" where we have no idea what went on in the world. Daniel's prophecies tell us exactly what was going to happen, including the little goat who went so fast his feet didn't even touch the ground. That was so accurate that it's said Alexander the Great did not destroy Jerusalem because he was impressed with the description of himself and his speedy world conquests in the words Daniel wrote at God's direction.

One of the ways God declares repeatedly that people will know He is God is by His telling them what is going to happen before it happens. He put Cyrus in the book of Isaiah, and when King Cyrus read his name in the ancient scroll, he let God's people go back to Jerusalem with supplies and riches and his blessings too. Accurate prophecy is not difficult for God. He's outside time. We live in sequential *chronos* time. He's in the Eternal Now. For Him, past, present, future—all of eternity is Now.

And Jesus confirmed Daniel wrote it. He also quotes Moses and Isaiah as the authors of the books some scholars have tried to say they didn't write. Once again, Jesus confirms their authorship, and I figure he'd know. All the answers are in the Bible. Chuck Missler says it's as if the Holy Spirit anticipated these controversies over the authorship of these crucial books of the Bible and made sure to leave the proof in black and white and plain sight.

A word of caution about new discoveries. There are always extra books that people claim are divinely inspired but were left out of the Bible for various reasons. Don't believe it! God is perfectly capable of making sure His Book is complete and accurate. There are immense riches in our Bibles, more than we can ever mine in our lifetimes. Don't get sidetracked with these fake missing parts of holy Scriptures.

The other thing I want to say is, with all these proofs that the Bible is true, that it's what God wants us to know, we can trust it. And we need to read it. It's life-giving and supernatural to us when we take it seriously—all of it. That includes the Book of Revelation. The word is "Apocalypse" and it means (amazingly enough) "revelation." We tend to connect "apocalypse" with disasters. That's not it. Nor is it "revelations." No "S" because it's the revelation of Jesus Christ—not what He's telling us is going to happen, but Who He is. People get stuck in the seals, the trumpets, the bowls, the plagues, the creepy beasts, the giant hailstones. That's not the point. The last book in the Bible lets us know God is not asleep, weak, or permissive. He's giving people multiple opportunities to choose Him, and as in the ten plagues in Egypt, He's challenging and destroying each of the false gods so people can see true reality and choose life instead of all the dead ends that finish in the garbage heap. The long-term perspective helps us keep on track because we can see the End, the intended End. We know what to expect and how to get there whole and participating in the Great Adventure. It also reminds us there is a judgment, and end to all evil, a completion to this part of human life. Peter says it will end in fervent heat and everything will melt. That's not poetic language. It's incentive to keep on walking in the Light, bringing forth the fruit of the Spirit that draws others to Jesus through the sweetness of our lives. Things are messy now, and evil is going on seemingly unchecked, but it *will* be destroyed. In the meantime, Jesus tells us, "Take heart. I AM! Do not be afraid any longer." (Mark 6:50)

MORE PROOF

There are more than 300 fulfilled prophecies about the incarnation of Jesus and His time on Earth, from his place of birth, which He had no control over, all the way to His manner of death, which had not been invented at the time the prophecies on His crucifixion were written. There are three times as many prophecies about His second coming as there are for His first, and a whole bunch about the Day of the Lord that are yet to come. Some are so hard to fathom that people say they're symbolic, but there are quite a few statements in the Bible that have to do with supernatural interventions. God wants us to know what we see is not all there is, and His fingerprints and messages are everywhere in the Scriptures, sometimes practically shouting to get our attention so we might see and believe what He's telling us. He wants us to know, and to not be afraid.

Here's one of the most stunning examples, What did Jesus cry out from the cross? "My God, my God, why have You forsaken me?" It's not a random statement; it's the first line of Psalm 22, written by David a thousand years before Jesus was crucified. Just to give you a thrill, here are some of the words of the psalm:

¹"My God, My God, why have You forsaken Me? Why are You so far from helping Me, and from the words of My groaning?

² O My God... ⁶ I am a worm, and no man; a reproach of men, and despised by the people.

7 All those who see Me ridicule Me; they shoot out the lip, they shake the head, saying, "He trusted in the Lord, let Him rescue Him; let Him deliver Him, since He delights in Him!"

16 ...The congregation of the wicked has enclosed Me. They pierced My hands and My feet;

17 I can count all My bones. They look and stare at Me.

18 They divide My garments among them, and for My clothing they cast lots.

19 But You, O Lord, do not be far from Me;"

Pretty amazing, don't you think? When I read that and other prophecies of the crucifixion, I can't imagine how these descriptions could be more precise. Can it be anything but supernatural inspiration? In Paul's letter to Timothy, he says this Book is God-breathed. It can be trusted to guide you. It tells you Who God is and what He intends us to know about His purposes for human beings. And everywhere there are hidden treasures, such as this line which gives the response to the first cries in Psalm 22: "24 For He has not despised nor abhorred the affliction of the afflicted; Nor has He hidden His face from Him; But when He cried to Him, He heard."

Many Bible scholars have said God turned His face away from Jesus when He was on the cross, saying God cannot look upon sin. I'm not going to tackle that theology. All I can say is Jesus has experienced everything we humans go through, and that desperate hopelessness of feeling totally separated from God is one of the deep horrors of human life. Whether Jesus was actually separated from the love of Father God at that moment, I'm pretty sure He was feeling that He was. I also believe He intended us to read the revelation of the heart of God in the words that David wrote a thousand years before and be assured that, because of what He did on the cross, nothing can now separate us from the love of God—ever. As christian philosopher Francis Schaeffer says, "In view of this, how shall we then live?"

Psalm 22 ends with these lines: "It will be recounted of the Lord to the next generation, they will come and declare His righteousness to a people who will be born, That He has done this." That's us—born more than two thousand years after. He is declaring to us that He has done this, and because He did, Father will never ever turn away from us. Nothing can now separate us from the full, extravagant love of God.

These are wonderful truths—the peace and love of God that we need so much, especially these days, the promise of guidance and divine presence that rings all through the Bible, but sometimes the Word just bounces off my head. Jesus has an answer for that. It's in Mark 8:13-21, when the disciples were worrying about having forgotten to bring bread. Jesus was telling them to beware of the leaven of the Pharisees. But they didn't get it. Jesus said their hearts had grown dull even though they'd seen Him multiply loaves and fishes for more than 9,000 hungry people. Sometimes I feel that unresponsive, as if I'm in a spiritual coma. Like today.

When I asked Him about it, Jesus reminded me of this part of the parable of the sower. The seed is the Word of God. In the second group are those with rocky soil who at first receive God's truth with joy, but they accept it only superficially. With no real root in themselves, "they endure only for a little while; then, when trouble or persecution comes because of the word, immediately they [are offended and displeased at being associated with Me and] stumble and fall away." (Mark 4:17 AMPC) As for those in the thorns, "these are the ones who have heard the word, but the worries and cares of the world [the distractions of this age with its worldly pleasures], and the deceitfulness [and the false security or glamour] of wealth [or fame], and the passionate desires for all the other

things creep in and choke out the word, and it becomes unfruitful." (Mark 4:18, 19 AMPC)

I know about seeds. Fifteen years ago, my dad gave me
some for *gow choy*—dog grass. They came up and have continued to fill the big planter with long, slender, deeply green
garlic chives, plus puffy white seed flowers once a year. Seeds
want to grow. It's their nature. They have life in them and it's
persistently powerful for something so small.

The Word of God is living. It produces life if we let it, but
first we have to let it. We have to let it get inside and have a
root-hold deep enough to withstand scorching heat and chok-
ing weeds. Reading the words above, I would add to the list
of distractions: worries, uncertainties, things breaking down
(health, relationships, communications, supply lines, truth,
morality, justice, education), prices going up (taxes, gas, gro-
ceries, insurance, medical care), etc. Even listing them makes
me anxious. The cares of this life can wear us down to the
point our hearts are dull and we forget to trust God. We forget that faith cometh by hearing and hearing by the Word of
God. Then there are times I open my Bible, and I can't comprehend the words.

But there's something about seeds. If you give them even
a little soil, water and sun, they *will* sprout. My son Thomas
has made a practice of reading five minutes of Bible first thing
in the morning. He says sometimes he doesn't get anything
out of it, but he does it anyway, adding that he doesn't always
remember what he ate for dinner either, but it still gave him
nourishment.

One of the greatest weapons Jesus has given us to protect us and enable us to destroy the workings of darkness
that creep ever nearer is His Word. It's Himself, the Word
of God. It's His essence, His messages, His reassurance, His

secret counsel. But it won't do a thing for us unless we take it in, let it take root and grow. Jesus defeated the devil with "It is written." He silenced the Pharisees and Sadduces with the righteous application of the Scriptures they were trying to twist. Knowing that, I open my Bible and sometimes implore the Holy Spirit to speak to me in my dull-hearted inability to comprehend the truth that would set me free from the cares and distractions that can make my life unfruitful.

I want to end this chapter with something my grand-daughter Anna sent me when I asked her why she reads her Bible. Perhaps this is the best way to approach that holy Book, not as a chore, a spiritual discipline or requirement, but as a vital necessity for life itself.

"When I was little, my dad used to wake me up in the morning. Even if he had to go to work before I was fully awake, he rarely failed to say goodbye just so I knew he was still there. Knowing that alone could make or break my day because his presence meant I was safe and loved. All was right with the world. Reading the Bible is like that for me. Reading the stories about God and how He interacts with mankind through any number of situations, both normal and crazy, reminds me that He is still in control and that He loves me. Of course His word also offers wisdom, correction, comfort, guidance and a whole slew of other things, but mostly, I read because the world is just too big and scary to face without my Father and King's daily presence in my life."

4

THE WORD-BASED UNIVERSE

"CQ DX. CQ DX. This is W6MVK. CQ DX. CQ DX. Anybody want to talk?"

In ham (amateur) radio, CQ is the universal invitation for contact, and CQ DX is a call for long distance contact. That means, "I don't want to talk to local stations. I want to reach far away—Thailand, Antarctica, etc. DX means distance.

My dad was a champion DXer, an avid amateur radio ham who really did reach Antarctica and talked frequently with the King of Siam (now Thailand). In 1938, he made history, the first West Coast ham to win the prestigious Sweepstakes Contest for contacting the most and rarest stations across the world in the time allowed.

How did a poor twenty-four-year-old from California's Central Valley overcome the handicaps of a lousy location and no money for equipment? He read all the radio magazines cover to cover, scrounged junk yards, wound coils around oatmeal boxes, and built his own equipment—with improvements. And then he spent countless hours tuning around, listening for signals. He got to the point he could hear the faintest sound, his fingers moving the tuner precisely, delicately, deftly homing in on that barely audible signal.

When it came time for the Sweepstakes Contest, eager hams hit the airwaves hoping to go farther faster than all the rest. East Coast hams had dominated the field, their powerful signals making them loud and easy to find, and their location on the planet gave them a considerable advantage. But this contest isn't just about who has the best signal or location; it's about DX, and for that, you had to find the farthest and the faintest. My dad had trained himself to pick signals from the noise, rare stations that brought him the prize, while others passed right over them, never hearing them at all.

God is always calling to us: CQ CQ. Anybody want to talk?

God is not hiding. But neither is He shouting. You do need to want to hear from Him enough that you'll sift through the noise of normal human life in search of what is extraordinary and rare. It's fingerprints He leaves, not gouges in the sod from big, heavy, stomping boots.

It's not that He's lonely or lacking; it's one of the most astonishing realities of the Judeo-Christian faith. God wants to talk. And He wants to hear what you choose to say back. Why? How else do you build a relationship? How else can you become friends?

If you scanned my brain, you wouldn't know me. I have to reveal myself to you with words. You can look at my photographs and paintings and see how I translate beauty, but you can't know who I am, how I think, what my life has been like. After you've read this book, you'll have a pretty good idea of how I got where I am in these seventy-four years, though there are some surprises yet to come, and I'm excited to share them with you...later.

Now that we've established the veracity of the Bible through Divine Authorship and the historicity proven in archaeological finds, we can examine it to find out what God wants to communicate to us—what He wants us to know about Him, His purposes for creating everything, and the wonders He has in the length and breadth and heights and depths of His love for us. The Bible is like a globe showing the entirety of our world in three-dimensions with continents and oceans in relationship with one another. It is also a map to help us get where we need to go, and turn-by-turn guidance that will never lead us wrong. The entire revelation together gives us a splendid, rich, and expansive worldview. It contains the directions for flawless navigation to our Destination, and our destiny.

In the early 1950s, my father led a group of avid researchers in an attempt to prove UHF (Ultra High Frequencies) could be used to provide uninterceptable, uninterruptible signals for emergency communications. And they did. From then on, even into the war in Vietnam, the enemy could see them, but not hear them. They could not distort the messages or stop them from reaching those who could send help. The enemy wants to jam our signals, distort our understanding of who we are, disconnect us from the Source of life and help, and disable us from fulfilling our purposes in life. The Bible has the answers to all of these issues and More, and when we read it, we receive a supernatural revelation of life lived in deep and abiding connection with the Creator of it all.

LANGUAGES

Language is the first way to discern the intent of the author. When C.S. Lewis wrote his *Four Loves,* he'd slip in and out of several languages—not to prove how smart he was, but because that was the best and most succinct way to express what he was trying to get across. I, however, did not know those languages, so I gave up and read his children's books instead. In *The Chronicles of Narnia,* I could grasp the complicated theology he was so good at understanding, but the way he said it was accessible to my own little pea brain. So the first thing we're looking at in the message of the Bible is its languages.

The Old Testament was written in Ancient Hebrew. The New Testament was written in Koine Greek. Wait! I thought the disciples and apostles were Jews (except for Luke, who was Greek) so wouldn't it make sense that the New Testament would be written mostly in Hebrew? Well, by the time Jesus walked the earth, some people spoke Hebrew, but few could read Ancient Hebrew. For the most part, everyone spoke Greek. Why? Because about 300 years before Jesus, Alexander the Great conquered all the known world and made his native language the official one, thus creating a wide-spread use of Greek, the language that would later carry the Good News across the civilized world in the words they would be able to understand. During the reign of Ptolemy II, the Greek king of Egypt, scholars labored fifteen years to translate the Old Testament into Greek. In 270 B.C., it was completed. That's how we got the Septuagint translation, meaning "seventy," so-named because it is reported that seventy (or seventy-two) scholars worked on it.

Some of the Bible is written in Aramaic, the language of the Babylonian Empire. The Jews were captives there for seventy years, so it's not surprising they would use that language. Some of the Book of Daniel, who was a teenager when he was carried off and chosen to serve in the court of the king is written in Aramaic, as are some court documents in the Book of Ezra. Jesus spoke Aramaic, Hebrew, and Greek, but when He quoted the Old Testament, 10% of the time it was in Hebrew, and the other 90% He was quoting in Greek from the Septuagint.

The New Testament was written in the language of the common people, not the formal, academic, classical language of literature and scholars. If it were not for the New Testament, Koine Greek would not be studied today since it was not used for important literary works. "Koine" means "common." Isn't it interesting that God chose to present His mysteries, secrets, and revelations of his heart, ways, plans, deep truth, and things yet to come, in a lowly language whose words would become the most treasured in human history?

There's a message here. God wants to communicate with everyone, no caste system, no hierarchy, no preference based on circumstances or worldly worth. "If anyone is thirsty, let him come to Me and drink."

Notice how often the Bible uses words having to do with speech, words, reason, communications, commands, shouting, calling, pleading, praying, questioning, and making connections.

The heavens declare the glory of God. The firmament proclaims His handiwork. Day after day pours forth speech, and night after night shows forth knowledge. There is no speech or spoken word, yet their voice goes out through all the earth. (Psalm 19: 1-4)

Why does this matter? It's about communication. To me the most obvious message of the Bible is God wants to communicate with us. He wants us to know Who He is, first of all. Then He wants us to know how and what He created and why. He wants us to know what He intended for us, how it was lost, and the extremes to which He has gone to get it, and us, back from eternal separation from Him. He wants us to know why we're here and what our individual lives mean to Him personally. He wants us to know where it's all going and why. And He wants to tell everyone. No elite, exclusion, or secret pass codes.

There was a time in the past when a person could be burned at the stake for translating the Bible into the common language. Religious leaders thought the ordinary, common person wasn't capable of comprehending anything so sacred and holy; they needed an interpreter—themselves. Of course, that also gave them a lot of power, prestige, influence, and wealth, but that's another matter. The point is, God never intended to exclude anyone. In fact, when King James ordered the translation of the original text into English, it was translated into the language of the streets. Where we feel distanced from the lofty-sounding Thees and Thous and the stiff and difficult grammatical structures of that day, it was not so for the people of that time. Thee and Thou were terms of endearment used between engaged couples, not the formal titles of dignitaries and authorities who were never addressed in familiar and casual ways. So we have Koine Greek and the language of the English streets to show us that God intended to bring us into relationship with Him in the most unintimidating words possible. And we have God being addressed in the fond and familiar terms of couples who intend to join their separate lives to spend the rest of their time creating something new through their intimate, deeply committed relationship together.

PRINCIPLES

When you're reading the Bible, there are various patterns that scholars have used throughout the ages to understand better what God is trying to convey. One is the Principle of First Mention. The first time a word, a type, a symbol, a concept, a phrase is used, that's something to notice. For example, the first time the word "lamb" appears in the Bible is when Isaac says to his dad, "I see the fire and the wood, but where is the lamb?" (Genesis 22:7) Abraham replies, "The Lord will provide himself a lamb…" The first time you see "lamb" used in the New Testament is when John the Baptist sees Jesus and says, "Behold the Lamb of God, that taketh away the sins of the world." (John 1:29) That connects both Testaments and the significance of the lamb. The first mention is when Abraham does not have to sacrifice his son. The first New Testament mention identifies Jesus as the Lamb God would provide for Himself, as Abraham prophetically declared. There was the immediate provision of the ram that was tangled in a bush nearby, and the fulfillment of the "type" by Jesus two thousand years later. It's significant that the first time the word "love" appears in the Bible is Genesis 22:2 when God tells Abraham, "Take your son, your only son Isaac whom you love..." It's a foreshadowing of a time on that very same land when He will sacrifice His own only Son, Whom He loves. Here we have "love" and "lamb" and "Lamb of God" clustered together, one aged father's breaking heart spared the death of his son, and the Ancient of Days going through with the sacrifice breaking His own Father-heart on Calvary—for love.

Another tool for understanding biblical truth is repetition. I especially love when God says the same thing in both Testaments. My favorite is "I will never leave you or fail you or forsake you." It's in Joshua 1:9 and again in Hebrews 13:5, but it is also there other times, I just don't remember exactly where.

Another language thing is the meanings, the overtones, in the originals. I love the Amplified Bible because many of the Hebrew and Greek words are too rich to be adequately expressed in a single one-to-one word translation. My favorite word in the Bible is "good," which is *towb* in Hebrew and *kalos* in Greek. Wait till you see what "good" means when God says it! As a lover of words, this one truly blows my mind, tweaks my circuits, delights the cockles of my heart.

The Hebrew word *towb* is used to describe that which is good, pleasant, beautiful, excellent, lovely, delightful, convenient, joyful, fruitful, precious, sound, cheerful, kind, correct, and righteous. Astonishingly, the Greek word for "good" has the same overtones. *Kalos* contains, not only the sense of moral goodness, but also nobility, loveliness, charm, delight, winsomeness, and a kind of attractiveness, as in the beauty of holiness. In *New Testament Words,* author and Greek scholar William Barclay writes *kalos* is used in secular Greek papari to describe animals that are in good condition and gentle in nature, and grapes that are fully ripe, sweet to the taste, and beautiful to look upon. He says it's used for that which commands love and admiration, is useful, and honorable.

In the New Testament, *kalos* is used for goodness which is a lovely thing, useful for all the purposes of life and pleasant to see. It satisfies the conscience but also delights the heart. Greek scholar Spiros Zodhiates says it's harmonious completeness. Embodied in these two words is the idea that this kind of good always has a lovely face.

What does it look like in the text? Try this one on for size. It's the meanings of *kalos* in Matthew 11:30. "My yoke is wholesome (useful, good—not harsh, hard, sharp, or pressing, but comfortable, gracious, and pleasant), and My burden is light and easy to be borne." Changes our view of the Good Shepherd, doesn't it? It certainly adjusts my thinking about getting into yoke with Jesus no matter what the load may be.

THE MESSAGE IS TRUE

Two things ring loudly in my heart as I write this book. One is how many times God specifically states He is the Lord, the One Who made everything. Bible scholars emphasize the significance of the first time something is mentioned in Scriptures. They also note the signaling of significance through repetition. The first thing in the Bible is God's account of creation. And then He identifies Himself as Creator throughout the subsequent pages, all the way to The End. Apparently, it's very important to God that we know He created everything—deliberately, purposefully, carefully, lovingly. And why. In Revelation 4:11 it says, "And for Thy pleasure Thou has created all things." My friend Dan says God doesn't create anything He doesn't love.

The universe is glorious. It has been called The First Book because anybody can read it, whether you know language or not. Calvary Chapel Founder Pastor Chuck Smith says, "There's one thing you can learn about God from seeing His creation: He loves beauty. But it doesn't tell you about salvation." It also doesn't tell you about the principles of life that bring insight into how best to align with the Mind of Christ. That requires words. You can also see what matters to God by how much space He dedicates to it in the Bible and what it cost Him. There's a lot about creation, some fabulous descriptions in Psalms and Isaiah and Job: 38-41, but when it comes to Redemption, you'll find that on every page. From Genesis to Revelation, it's all about Jesus. It shows Him fully God and fully human. It shows His divinity and His humility, His revelation as King of Kings, and His vulnerability as a spotless lamb who does not open His mouth in His own defense or to stop the stripping of all dignity.

There is a lot of confusion about Jesus. The Gnostics believed matter is bad so Jesus, as God, could not have been a real human. They say He didn't even leave footprints. Others say He was just a man, a human being deified by His followers though he never claimed to be God. Of course, that's silly. If He didn't make Himself equal with God, the Pharisees wouldn't have been so enraged, accusing Him of blasphemy, punishable by death. Of course, "Jesus" is the name by which He revealed Himself to us in the most significant relationship He would have with humans. It means "Savior." Before that, He was called "The Word." He was fully God—always was and always will be. Names are important. They tell us things we couldn't otherwise know, especially when it comes to understandings we could not ever get except by divine revelation. They're kind of hand holds we can hang onto as we try to grasp concepts from supernatural realms.

In the beginning [before all time] was the Word, and the Word was with God, and the Word was God Himself. He was present originally with God. All things were made and came into existence through Him; and without Him was not even one thing made that has come into being. In Him was Life, and the Life was the Light of men. And the Light shines on in the darkness, for the darkness has never overpowered it [put it out or absorbed it or appropriated it, and is unreceptive to it.] (John 1:1 AMPC)

In the old days, I hadn't a clue why Jesus was important. He always seemed kind of a middleman. God is too holy, so you have to go through this elder brother buffer zone who can protect you from a rather demanding Father. But, I figured, since Father God made it all, He had a right to be demanding.

That's before I understood that the word "God" in Hebrew is Elohim, a uni-plural noun that always means a unity among more than one. In English, a plural is two or more. In Hebrew, a plural is at least three.

So They were all there at the very start, and Jesus, far from being a spectator, turns out to be the Word through Whom all things came about, and, Scripture says later, through Whom all things consist (hold together). I like the part about the Light and the darkness because of how thoroughly darkness is always overcome by Light. Important to keep in mind as things get stranger and darker in these uncertain days.

We get confused by certain terms. There's Father, Son, and Holy Spirit. We read "only begotten" and we think Jesus is derivative, a product of Father God, lower, and inferior. We get confused by the terminology. God gave us certain names that indicate relationships so we would understand how He wants to relate to us, and how we are to relate to Him. Think of it as roles. When Jesus calls Himself the Son of God, it's one kind of revelation. When He calls Himself the Son of Man, it's another. When Jesus says the Father is greater than Himself, He's talking about his relationship as a human being with Father God. In humility, Jesus took on the form of a human being to live the sinless life and pay the price to buy us and Earth back, but also to show us how we were intended to relate to God in the sonship that was God's original design for every human being. "Begotten" also causes problems because we think of the begats in the genealogies and think it means engendered or created or birthed. In those lists, it does, but "begotten" in the original Greek is a different word. It means unique, the only one of the family,

Jesus is never called *teknon* (child) as believers are called the children of God. Zodhiates says the word in Greek is *genos.* Jesus Christ is designated as the Only One of the same stock in the relationship of the Son to the Father. He is not to be understood as eternally born of the father, but only in his humanity was He born. Jesus was the only such One ever.

The whole idea of the Trinity is not something anyone can explain, and I'm certainly not going to try. I just want to offer some thoughts on how to understand what God wants to get across to us. For now, the most important thing I want to share is Jesus is fully God. On Earth He was fully God and fully human, but before all time, He was The Word—the Logos—God.

Another important distinction shows up in the passage, "In Him was Life, and the Life was the Light of men." The word "life" that's in Him is *zoe*—spiritual life. It's much higher and noble than "*bios,*" which is the life of grass and bugs. In scientific materialism there is no *zoe* because it can't be discerned, whereas with *bios,* it's either alive or it's not.

We have had revelation through names. Now I want to look at the revelation of God's intention for our material world through the phrases. All this is purely structure. It's not theoretical.

In Genesis, we have a series of repeated phrases: And God said. On the third day He spoke and land was separated from water. Then He spoke again and vegetation appeared—trees and grasses self-replicating in distinct forms from one another.

Life (*bios*) is distinguished from matter by an act of God. On the fifth day, we have God speaking creatures into the seas and skies filled with birds. It was teeming—abundant life. So now you have life with blood in it as distinguished from plant life.

On the sixth day, God spoke into being animals that are on the earth. Some are wild and some domestic, another distinction in created purpose and relationship with human beings. I think it's lovely that God designed some creatures to be comfortable with people. Partnerships with animals are so wonderful. Then God said, "Let Us make Man in Our own image." There is a separate word of creation, a distinction between animal life and human life. A BIG difference. People did not evolve from lower-level sentient beings, gradually standing more upright, the thick bone of their foreheads thinning to make more space for a prefrontal cortex and better analytical thinking. In my mind's eye I have a picture of God's hands lovingly forming Adam from the clay, and then bending close enough to breathe into his face. For a moment, they share the same breath. That's a feeling I get from reading that account in the way God has personalized it for me. That's how He feels about every one of His children. Maybe this is too anthropomorphic for some. To best explain how this works, I cite what Mathematician John Lennox said when a famous astrophysicist said to him, "God doesn't communicate with a voice box and lungs."

"That's ridiculous." Lennox replied, "You're being ridiculous. This is simple language, but it's expressing it in the only way we would understand it."

Yeah, we have pretty puny brains compared to His! We're like goldfish in a bowl trying to figure out why the water shakes when a garbage truck at the curb outside dumps the recycle at 5 in the morning.

So God created human beings in His image, and then He talks to them. Genesis reports, "God said to them." Immediately you have communication, contact, meaning, personality. Lennox says, "You have the creation of men and women in the image of God—*Imago Dei*. For centuries people have asked what that really means. Here's one thing it means: We are creatures so special that God can communicate with us." Lennox adds, "We understand the universe and we can describe it in words, particularly in mathematical words. Why is the universe like that? The biblical claim is it's like that because God, the Word, created it. And God, the Word, created the human mind in His own image."

Astonishingly, God gave us the capacity to see more than what is good to eat, where is safe to rest, where the sweetest waters flow. He gave us the capacity to perceive different realms and realities, to reason and understand what is immaterial, to exercise logic, to conjecture, to imagine, and to communicate with God. All through the Bible you see people talking with God—with words. He still does, too, though many of our civilized societies chalk that up to wishful thinking, overactive imaginations, or delusion. As one who has heard from God in words, I can tell you there's a very big difference between what I can conjure in my imagination and what He says. I always know when it's He, not me, because it isn't anything I could have thought up on my own, and it always gives me insight into His heart and causes me to love Him more.

THE LONGEST WORD

Now for a look at the physical universe itself. It, too, is based on words. God built language into this universe. Besides the speech that Psalms 19 says is uttered by the glories in the skies, there are even more remarkable words in tiny places. When it comes to life itself, it's word-based on the DNA code—the human genome. What impresses me, however, is not just the 3.4 billion four-chemical-letter word that is the DNA. When Frances Collins announced the decryption of the DNA molecule, he said. "This is written in the language known hitherto only to God." But DNA is not the whole show. The body plan is not in the DNA. One biologist said DNA is just a supply list. What? I thought DNA was the big star of the age. Nope. There's more. You may have a bunch of building materials for constructing a house all neatly laid out and ready, but you need a floor plan and a particular order for assembly—foundation, structure, wiring and plumbing, etc. If you try to attach the roof before the walls go up, you have a big problem. All of this requires information. Data. Sequence. And that's not in the DNA. Something else is directing the show here. You've got epigenetics going on, overseeing gene regulation. Life is much more complex than we thought, and Darwin, himself, hadn't a clue. He said if the cell is more complex than a blob of protoplasm (I'm paraphrasing) his whole theory falls apart.

We are in the Information Age. We know information is not material. When you reduce everything to physics and chemistry, you empty it of meaning. A piece of music becomes just marks of ink on a piece of paper—no thought, structure or artistry. Try to imagine the best works of Bach happening by accident.

NAMING

Our navigation system needs to be aligned with God's coordinates, pathways, and boundaries. Our worldview will be accurate only to the degree we're in agreement with Him, not the opinions around us. The worldview that insists on absence of meaning is one of the most deadly of the faulty programming that will direct us to the garbage dump. And it's such a lie! If there's one thing that's emphasized in the Bible, it's the abundance of significant revelation and the absence of futility. God Himself says He didn't make things to be empty, formless, inert, unproductive, insignificant, barren, futile, ineffective, meaningless. Over and over He says, "Then they will know…" Significance will become clear. Purpose is revealed. Patterns and relationships and interactions will be recognized and put into formulas and words. Descriptions contain observations of process. We give things names. Just take a look anywhere in the Bible and you will find names, and within those names, there is even more meaning. I'm not talking about endless genealogies; I'm talking about God giving things names. Here's one of my favorites.

The Hebrew word for "evening" is *erev* (or *ereb*). In addition to meaning darkness, dusk, and sunset, it also carries with it its original concepts of obscurity, mixture, chaos, and increasing entropy. As evening begins to darken the earth, it's harder to see. Things become obscured, and all the color is changed to shades of dimming gray until, when the approach to darkness is complete, there is no color left at all.

Boker (or *boqer*) is the Hebrew word for "morning." It means "the breaking forth of the light" and "the dawn," but its original meaning includes the reduction of entropy. As light brightens the sky and spreads out across the earth, things become visible, then increasingly discernible. What was confusing becomes easier to understand. What was chaos becomes more orderly and color is restored to the world.

When God relates to us the specific details of His creation, He chooses to go from darkness to light, from chaos to order, from confusion to comprehensibility. He also makes divisions, boundaries, limits. Genesis says God called the darkness Night and He called the morning Day. The first named distinction we hear is the separation of light from darkness. It's as if He is telling us, "That was then. This is now. You have a new day. My mercies are new every morning." And it isn't a generic allotment of mercy, it's specifically new according to your needs on that particular day.

Every detail in the Bible is full of message and meaning. The order in which things are mentioned, the frequency of repetition, the overtones of the words. There are treasures everywhere. God moves us from darkness into light, not the other way around. Life is not about steady deterioration and loss. There are glories ahead. He has exciting revelations for us to see as he brings illumination to what was previously incomprehensible. His is the Mind that invented physics. He can handle your present darkness. And in the midst of it, will reveal Himself to you in ways you could not know under any other circumstances.

Proverbs says it's the glory of God to conceal a matter and the glory of kings to search them out. There's an intrinsic human joy in finding things—a vein of gold in the earth, a missing earring we thought we'd lost forever, a new star, a new complexity in the cell, a truth in the Word that suddenly comes to life for you and sets you free, a new view of Himself we could not otherwise ever see—God gifts us that way, and He loves it when we discover the wonders He has placed for us everywhere in His Word.

Naming is a big deal. One of the first things God did was bring the animals to Adam so he could give them names. That took a very big intellect on Adam's part, but, after all, he was in the untainted image of God before sin started the deterioration of brilliant, insightful thought. So, first, let's do away with the picture of early Man as a lumbering caveman grunting and making up words beginning with nouns and sign language. Sorry. If we're going to understand ourselves from God's purposes and point of view, we have to let go of illustrations from early childhood text books and murals painted on natural history museum walls.

Adam was given dominion of all Earth—animals, plants, waters, land, seas, air. He and Eve were to make it fruitful and fabulous, and God brought Adam the animals to name. According to Spiros Zodhiates, the act of naming is sometimes an assertion of sovereignty over the thing which is being named (Genesis 1:5). God wanted Adam to assert his own authority in this world (Genesis 2:19).

The most amazing part of this whole naming of the animals-thing for me is the honor God gave His created being. Whatever Adam called the creature, that was its name. God, Creator of everything, the greatest Mind of all, accepted Adam's choice of what each of those creatures would be called. Wow! Does that tell you something astonishing about God and His relationship with human beings? My parents let me name my goldfish and the Pontiac station wagon I drove to high school, but not their corporation. Adam was given a huge responsibility, and I believe God was pleased the way we are pleased when one of our offspring is particularly wise and insightful. God, Creator and designer of everything, Supreme Intellect and Name above every name, delights to honor human beings with this level of authority and privilege. Really? I had no idea that is how He relates to us. My thinking tends to be too small. I'm starting to realize in some ways I'm still relating to God on the level of a very young child whose biggest thrill was getting to clean the erasers for my second grade teacher!

In the Bible, we see a lot of naming going on, the most significant of all being the revelation of God Himself through names.

My father is Dr. Thomas W. Wing. He was Kay Wing's husband Tom. He was my cousins' Uncle Tom, my sons' Grandpa Wing, and my beloved daddy. He was an herbalist, chiropractor, acupuncturist, inventor, scientist, and avid amateur radio ham. His California license plates proudly displayed his call letters, W6MVK. Once when he was driving in San Francisco, a car load of young men jockeyed their car to be alongside his at a stoplight. Out the window one shouted, "Are you really W6MVK? *The* W6MVK?" It had been forty years since my dad won the Sweepstakes Contest, but he still had a reputation among the youth of radio enthusiasts generations later. They knew him by his call letters. They didn't know him by any other name.

But God has revealed Himself through many words—compound names and titles and relationships (strong tower, hiding place, Rock, buckler and shield, Bread of Life, Living Water, Alpha and Omega…) And we know Him through the incredible revelation from the burning bush when Moses asked to know the name which he could tell the suffering Hebrew people had sent him to lead them out of slavery. It's translated "I AM," and the Hebrew carries a sense of having always been and being ever present and without end. It has the huge idea of being Himself—YHWH—the sacred name of God so holy His people refused to speak it aloud, and over the years they forgot how. They were being respectful, not wanting to offend Him by mispronouncing his name, but everything I see in the Bible makes me think He wants a close, deep, intimate relationship with us, not a distant one, no matter how respectful it is.

Whenever you see "LORD" in the King James version, those caps let you know that's the I AM name of God.

"I AM. I AM Who I AM." Hebrews 11:6 says he who comes to God must believe that He is. Some translations say "must believe he exists," but that can't be right. James 2:19 says, "You believe in God; you do well. So do the demons, and they have the good sense to tremble."

No, just believing God exists is not big enough. He who comes to God must believe He is. He is His own definition of Himself, not a name that tries to take dominion or authority over Him or makes Him smaller. It's really important for us to know our God is not small, because sometimes we get to looking at our bank account or our waning health, or our troubled families and we feel hopeless and overwhelmed. YHWH is never at a loss. He spoke light into darkness, order into chaos, fruitfulness where there was nothing but bare land before, and the skies and seas teemed with life at His Word. His Word has not lost an iota of power since then, nor the slightest creativity in finding just the right solution to whatever troubles your heart.

Meaning, significance, connection, personal involvement—they are all present in God's names delivered to us in the pages of His divinely authored Book. Here are some of my favorite discoveries. YHWH, the covenant name Moses heard spoken from the burning bush—that's not the first time it shows up in Scripture. I found it by looking for the word LORD in caps in the King James Version. The first time it appears is in Genesis 2:4. In Hebrew writing, they often state something once and then state it again with additional information added. All through Genesis 1, Creator is Elohim, the Godhead, the Trinity, but when we see creation described the second time, it reads, "These are the generations of the heavens and of the earth when they were created, in the day that the LORD God made the earth and the heavens." There, at the very start of everything we would ever know or need to know, God reveals to us through his covenant name that He is actively involved in our lives. He is not off attending to more important matters than our puny worries, He is working, and it's on such a grand scale we cannot comprehend it all. Even his name, YHWH, emphasizes that truth. YHWH is actually a verb. It embodies the idea of action. There's energy and movement, effort already expressed on our behalf, and covenant to be revealed in the fullness of time.

The next time is three verses later, when God forms Adam from the dust. In all the other creative acts, God spoke them into being, but Genesis 2:7 specifies He formed him from the dust, the Potter shaping the clay. Touch is involved. Scripture says, "And YHWH Elohim formed man of the dust of the ground..." Right then we have the Presence of the Deliverer Who would rescue them from slavery, the One Whose innocent blood would cover what they lost in Eden even before they had ever seen the Tree.

GOD'S OPINION OF HIS CREATION

God went out of His way to emphasize the reality of His creation as a magnificent means for Him to communicate with us. His fingerprints are everywhere. His care is in the fine tuning so precise it boggles the mind. It's in the mathematical words that give us ways of comprehending the orbits and gravitational pulls of planets and moons and the relationships among stars. It's in the information of epigenetics that turns genes on and off in just the right sequences to bring about developments, functions, and consequences. It's in the impressions He speaks to our hearts in intuition, pictures, discernments, and the Word of God He quickens by His Spirit to leap off the page into our hearts as *rhema,* spoken revelation individually given.

So God looked at each day's work and pronounced it *towb,* except the sixth day when He gave Adam and Eve each other and moral law and dominion—the charge to care for all of creation and said it was *very towb.* In the Septuagint translation, the "good" God pronounces in Genesis 1 and 2 is *kalos*—beautiful, winsome, gracious, fruitful, noble, righteous, lovely, good. And He blessed all He made. And He blessed the man and the woman. And He pronounced them all good. That's God's opinion of matter, purpose, and how He feels about all of it. He said it was all good. He made it that way on purpose. He loved it. He made it fruitful and pleasant and beautiful. It was perfect. There was no suffering or sorrow or misunderstanding or division or strife. And then God gave Adam and Eve authority on Earth. They were free to expand the garden in any way they chose, and there was no death. They had day-to-day fellowship, the man and the woman and their Creator. God gave them meaningful work, harmony with animals and their environment, a superb intellect, one command, and free will.

Then came the temptation that has been repeated billions of times since then—"Has God said…?" Eve fell for the temptation that questioned the Word of God, the wisdom and goodness of God, and decided to take matters into her own hands. Adam didn't even need to be tricked. He just took the fruit and instantly there was division—shame and blame and hiding. Even so, God had prepared a way back for them. He covered them in tunics made of the skins of innocent animals, the first of many deaths that would follow. The coverings represented the sacrifice of the Lamb of God that was yet to come, and, Scripture tells us, had already been established before the foundation of the world. God gave free will. He understood the risk. He knew the consequences, and He made a way to restore human beings to Himself. Though Eve had released what would become compounding horrors upon His beautiful, perfect creation, the Lord would bring through her offspring the One who would redeem everything that was lost. He told her the serpent would bruise the heel of her seed, but the Savior would crush the serpent's head—forever.

In faith—the leaning of the entire human personality on God in absolute confidence and trust in His power, wisdom, and goodness—that's the way Jesus did it. Hebrews says without faith it's impossible to please God. He who comes to God must believe that He is. Is what? Is Who He says He is—not our definition or our judgment of what He should be. We must believe He IS—the I AM, the unlimited, the fullness of power, wisdom and goodness. He is Himself, and He wants us to know there is reward for those who seek Him. The reward is a supernatural life that transforms us and everyone and everything around us. Jesus did it, and He said we are to do the same. This that we see—it's not all there is or all that can be. *Zoe*—God life—is ours now, not just after we leave for our eternity with Him and loved ones who have gone before. When *bios* is over, *zoe* is just beginning its full, unhindered, unobscured expression in the reality that is God's intended life for us forever.

"Now faith is the assurance (the confirmation, the title deed) of the things [we] hope for, being the proof of things [we] do not see and the conviction of their reality [faith perceiving as real fact what is not revealed to the senses]." (Hebrews 11:1 AMPC)

He has something for us to do now—to walk in a free-will choice to follow His will instead of our own sinful way, depending on Him in communion with Father, empowered by Holy Spirit, with a charge to transform the world around us the way Jesus did, bringing the Will of God to Earth in the extraordinary life God intended for us from the beginning. And until we see Him face to face, He says He will never leave us or fail us or forsake us, and our turn-by-turn guidance will guide us unerringly to where we are meant to be—with Him in the fulfilling life He designed for us, bestowed on us, and we will someday continue to live in a whole new kind of heaven and Earth when everything is completed to the uttermost.

God is communicating and nothing is arbitrary. He wrote it in His Book. He reveals it to our hearts. Repetitions matter. First mention matters. Details matter. Words and names and individuals matter. It all has meaning, significance, purpose. And it transforms us into His image as we express His heart and spread His blessings to all those around us wherever we go.

"CQ CQ," He calls to us from the heavenlies. "CQ CQ. This is YHWH. Anybody want to talk?"

5

HOW DO WE SEE OUR WORLD?

Lake County has been praised for great air quality—the best in California—but for the past five years or so, high temperatures, low humidity, drought, and powerful winds have set our world on fire. We have been surrounded by raging wildfires that kept every day gray for weeks and weeks at a time. The smoke was dense with particles from burning trees, buildings, vehicles, glass, rubber, metal, carpets, furniture, and family heirlooms. We were advised not to go outside because the air was so toxic. From my deck, I could no longer see the lake. The sky was filled with poisonous smoke. It came in through window frames and doors. Even in my living room, my lungs hurt and my eyes burned. It was so pervasive we couldn't keep from breathing it. But after a while, it became normal. Every day was dismal gray. There never had been a lake. Beyond the few close trees, there was nothing there. Nothing at all.

The atmosphere of this present age is dense with the prevailing worldview. It's so pervasive and we're so used to it that we don't even realize it's affecting us.

In the last chapters, we explored the divine origins of our Bible with its miraculous hepatic structure, words hidden in equidistant letter sequences, the historicity of biblical accounts and people, and the messages God is communicating in His Word-based universe through patterns, repetitions, names, words, and even His choice of languages. One thing is clear: He cares. He's personal. He's present. And He loves us more than we can possibly imagine. Do we really know that? Do we believe it enough to base our thoughts, actions, and choices on it? My guess is that most of us, having grown up in contemporary culture, have absorbed concepts about the nature of life that contradict the messages that God wants us to understand. I think we can all use some examination of what we're being told is the origin and nature of reality because those fundamentals affect our own ability to believe God's truth and walk with Him in it.

WORLDVIEW

Worldview is the foundation from which people operate, the basics of their beliefs and orientation toward life, the lens through which they interpret reality. Here are some of the questions involved in worldview:

"Why am I here?"

"What's my purpose in life?"

"Is there a God?"

"What's the nature of a human being?"

"What is the meaning of life?"

"Where will I go when I die?"

"What is the thing or the entity or the process from which everything else comes?"

According to the prevailing worldview, the answer to the last question is scientific materialism—the reduction of everything to energy and matter. This belief system asserts that life came about by accident and continued through a process of random mutation and evolution by minute changes over time. This process is entirely arbitrary, undirected, and inadvertent, with no design, intention, meaning, or purpose. It's random. Nothing has significance. So let's take those worldview questions and answer them in the context of scientific materialism.

"Why am I here?" Sperm, egg, sex, chance.

"What's my purpose in life?" There is none. You can make up your own.

"Is there a God?" No.

"What's the nature of a human being?" animal

"What is the meaning of life?" There is none. You can make that up as well.

"Where will I go when I die?" Nowhere. There is nothing after death.

The most important aspect of the theory of evolution that you need to know is it insists there is no deliberate, intentional, purposeful Cause for life. In other words, there is no God. Without God, there is no spiritual realm, creation, design, eternal life, heaven, hell, or reason for anything, no right, wrong, or intrinsic value. The materialistic view of life completely rejects God and considers the Bible fables and fairytales. Grownups don't need God. They have science. And science has the answers to everything. Here is a quote from a popular university text book on evolutionary biology that is currently in use: "By coupling the undirected, purposeless variations to the blind, uncaring process of natural selection, Darwin made theological or spiritual explanations of life superfluous."

Okay, so they don't believe in God. It's their choice. God gave to every human the ability to say "yes" to Him—or "no." But some scientists have taken this on as a war where one or the other must lose, and they hope it's belief in God. Why? Darwinistic Atheist Richard Dawkins says it's to save the naive and ignorant from their "primitive superstitions."

There are lots and lots of really good scientists who believe in Jesus and creation and the veracity of the Bible, but rather than present what they express so well in their own talks and books, I want to concentrate on the parts of scientific materialism that affect us subtly and destructively. The first is the assertion that evolution is absolutely true and only ignorant fools don't believe it because, as one spokesman said, there's such overwhelming evidence for evolution that it's obviously proven to be true. They're also claiming everything came from nothing, and that life itself is included in the mechanical appearance of the foundations of what has become our universe, our planet, and all the complexities upon it.

First, the scientific method is based on observation, suppositions, and repeatable verifications. Since nobody was there to observe creation, and it cannot be duplicated in the laboratory, any suppositions about the origins of life are theories. Any claims to the contrary are not scientific.

The big problem with these materialistic theories is their inadequacy to explain all the realities in the world around us, especially the presence of information. Data is not an observable substance. As you read this page, you are receiving thoughts and ideas. How do the material substances of ink and paper produce that information? I'm not talking about the shapes of letters and combinations that make words. I'm talking the physical substances of paper and ink, their chemical components and molecular structure. This rather simplistic example is actually such a powerful contradiction to the beliefs of ontological reductionism (which says everything can be reduced to energy and matter) that it led a number of scientists—from Christians to atheists—to coin a new term, "intelligent design."

Intelligent design is not "warmed-over creationism," as many think. Dr. Paul Nelson describes it this way, "Intelligent Design is the study of patterns in nature that are best explained as a result of intelligence. It's a minimal commitment scientifically to the possibility of detecting intelligent causation." Proponents of intelligent design include scientists of various faiths and agnostics. Belief in Intelligent Design is not a commitment to the Judeo-Christian God. It only recognizes the principles of random natural selection and undirected evolution as inadequate to explain life on this planet.

Biologist Dr. Stephen C. Meyer states, "The postulation of intelligent design not only helps to resolve a long-standing scientific mystery, it also speaks to a larger question because what we see in the origin of complex life on Earth is not evidence of just undirected process. Instead we see that life was designed, that life was planned, that it was intended."

One of the big arguments for intelligent design is the complexity of our universe. How do evolutionists answer that? This is what Richard Dawkins wrote in his book, The Blind Watchmaker, "Biology is the study of complicated things that give the appearance of having been designed for a purpose." Dawkins' premise is that this seeming requirement of design is only an illusion. Later, he wrote, "The universe we observe has precisely the properties we should expect if at bottom there is no design, no purpose, no evil, no good—nothing but blind, pitiless indifference."

So far we have the assertion that everything came from nothing (which is an incredibly huge insult to God, Who created it all), that it all came about through random mutations and survival of the mutations that are most advantageous, and a rejection of Creator God, because that would require purpose and deliberate design instead of accidents. There is such an aversion to the idea of intelligent design that it is labeled "pseudo science" and competent scientists have lost their jobs for even implying it might have some merit in scientific investigation. To me, that kind of censorship is a completely unscientific way to approach any investigation of an area of study.

But moving right along, what is the message of the concept of a single common ancestor? This is one of Darwinian evolution's basic tenets. What does it tell us about all life on Earth, and how does that affect our understanding of ourselves as human beings? Let's go to the branching tree of species that is so often portrayed even in biology textbooks today.

Let's ignore the Cambrian Explosion with its sudden appearance of vast diversity in body plans including such complexities as articulated legs and compound eyes. Let's disregard the absence of transitional forms in the fossil record. Let's assume we all descended from a common ancestor with the internal sophistication of jelly, and see where that leads. It means we're all equal. From asparagus to alligator, we are all essentially the same—varying complexities and capabilities depending on random mutation and natural selection. And if scientific terminology categorizes things as animal, mineral, vegetable, we humans fall into Group 1. We're all animals.

What do animals do? They eat, reproduce, and fight to stay alive. They compete for territory, social privilege, and look for whatever provides security, progeny, and the best chance of surviving the long winter. If there's mother-love, it's hormones released from pregnancy. If there's loyalty to a mate, it's a function of the particular variation in the type of animal you happen to be. And everything is about instinct, chemical reactions, and survival mechanisms hardwired into the brain because that's a random variation that had good results and has been passed along to subsequent generations who get to benefit from that chance advantage. No wonder so many people these days act like animals! That's what they are taught they are.

Of course, not all people who believe in evolution are atheists violently opposed to the Christian faith. I have cherished friends of many years who are agnostic or adhere to other faiths, and they don't talk like Richard Dawkins. But the truth remains that the basic tenets of Darwinian evolution affect us and our society. Most of us have grown up with these views of how life originated and how it functions and they are diametrically opposed to what God tells us about what He made and how it works. How can we align with His values when we don't even notice we're accepting a false reality?

CAN SCIENCE EXPLAIN EVERYTHING?

I guess there is the appearance or the assertion that science has the answers to everything—or that everything can be eventually explained by science if we keep looking long enough. Eventually everything will give up its secrets to the power of scientific investigation. But does it really? Einstein said you can talk about the ethics of science but you can't talk about the scientific basis of ethics. Science doesn't tell you what you ought to do and it does not answer the question of meaning. To find those, you need philosophy, history, music, art, and literature.

Scripture says without a vision the people perish. They cast off restraint. They flounder. They can't control themselves. Darwinism says there is no purpose in anything in general, and certainly none intrinsic in a human life. So I asked my granddaughter Gracie (Thomas' second daughter) if she thought God has a purpose for her life. In response, in-between classes that she said had already made her lose her mind, she sent this deeply compassionate and beautiful answer, and I'm so proud of this young lady who shows a spiritual maturity you wouldn't necessarily expect to find in a person still in college.

"I know God has a purpose for my life. I'm not exactly sure what the specifics are, but I think it has something to do with helping those around me and reminding them that there is a God who is capable of great things and kindness. Growing up, I've been around a lot of people with tragic lives and who don't believe God can exist because of how lonely they feel. I especially feel this among the youth kids at my church who have grown up with the church. I believe that God has given me the heart and the ability to share my own experiences and God's love with these kids so that they remember they aren't alone or abandoned.

Lots of love, Gracie"

Let's get a new vision for our lives. Scientific materialism leaves out the most important part—God. His ways are wonderful. His creation is good. We are created in His image. We have language and the ability to postulate the existence of planets we cannot see, based on mathematical calculations covering distances only a divinely-created intellect can comprehend. We are like our Daddy. He gave us intelligence, but knowledge was never meant to be a god. Our mind is gifted with the capacity to receive direct communication and revelation from One Who desires to share His secrets with us, His children. Then, with His life moving through our beings, we can see the needs of those around us who are floundering in darkness, and, like Gracie, reach out with the transforming love that comes from heaven alone.

How does belief in purposeless, meaningless, random undirected process express itself in real life? Ontological Reductionism says everything can be reduced to energy and matter. What passes for free will is just pre-programmed neurological patterns interacting with the pre-programmed patterns of other people. So do we have free will or don't we? The Bible says we do. In fact, of all the gifts and unique blessings God conferred on His children, free will is the most powerful. He gave us the ability to tell Him No. He gave us the choice whether to love Him or ignore Him. Why? Because only love that comes from free-will choice is real, and God risked losing many of His special creations to their free-will choice to please themselves and do "what is right in their own eyes," because only freely given love is real, and that's the only relationship worth having with Him and one another.

What you believe about the origin of life affects everything. You either believe there's a God Who created all life (including you) for His purposes, or, if you believe the ontological reductionist worldview, you're a random convergence of chemicals and biological functions—just another one of the many species trying to survive. This one foundational belief affects everything you think, do, become, and, ultimately, where you will spend eternity.

The prevailing worldview obscures the reality of God's truth subtly and pervasively, which is why I wanted you to have the information on science that I've written in this chapter. There is much, much more, and I recommend that you revel in the wealth of wonderful teachings of such godly men as mathematician John Lennox, information scientist Chuck Missler, nano technologist and chemist James Tour, astrophysicist Jason Lisle, biologist Stephen C. Meyer, physicist Barry Setterfield, and creation scientist Carl Baugh. They're smart guys who know their stuff and, more importantly, are thrilled that their names are written in the Lamb's Book of Life. But to end this chapter, God gave me four things you need to know about science and the Bible.

1. God created everything. It took intelligence, design, intension, and forethought. Science verifies the requirement of information for everything to function. There is nothing arbitrary, inadvertent, or accidental in what God created.

2. God made it good. There was no suffering, division, or death until the Fall. Why is this important? Because people look at all the suffering in the world and blame God, or decide He doesn't exist. They don't factor in the Fall because they believe Genesis is a fictional tale. They look at the huge skeleton of Tyrannosaurus Rex and conclude the prehistoric world was full of violence and fear—the big and powerful preying on the gentle and peaceable. Obviously there was no safety or security for anything weaker or smaller. Survival of the fittest. But that's not how God designed it. Dr. Jason Lisle, who founded the Biblical Science Institute, provides extensive

evidence in this regard. It's so significant that I'm including a few of his insights to help you rethink what we've been taught.

Please consider this different way of seeing the pre-Fall world. According to Genesis 2, animals were created on the fifth and sixth days. Dinosaurs included. All creatures lived in harmony with everything and everybody in the Garden and they all ate plants (Gen 2:29). Yes, some had sharp, serrated teeth, but so do fruit bats. Rinds and shells can require that kind of equipment. And some dinosaurs were very large, but "big" does not equate with "carnivore" or "mean." Elephants are big, and they eat plants.

Science tells us dinosaurs appeared on Earth millions of years before humans. Think about it. That would mean there were countless terrors, fears, sufferings, pain, devourings, and deaths. Meanwhile, other life forms were finding their sweet spot, the point at which they could stop evolving because they were successful enough to survive. All this went on for eons before humans evolved to the point of standing upright and meriting the label "*homo sapiens*," "wise (or knowledgeable) man." But wait! Genesis 3 says death did not enter God's perfect creation till after the Fall. How could *homo sapiens* be predated by millions of years of agonizing deaths as well as trillions of experiments in life forms (most of which failed), the genetic roulette going on until life in its present complexity was established. Looking at this model of the history of Earth, would you call this view of creation "good"?

3. The Bible is not myths, legends, and fairytales. Noah's ark has been the target of a lot of ridicule, and even Christians tend to think of it in terms of Sunday school stories with cartoon images of a little fat boat with animals sticking their heads out the windows. Dr. Lisle has done the math. The capacity of the ark is the equivalent of 522 railway stock cars and, considering all the kinds of animals, he calculated

there would be room for every one. In fact, they would inhabit only half the space, which would leave ample room for other things, such as food. Noah's ark is not a fairytale. Which brings us to the fourth thing God wanted you to know.

4. The story of the ark and the evidence for the world wide Flood are proof that the account in Genesis 6 is not symbolic, ancient literary fiction or even a legend. Why is this important? Because it was a severe judgment on rampant, widespread, unremitting wickedness, a time when people were flagrantly disregarding God.

Hold on a second! In Genesis 4:26, it says, "Then men began to call on the name of the LORD." Doesn't that show not everyone deserved to be destroyed? A lot of Bible readers have wondered about that, me included. I'm so grateful for Chuck Missler, who helped design The Blue Letter Bible with its easy access to the original languages and accurate translations of each word. He explained that "call upon YHWH's name" didn't mean they were crying out to Him for help, mercy, or communion. It meant they called Him by other names or by His real name, but attributed to Him wrong characteristics. It is better translated, "Then men began to blaspheme the name of the LORD." The reason I mention this is because there are many these days who call God by other names. Others attribute to God characteristics that do not represent His true character. They are using His name in vain. That means they have emptied it of meaning, significance, power, and truth.

Jesus said, "And as it was in the days of Noah, so it will be also in the days of the Son of Man: They ate, they drank, they married wives, they were given in marriage, until the day that Noah entered the ark, and the flood came and destroyed them all... Likewise as it was also in the days of Lot: They ate, they drank, they bought, they sold, they planted, they built; but on the day that Lot went out of Sodom it rained fire and brimstone from heaven and destroyed them all. Even so will it be in the day when the Son of Man is revealed." (Luke 17:26, 27, 29, 30 NKJV)

If we are to align with God in these times, it's crucial that we accept the reality of the Flood, the ark, and the judgments He has already executed on Earth. Jesus tells us there will be another judgment, the final one, but there's something more He wants us to know. Notice that Jesus refers to the time when Lot went out from Sodom before the fire fell. Remember the conversation Abraham had with the Lord? God said, "Shall I hide from Abraham, My servant and friend, what I am going to do?" (Genesis 18:17) Precisely because Abraham is His friend, God tells him, whereupon Abraham has that amazing exchange with the Lord of the universe, gradually reducing to ten the number of righteous men required to avoid annihilation. Of course, we know there weren't even nine, and Lot, himself, wasn't all that pure, but God made sure Lot was safe before the fire fell. Now here's what touches me. In Genesis 19:29, it says, "When God ravaged and destroyed the cities of the plain, He [earnestly] remembered Abraham [imprinted and fixed him indelibly on His mind], and He sent Lot out of the midst of the overthrow when He overthrew the cities where Lot lived." (AMPC)

It's significant that Jesus connects these two judgments with his imminent return. In the account of the ark, Noah preached all the years that he worked on constructing the boat, but apparently nobody believed him. Only those whom God had called (including animals) went in. However, in the story of the judgment on the cities, Abraham interceded for Lot and God honored His friend by making sure Lot was safe before the fire fell. I think God wants us to know we can make a difference. We can intercede for people and they can be saved. It won't be angels dragging the reluctant ones from their homes, but us—you and I—partnering with the Savior of their souls in ways He will show us, ways that will prepare and reach their hearts with the truth that will make them free. Remember, Jesus is delaying His coming because He paid a terrible price for each human being alive on Earth today and He's not willing that any of them perish, wicked as they might be at this very moment. You know some of them personally, and there are others you don't know except through the news, and you may be tempted to hate them. I'm not saying God will have you pray for all of them, but please be open to the nudging of the Holy Spirit if He makes you aware of the drug dealers next door, the local big shot who picks on you, or professors who tell you God is unnecessary now that we have science. The Lord may be asking you to pray for them. There's still time, and I can tell you that more than one former Jesus-hater is deeply grateful for the prayers that opened her eyes and turned her around.

Creation, Eden, the Fall, the Flood, the ark, the people and events in the Bible—if these accounts are true, if the people in the accounts are real, they surpass mere illustrations of moral character and become part of a legacy of God's interaction with human beings—a legacy of which we are currently partakers, and the same God Who delivered Noah and his family from a society so wicked God mourned for their self-selected degradation, can get us and our loved ones prepared to make a difference when unprecedented calamities come.

6

DEFINING REALITY

To this point, we've compared the worldview that God gives us in His Word and we've looked at the prevailing worldview of scientific materialism based on the absolute absence of meaning, purpose, ethics, free will, life after death, or loving personal God. Let's look a little farther into the effects of a worldview based on the ideas of evolution, natural selection, and survival of the fittest. What does a materialistic worldview translate to in philosophical thought?

Not surprisingly, Darwin's theories deeply affected thought starting in the nineteenth century and continuing into today. It inspired Nietzsche to create the dismal worldview he called "Nihilism" (*nihil* in Latin meaning "nothing") "a viewpoint that traditional values and beliefs are unfounded and that existence is senseless and useless." Really? Who would want to believe in nothing? What a depressing way to see your life! As you can imagine, that kind of worldview can lead to a whole bunch of very unpleasant behaviors, beliefs, and dead ends. How sad that people would choose to believe there's no meaning in life rather than trusting there is a Transcendent Reality, one that gives each life incredible value and potential. Do you think this poisonous atmosphere of hopelessness could be empowering the increasing despair that manifests in alcoholism, drug abuse, and suicides?

In literature, Darwin's theories brought about a philosophy called "Existentialism" which emphasized the absence of meaning. You have to create your own, since there is no God to confer value on you or give meaning to your life. The literary works spawned by Existentialism were powerful and heartbreaking, making a very good case for futility and hopelessness. Sartre was one of the best at doing that, and I wish I had never read his plays. I was in college, being systematically taught that everything I'd believed to be true was not, including my own identity. I was faced with the daunting task of having to redefine myself in view of all the new realities I was being immersed into, and Sartre plunged me right to the bottom. But Jesus pulled me out of the Pit, and I am eternally grateful.

Philosopher David Hume is best known for his empiricism, skepticism, and materialism. He claimed there are no innate ideas, that all human knowledge comes solely from experience. He declared miracles impossible because they violate the laws of nature. This view of miracles was enthusiastically embraced as the last word on the subject, an indisputable argument that is still cited today. And, guess what? If there are no miracles, there can be no Christianity because it starts with the miraculous birth of Emmanuel, God incarnated as a human baby, fully God while being fully Man. Then there were all those miracles for three years—starting with water into wine, with healings, storms stilled, and resurrections of dead people, deliverances from demons, plus multiplications of bread and fish, and more, before the final and most significant miracle of them all—the resurrection and the empty tomb. After that, Jesus was seen by 500 people in the forty days He walked and taught and ate fish with those who had seen Him die, and then He ascended, lifted into the sky while they watched. How can that be? According to Hume, it can't.

But wait! We don't live in a closed system. In the universe God created, natural laws are not violated when a different energy is introduced from outside our reality. John Lennox explains it this way. A billiard ball rolling across the table doesn't suddenly begin to fly. That would violate natural laws. However, if I pick up the billiard ball, no natural laws have been violated. I've simply introduced a different energy.

The whole of our existence is supernatural—"super" meaning "above." Above the natural, the realm of matter and energy. There is the mysterious encoding of information, data in mathematical precision that allows everything to function synergistically, interconnected, intricately and brilliantly designed. From Beginning to End, our known universe and our beautiful planet with its wondrous features and life forms, is meticulously fine-tuned and maintained by the will of the One Who created it all for His divine purposes and pleasure.

SITUATIONAL ETHICS

Situational Ethics was introduced into schools during the time I was teaching in public schools. This worldview is best known for its lifeboat exercise. You're in a lifeboat with an elderly lady, a young boy, a drunkard—I don't remember the exact occupants—but the idea is there is only so much food and water and supplies are running low. You are asked to choose which of them you would throw overboard first.

In Situational Ethics, there are no absolutes, no right or wrong. Everything depends on the situation. What is immoral or unethical in one situation may be an appropriate action in another. It all depends on the circumstances. This is logical if your view of the world is that it happened all by itself and everything on it is the result of random, unguided process and natural selection—survival of the fittest with limited resources and no accountability to God. Without God, there are no absolutes, there's no intrinsic morality, and no ethics exist beyond what we decide ourselves.

I was not a Christian when, as a young teacher, I first encountered the lifeboat of situational ethics. I worried about who would be best to throw overboard. It created an underlying anxiety in my heart. There are many situations in life where society makes it seem as if we have to assign value and decide whether we will try to keep things intact or throw something away—a spouse, a child, our standards of right and wrong—in order to survive. Without absolute Truth to anchor our souls, choices become arbitrary according to who is making the value judgment.

REAL PEOPLE

It's one thing to read about Daniel continuing to pray though it got him thrown into the lions' den, and quite another to see ordinary people living in much more recent times who looked into the face of their own deaths and made hard choices. If this life is all you have, it makes sense that you would do everything you can to prolong that life, but not everyone is given over to survival of the fittest. There have been those who put themselves at risk to help Jews escape the Nazi camps, such as Schindler and the family of Corrie ten Boom. And there were the musicians on Titanic, who chose to continue to play music from the top of the Grand Staircase to calm passengers as they were being loaded into lifeboats. When faced with a real lifeboat dilemma, they made their choice, and passengers in lifeboats reported hearing "Nearer, My God, To Thee" floating over the icy waters as the ship went down.

Nate Saint was a missionary in Ecuador. When he was getting the little yellow plane ready for what he and four other men hoped would be their first physical contact with the most violent tribe in the jungles of Ecuador, his young son Steve watched anxiously. "Are you going to take a gun?" he asked.

"Yes."

"If they attack you, will you defend yourself?"

Nate Saint paused and looked at his boy, "No, son. Because we're ready for heaven and they're not."

Only a short time later, all five of the missionaries were dead, speared by the men they had gone to befriend.

After I became a Christian, I thought again about the life-boat exercise. And, sharing Nate Saint's worldview, I knew immediately who I would throw overboard. Me. And I would let the others know where I was going to be after I died, and encourage them to choose for themselves a relationship with the God of the Universe in whatever was to come.

It's inspiring to hear there are well-documented historical accounts of those who exercised their God-given free will to go against overwhelming powers and pressures because they lived by a higher standard, knew their destiny was Heaven, and refused to compromise.

BECK WEATHERS

I find it really interesting that Christians aren't the only ones who choose for the well-being of others. There is an internal moral compass that tells every human being what's right and what's wrong. I bring this up because Situational Ethics tries to disconnect ethical choices from any external values, but Romans 1 says God wrote them on each human heart. Call it conscience or exposure to influences, it still belies the capability of situational ethics to bring about a secure and satisfying life.

Here's my favorite example of a man operating from a strong moral compass in an extreme circumstance.

In 1996, Beck Weathers was left for dead after passing out in a blizzard on Mt. Everest that stranded a group of climbers. Miraculously he woke up the next morning and managed to find his way back to his group, and they helped him down to Camp 1, which was still very high—2,000 feet above where any helicopter had landed before. Back home, Beck's wife was determined to get him rescued. She and her friends called everyone they could and finally reached a secretary at the Embassy who said, "I know a man. He's always believed that he has a brave heart, but never has had the chance to know."

They asked him to do the rescue. The pilot said he would try, but no promises.

While Weathers waited for the helicopter, another injured climber was brought down. "It was clear that the helicopter was there to pick me up," Weathers said. He discussed it with the others there and Beck made his decision. He said, "I couldn't go in the helicopter and leave him. I would have spent a lifetime regretting that decision. You want to survive these things but you want to come through it with some sense that you've behaved well—that you've done the right thing. So I gave the position I had to him and they took off."

Weathers was sure the pilot would not try it again, but he did. And this time Weathers did not hesitate. He jumped in and the pilot tipped the helicopter off the icy edge, dropping like a stone through the impossibly thin air till the valiantly rotating blades caught denser air and they made it safely back. Weathers said, "The pilot didn't do it because there was any kind of fame or glory. He just did it because it was the right thing to do. And I think he did it because he does have a brave heart."

I was so moved by Weathers' remarks that I watched his interview multiple times. Though he was severely injured by his ordeal and would lose crucial body parts, he chose to give up his place because he didn't want to spend a lifetime regretting that he had gone to safety while leaving another man to die. Weathers' actions demonstrate His strong moral compass and exposes the inadequacy of Situational Ethics to guide a person's choice in ways that bring life, peace, and no regrets. The act of declaring yourself justified in how you decide to survive does not protect you from experiencing the consequences of your choices. That's the part that gets left out. You still have to live with yourself afterwards, and it's hard to shut off the truth in your heart. Weathers is not a Christian, yet he showed by his actions that he would rather die than spend the rest of his life regretting his choice not to behave well, or do the right thing.

Perspectives

Psalm 135:18 says you become like the god you worship. The only One you can worship Who is not an idol is God. If what you believe, cling to, trust in, rely on, and give absolute devotion to is faith in the absence of God, design, purpose, with no evil, no good—nothing but blind, pitiless indifference, is that what you become?

If you believe there is nothing beyond this material world, you are free to create your own meaning, significance, and reality. And anything you decide to do to improve the species, including yourself, is acceptable. Since you are not designed by a purposeful, loving God, you are free to change anything you don't like—your figure, your face, your gender. You may redefine marriage, do whatever pleases you to give you pleasure, power, more influence, bigger territory. Everything you see is fair game for your purposes. Everything is a potential resource—the land, the water, the seas, the plants, animals, and other human beings.

Since human life is not intrinsically valuable, you may eliminate what does not advance your agenda. That includes getting rid of anything that hinders your own satisfaction. Since marriage is a man-made institution, and the limitations it imposes on sexual expressions are cultural, monogamy and fidelity really don't apply to enlightened human beings. Sadly, even Christians fall into this one, ignoring the many Scriptures that specifically address the importance of sexual purity in a life that is given to Jesus. All through the Bible, worship of sex was one of the forms of idolatry that brought God's judgment on cities, kingdoms, and people groups, including God's own. Is God a huge spoilsport? No. He's the Creator and He knows what sexual immorality does to the human heart, not to mention the damage to relationships and all the unwanted children who are born…or not…because of this lust for physical pleasure. God created us to do what Jesus did on Earth and more, but we have to take Him seriously—about everything He said. This is such an insidious trap and it works so easily and well on God's people. Purity is so powerful—pure water, pure air, pure light. In these dark days, God wants to pour His pure power through those who take Him seriously and do not walk in the ways of the world that tell us we can do whatever we like no matter who it hurts because it's survival of the fittest and there are no external absolutes and no one to account to afterwards because there is no Afterwards.

Moving right along, because there is no eternal soul or destiny for each individual life, you may also freely conduct experiments in genetic engineering, deciding who is fit to live and who is not, who is fit to breed and who is not. Who is inferior and who is not. And who is to say you are not qualified to make these judgments? There aren't any standards, external absolutes, and no life is intentional. It's all random genetics with absolutely no destiny intrinsic in any human being. In this framework, you can see how situational ethics makes perfect sense. There is no God so you get to decide who matters and who does not. And if this life is all there is and then you rot, the most important thing is to keep yourself alive.

But what if you believe God is personal and deeply committed to you? What if He says He will never leave you or fail you or forsake you, that He has engraved you on the palms of His hands? I wonder if that engraving has anything to do with nails.

What if God is not pitiless, capricious, indifferent, tyrannical, or vicious? What if He's kind, generous, patient, loving, protective, a provider of all our needs? What if He has purpose for us here on Earth and a place for us after we leave it? What if He paid the ultimate price in blood so we could have all these things and more? If that's the God we believe in, what will our lives become as we worship Him?

THE INVISIBLE WORLD

We've looked at the philosophy and literature that results from an atheistic worldview, from the perspective that says we're all animals—-matter and energy. If you can't feel it, smell it, taste it, hear it, experience it, it doesn't exist. Except there's this thing about consciousness. What is it? Are we merely molecules, or is the real person invisible—and eternal? I keep thinking of the hundreds of stories about people who have died or been in surgery and left their bodies only to return with startlingly accurate accounts of what was done during the surgery or what was going on elsewhere. One woman who had been in an automobile accident went to see what was happening at her church. They were praying for her, and she peered over the pastor's shoulder to look at the Bible from which he was preaching that morning. Later he went to visit her in the hospital and she told him what he had preached and the Scripture he was using as his text. He opened his Bible and showed her the passages that were marked just as she had recalled.

What do atheists do about those multitudes of verified experiences? The Bible is full of references to the invisible realm—the realities that cannot be seen. Peter says this material world is going to melt with fervent heat. Revelation records a destruction of the world as we know it, all evil and defilement decimated, replaced by a new heaven and a new Earth. What we see now is not all we get, and Christians these days will be much better able to navigate the coming storms if our lives are built on the truths of God's Word, anchored on the solid Rock, with a future that includes Eternity.

Now let's look at life lived from a Christian worldview.

WHAT JOHN LENNOX LEARNED

John Lennox grew up with very unusual parents in Northern Ireland, a highly sectarian country. They were Christian without being sectarian. When John was a boy, his father had a store that employed thirty or forty people. Hostility between Catholics and Protestants had been fierce and violent for decades, yet John's father made a point of hiring equal numbers of Catholics and Protestants. For this, his store was bombed and it almost killed John's brother, who needed 300 stitches in the face and it damaged him psychologically.

When young John asked his father, "Dad, why do you do that?"

His father said, "It's very clear. Think about what Genesis says about all human beings—they're made in the image of God. And that means that they all, whatever they believe, are of equal value and we need to respect them."

Lennox said, "That's the first big thing he built into me. It's stuck with me lifelong, especially when I'm debating people I disagree with profoundly."

Today, John Lennox is known for debating the world's most famous atheists, brilliantly showing through logic and reason that science richly supports, not only creation, but the existence of the God behind it. To me, the one thing that distinguishes John Lennox in these debates is his gentle kindness and unflappable good humor. He is disarming in the true sense of the word. He is not overcome by evil, but overcomes evil with good—good science, good humor, and goodness as a gracious, God-honoring human being. We do not need to be afraid of any of the world's arguments, no matter how powerful they seem, no matter how forcefully and convincingly they are asserted. Jesus was not insulted and retaliatory when various religious leaders tried to trap Him under the guise of asking spiritual questions. He let the Holy Spirit which dwelt within Him, His knowledge of Scripture, and His relationship with Heavenly Father inform His every word. The answers

He gave still astonish us today. And, you know what? When we are connected with God in these same ways—indwelt with the Holy Spirit, confident and trusting in Father God, full of the Word of God which is Jesus, we will do the same.

Dave's Daughter

My friend Dave had a little daughter. Let's call her Linda. She was sweet and smart, and a little homely. One day when Dave and I were talking, Linda came in. Immediately Dave stopped and exclaimed, "Is that my daughter? Oh, my! Is that my Precious daughter, Linda! You're just so beautiful!" The little girl made kind of an "aw-shucks!" sound, and looked shy and immensely pleased. This was their usual type of exchange.

Years later, I was invited to Linda's wedding. When she walked down the aisle, I about fell over. I hadn't seen her in fifteen years and she was, without doubt, one of the most stunningly beautiful women I had ever seen. At the reception I had a chance to visit with her, and I watched her interacting with other guests. What I noticed was how unself-conscious she was. She was a gorgeous woman, but she didn't act like one. Early on, her dad had made her so secure in her value to him that she had no insecurities at all about her worth. She knew she was beautiful in every way because her daddy had told her every day of her life—and meant it.

We do not need to align with the world's values. We are created for an astonishing life of deep fellowship with the Lover of our souls. We have a beautiful invitation to walk and talk with the Creator of the Universe, to be His friend, and be transformed from glory to glory by the renewing of our minds, not blinded by the smoke screen of a worldview of life without meaning.

Furthermore, we are designed for this particular time in history. Our Father God is neither arbitrary nor inadvertent. The very fact that we are alive now indicates that He considers this the optimum time for us to be on Earth. He has a destiny for each of us, and is committed to bringing about careful re-finement in our lives that we may be totally fulfilled in all He created us to be. If we could only understand how valuable we are to God (that He loves us so much that He would "rather die than be without us"), perhaps we would realize that our presence is His gift—deliberate, meaningful, significant—in-tended to make a difference during these troubled times.

In the rest of this book are many areas of More that we have in God that make the kingdoms of this world seem pale, dull, and insignificant. Like Linda's dad, Father God wants to bring us into a lifetime of security and confidence in who He created us to be, filled with precious treasures He designed specifically for us. He intends us to move in bright, unselfcon-scious beauty, a blessing wherever we go.

7

VALIDATION

"Chun Shee" was the name my father told me. He never mentioned her personal name. Perhaps he didn't know it. "Shee" is a generic term like "Miss." "Chun" is a family name. It means "dust." This is the story she told my father. When she was just four years old, there was a terrible famine in China. In desperation, her parents sold her to a wealthy Chinese woman who took her across the ocean to San Francisco to serve as a maid in her house. Chun Shee said her parents told her they were not selling her so they could survive, because there was nothing to buy to eat. They were selling her because she was beautiful and the only one the woman wanted. She would go to another land. Back in China, they would all die, but she would live—Miss Dust.

Whether that story is actually what happened, we'll never know. What we do know is Chun Shee did serve in the wealthy woman's house, where my father said she learned survival tactics and eventually ended up with two different husbands and thirteen children, one of the last of whom was my father.

Survive. She learned how to do so with great skill that my father said included lying, stealing, deceiving, manipulating, scheming, and making others look bad. She had an altar with various gods that she honored with incense and promises of gifts if her prayers were answered. My dad recalled seeing her make good on one of those promises, presenting the god with a gold badge. But later, when finances got tight, she explained to the idol that she had kept her promise, and now things had changed and she needed to get some money. Then she took the gold badge and sold it. She also threw the yarrow sticks every morning to look up her fortune in the *I Ching*, and had

89

a picture of Jesus she kept in a closet (with the light on so He wouldn't be in the dark). My dad said she wasn't taking any chances.

While I was in my mother's womb, my father took my mom and my sister and left his family with their Confucian demands and never spoke of them for fifty years. I knew nothing about any of this until I started writing books on my parents' early lives. That's when I found out what my dad had suffered in the turmoil of his family. I wish Chun Shee had been able to embrace her value as a cherished child of God. I don't think she ever felt secure. She was always trying to figure out ways to make things come out advantageously for herself, even if it meant turning her back on her youngest son.

Why am I telling you this? Because I think a lot of us never realize our true value and spend our lifetimes trying to get validation from what we do or have, not realizing our value has already been set by the King of kings who paid such a high price to take us to a different land where we would be able to live in new ways not possible in the desolate place from which He rescued us. We feel the poverty of being dust. And we strive to validate ourselves by aligning with the values of the world in which we're trying to survive. We do what seems advantageous, too fearful to take any chances of offending any of the powers that could make our lives fortunate. It's so much less than what God has intended for us.

WALKING AFTER THE FLESH

Chun Shee lived her life according to the dictates of the flesh, doing whatever seemed expedient and advantageous for herself and her firstborn son. What she sowed was discord, mistrust, jealousy, favoritism, and a lot of conflict within the family, and it left a huge hole in my father's heart. I think he strove all his life to prove to himself that he was worthy of her love.

The Bible says to walk after the Spirit, not after the flesh. It says to be carnally-minded is death. He that sows to the flesh reaps corruption. Be not deceived. God is not mocked. It may seem to have gotten you what you wanted, but there's a whole lot of stink that goes along with it. That's what happens when there's rotting flesh lying around. Chun Shee did it, and it passed through my father directly to me.

In this chapter, I want to talk about things that might not seem to be all that fleshy, but I have biblical proof that they are. The example is what happened with Abraham and Sarah. Abram received a promise from Yahweh and He believed Him. Even though he and his wife were pretty old. But after the years went on, they must have wondered. You know the story. They decided to do what made most sense to them. In those days, an heir could be brought about by giving one's husband a substitute woman who would bear his child, but it would be attributed to his wife. It was legal, moral, ethical, reasonable, legitimate, socially acceptable, culturally comfortable, and normal. By the standards and mores of the day, it was a common way to solve the problem. That's what results from human reason. It's very effective in its own way, but it will never get you where the Spirit wants you to go. Flesh never lifts you to the miraculous. It can't. Different dimension. Different world.

The world says you are what you do. If you're really good at it, you can become powerful, influential, even adored. You might even be given the title "idol" to validate your talent and your value. There are more, but you get the point. I've lived those values and based my choices on them. Even after I became a Christian, those continued to be aspirations. I did think more about Jesus, and everything I did was legal, moral, ethical, reasonable, legitimate, socially acceptable, culturally comfortable, and normal, but my validation and values were still the world's. It was flesh. I'm not talking about strip clubs or hanging out in a crack house, but life aligned with the world's standards, possibilities limited to human reasoning. I didn't understand that belonging to God's family means living God-life—*zoe*—starting now on Earth the minute you're born again I had no idea God had so much more for me. What I was doing was working just fine, and I was, in the world's eyes, pretty successful.

That was Before. My future was predictable. The Book of Revelation was far away. The private briefing on the Mount of Olives with information for disciples on the End Times was a very distant possibility, something that didn't really apply to me right now, like trying to picture yourself at 80 when you're 5. I don't think that anymore. I never could have imagined how technology would change our world and how many of the descriptions in the prophecies would be realities this very day. It changes how I see my life, my role, my responsibilities to the One who bought me with his own blood.

Some people are resenting this intrusion on their plans— Christians included. It reminds me of the countries that chose to believe Hitler could be appeased if they cooperated with him. Things are changing whether we resent them or want them to or not. But we're still at the start, at the first of the birth pangs. We still have time to realign our priorities, review our view of who we are and reconsider why we're here on Earth at this specific time. All things considered, how shall we then live?

Scripture says not to walk after the flesh but after the Spirit. What does that mean? It means following the ways of the Lord, harmonizing with His heart. You know what they are. The Bible is full of them. Matthew is especially packed. You have the Beatitudes. Then you have those things about letting yourself be slapped on the other cheek, not obsessing on the speck in your brother's eye, and, horror of horrors, blessing those who curse you, doing good to those who hate you, and, worst of all, loving your enemies. There are really awful things in that holy Book. James, for example. "Wherefore, my beloved brethren, let every man be swift to hear, slow to speak, slow to wrath;" (James 1:19 KJV) Not to mention counting it all joy when we face trials, and 2 Peter with all those things about submitting to wicked authorities. Really? Is that what it takes to align with Your values, Lord? I don't think I can. It's too difficult.

I'll be addressing the "too difficult" part later in the section called "The Straight Wall." For now, I'll just say God created us. He knows what we can do and what we can't, and He knows we can't do these things that are His will—not in our flesh anyway. It's not a matter of will and determination; it takes supernatural help—divine help, *Spirit* help. And surrender. Here's a little verse that puts it in perspective: "But now, O Lord, thou art our father; we are the clay, and thou our potter; and we all are the work of thy hand. (Isaiah 64:8 KJV)

If you've been a Christian for any length of time, my guess is you know what God cares about. Mostly it looks like the exact opposite of what the world values. But it's one thing to know the principles and another to see them in practice. In the coming chapters there will be examples of real people living God's heart and they will be offered to you in depth. We are so used to flashes and bits and images only milliseconds on the screen that we miss the fullness of what we would understand if we were given longer to soak in the significance of what we're seeing.

DIVINE RESET

Many of us need a divine reset—taking a look at what we've accepted in our normal walk through this current world. A big part of the confusion is dissatisfaction with God's original designs. I fell for this one too, so I want to spend some time on it because it makes such a huge difference if you fall into this destructive and damaging deception. God designed each person very specifically for a very specific purpose that only that person can bring about. He chooses their time, race, place, abilities, gender, hair color, body plan, position in the family, etc. There are treasures in each parent's family line, and traumas and ugly things as well, but each part of that carefully chosen lineage has a purpose. When society tells us to choose to redesign ourselves, we are focusing on the flesh and completely missing the wonders He wants to reveal to us of the unique individual He created us to be. If we start changing our fundamental design, who knows what we will dismantle of the destiny He wants to open before us? Here's how it looks in just one life—mine.

Not long after I became a Christian, someone said, "If there's anything you don't like about yourself that you can't change, take it up with God. He's the One Who made you like that." So I told God, "I don't like my nose."

He said, "Why don't you like your nose?

I said, "It makes me look Chinese."

He said, "I could have put you halfway around the world with a billion people who look like you, but I thought you'd be better this way."

And then He gave me ten reasons. At the top of the list were my parents. If I were not Chinese, I wouldn't have those parents. At the time, I wasn't all that thrilled about that reason, because I didn't want to be "different." I still wanted to fit in and be like everyone else. However, there were things hidden from me at age thirty that would become blazingly clear in subsequent years, and the blessing of having those specific human beings as my parents continues to be revealed to me as my life goes on.

However, there were some things about being Chinese I really didn't like. There's this firstborn-thing. And there's this thing about boys. My mom went through it. She was practically a slave in her parents' hand laundry, an eight-year-old spindly little girl ironing with an 8-pound sadiron heated on a coal-burning stove in the horrid heat of Central California summer while her brothers went swimming and fishing, and hung out with their friends.

In my family, I had no status at all. I was the inferior gender and I was born second. Since my sister was first, she was automatically the favorite. She was a girl, but she was first.

"Why didn't You make me a boy?" I complained to God. "At least then I'd have my father's attention." Once more the Lord told me He chose my gender on purpose because there were things I'd be able to do as a girl that a boy could not do—things He designed me specifically to do. I am now almost seventy-five years old. Many things I longed for in my youth seem pretty silly to me. I now see how absolutely perfectly God designed me, every aspect working together in ways that make my life fruitful and fulfilling.

But that's not the message we get from our world. There's a standard, a model, an ideal. We're not taught to discern our blessings and purposes for the Kingdom.

Back to the Lord's list of reasons for making me Chinese. Remember what was on the top of the list? My parents. You know what my parents had that was unique? The same rare recessive gene for Retinitis Pigmentosa. I'm telling you this because I asked God. "Since You say You wrote everything about me in Your book, every member and part of my body, before I was born, before there were any of those epigenetics and chromosomes and metabolic inheritances, did You also know I would be blind?" You can probably guess the answer. I'm telling you this because I've had to deal with the details of what God chose for me and make peace with them. I had to come to terms with what I have and what I didn't get, and accept them with gratitude as being good. I needed to understand that in some profound way He intended them to be blessings.

In the matter of the RP, there is a lot about it I really don't like, but what worlds have opened up to me because of it! Have you ever met a puppy raiser for service dogs? They are some of the most wonderful, generous, loving people on the planet. They take an eight-week-old puppy, do all the hard work of giving it house manners, teaching it to be relaxed in all situations, and then when the dog is just about perfect, they give it back to the school to be trained for service. Nearly two years of their lives they sacrifice so a person in need can have a dog to help them be more independent, confident, and free. They may never meet the person. They may never get a thank you. They may never see the dog again. And yet they do this wonderful work—some of them raising more than thirty dogs. They are among my favorite human beings and, because of my blindness, I know a lot of them. In fact, I'm now working with Matt and Amie Chapman in a really fabulous project that I'll tell you more about a little later. And then, if it weren't for the blindness, I would not have known Hedy, my precious guide dog. My relationship with her has been so extraordinary that I have said more than once it is worth being blind to have her. Am I upset with God because my parents were from villages too close together? No. I'm so grateful for all that I have because of, not in spite of, the RP.

Scripture says we were in God's heart and mind from the start. Then, reviewing the thousands of years of humans on Earth, He chose the perfect time for our birth. My Scriptural basis for that idea is this statement by the Apostle Paul.

"For we are God's [own] handiwork (His workmanship), recreated in Christ Jesus, [born anew] that we may do those good works which God predestined (planned beforehand) for us [taking paths which He prepared ahead of time], that we should walk in them [living the good life which He prearranged and made ready for us to live]." (Eph 2:10 AMPC) The Greek for "good works" is something we can't translate into English. It means that which results from the righteousness we have in Jesus. In Him we are new creations, and the things we do, say, think, believe, issue forth from that transformed, now spiritually vibrant life.

I love how this purposeful planting of the Lord is expressed in this line from the Book of Esther: "but who knows if you have come to the kingdom for such a time as this?" (Esther 4:14 NKJV) In Esther's case, God made her beautiful, and the king chose her to replace Queen Vashti. Esther ended up saving her people from annihilation. Moses was also very good-looking. His mom recognized it, and so did Pharaoh's daughter, who adopted him even knowing immediately he was one of the Hebrew children who had been intended for death. There are times when God designs a person's good looks for a specific purpose, and there are times He makes them ordinary and unremarkable, also for specific purpose.

I am reminded that Jesus wasn't good-looking, no matter what the movies and paintings show. Isaiah says there is nothing comely about Him that would make us desire Him. I think He was quite unremarkable physically. Why would I think that? Because Judas had to point Him out to the soldiers. He couldn't just say, "Look for the tall, handsome one." There are times God creates something or someone to not be stunning to look at, and He does it for a reason. Nobody gave Jesus special treatment because He was so handsome, and nobody could find Him if He needed to pass through a crowd unnoticed. We think of the absence of beauty as something not given, as if you have the normal, plain people, a few ugly ones, and then those endowed with special gifts that carry favor and advantage with them. We don't think of common features as a carefully chosen gift. When God designs a person, every minute detail carries its own advantage, though it may not look like that if we view it only through the lens of the world.

SUCCESS

The world says you are what you do, and your value is determined by how well you do it. Fame is the big thing these days. It seems to validate the person and establish not only the merit of their work but of their life. Famous people are elevated to unhealthy heights when they're really good at something. We even call them idols and act as if that's a desirable goal, a supreme achievement. So we have people whom others idolize, and it's really unhealthy for all of them. The only safe One to worship is God, but our current world has done a really good job of convincing people otherwise, hence the undue devotion to what is of vastly lessor value.

In actuality, each person will worship something. As Bob Dylan sang, "You gotta serve somebody." It's our nature. God created us to want to worship. Mathematician, physicist, and inventor Blaise Pascal wrote, "There is a God-shaped vacuum in the heart of each man which cannot be satisfied by any created thing but only by God the Creator, made known through Jesus Christ." And Augustine wrote, "Thou hast made us for thyself, O Lord, and our heart is restless until it finds its rest in thee."

This issue of worship is so crucial it's one of the three temptations Jesus had to overcome in the wilderness. Satan showed Him all the kingdoms of the world and said he would give them to Him if He bowed down and worshiped him. With the sword of the Word, Jesus slashed through this temptation. Worship God alone. (Luke 4:5-8)

What does it mean to bow down—bend the knee? It's an act of submission. Allegiance. Devotion. The world is always trying to get us to accept its leadership and align with its values. Jesus knew that it wasn't a physical act; it was a commitment. It's surrendering your will.

People can become idols. A career can become an idol, or a belief system, a consuming commitment to a cause (such as those who say science is the only truth and has all the answers). A passion can become an idol. God definitely designs people with gifts, and some are gifted extraordinarily, but this can become a disaster if the gift replaces the Giver in the heart of the gifted one.

A word from the Word about idolatry. An idolator is someone who gives supreme devotion to anyone or anything other than God. Psalm 135:18 has this sobering revelation: "Those who make idols are like them. So is everyone who trusts in and relies on them."

I want to mention that not all idols are persons we admire or want to emulate or be connected to. An idol can be a company or a career that demands compromise, or all your time. Even a ministry can become an idol. Attention, focus, even to obsession—whatever you bend the knee to satisfy, that's an idol.

God tells us idols can't help us. They have eyes but can't see. They have mouths, but can't talk. And those who worship them are like them. Not only that, if a person insists on relying on his idol instead of the living God, Yahweh says He'll let him. Scary! But worshiping the God Who created everything, the One Who loved us enough to come to Earth to rescue us, the One Who has purposes for every human being that will make our lives count in significant ways all the way into Eternity? It's worth bowing down to Him. All the rest is going to burn. Whatever we amass on Earth of goods, money, power, status—it's all going to burn—literally.

A little perspective.

A tour bus was making its way through the crowded streets of New York City. The guide was pointing out all the gleaming skyscrapers that Rockerfeller built with his vast fortune. One of the tourists asked, "How much did he leave when he died?" The tour guide answered dryly, "All of it."

BEFORE AND AFTER

Before, in the old days when we were young, the days when we could depend upon things being predictable, reliable and stable, people could make their plans and work to see them come about. Some had small dreams and some were much larger, but it was pretty much to be expected that the results would be connected to what we invested in it. What we sowed, we reaped. As I said, that was before. In early 2020, we were reeling from a shocking worldwide terror, but we were adapting, adjusting, figuring out ways to deal with it. It's now late 2021 and things are even more confusing than before.

If there's one thing I've noticed it's how ineffective our human reason is at times like these. It's kind of the point, if I'm hearing God accurately. Our self-reliant, can-do attitude won't save us when the demonic storm is bashing our boat and it sure looks like perishing to us. But Jesus is in the boat, and His first words to us after stilling the storm are, "Why were you afraid?" Our human reasoning can give Him lots of answers based on empirical evidence and past experience, but He says "Don't be afraid." He says that a lot in the Bible. Joshua facing Jericho, disciples huddled in a room with the door securely locked. It is especially significant that Jesus repeats that instruction in His private briefing to Peter, James, John, and Andrew on the Mount of Olives. They've asked Him about the end and He gives them details, repeating, "Don't be afraid," "Don't be deceived," and "these things must be." He says when they see these things, be aware. Understand what it means. These are the birth pangs, the beginning of sorrows, but the End is not yet.

Then He died. Then He rose. Then they understood. It changed how they saw their lives. From then on they lived in the context of the Big Picture—human history on the cosmic scale. They understood they had a part to play in it, something He had charged them to do.

Recently I was listening to a Calvary Chapel pastor teaching through the Book of Revelation. He said from Chapter 4 on, everything happens in the throne room of heaven, and it's all about the revelation of Jesus Christ—not what He's going to do, but who He is. If we try to understand what's going on in the context of Earth, especially with ourselves as the starting place, we will never understand what's really happening, or how to behave in it. We live in a me-centered world. It blinds us to the possibilities of what our lives are meant to be in the coming days. If we walk after the flesh, we will never find it, but Jesus is calling us to revel in the resources He has given us—spiritual discernment, divine wisdom, and our own carefully crafted individually designed lives able to do what the disciples did, able to do what Jesus Himself did on Earth—and more, just as He said.

8

WINNING

"What's the weather today," I asked my phone.

The pleasant voice replied, "It's currently foggy and 43 degrees. The high today will be 50 degrees and the low will be 37."

I went upstairs and looked out the window. It was sunny and blue and there wasn't a single cloud in the sky. The weather report on my phone is often wrong. One time it said to expect clouds in the morning and clearing in the afternoon. When I opened the door, it was pouring rain.

The report from my phone is probably right for the town that is being sampled, but I live on a mountain several miles away. The elevation here is 1,000 feet higher than it is over there. Forecasts will always be inaccurate because I live in a different place.

There are multitudes of measurings going on every day, from the number of views on a YouTube video to the statistics on unemployment, number of deaths from head-on collisions, popularity of a particular new movie or song. Data is collected. Internet searches are logged. Ratings can be accessed in milliseconds, and evaluation of merit and popularity and public interest goes on, numbers determining what's successful and what is not. It's a restless, changeable, data-driven calculation of worth, and it can confuse and derail us if we believe it.

It's liberating to realize we need not be driven to find our satisfaction and fulfillment in the values of the world. They will never satisfy us. C.S. Lewis said, "if we find ourselves with a desire that nothing on this earth can satisfy, the most probable explanation is that we were made for another world."

As Christians, our fulfillment doesn't come from what we can get from the world. Our value is not determined by its standards. The truth is this: no matter how sophisticated the measuring systems, they cannot give you accurate information about the value, success, and merit of your life when you live in a higher place.

WINNING

I remember commentators saying if the favored swimmer didn't get gold, he hadn't won at all. What's that all about? If you don't get Olympic gold, you're worthless and the public will soon forget all about you. So you'd better win. Otherwise, you know what you are? A loser. Well, nobody wants to be a loser, so you do what you have to do. Cheat on your exam. Lie on your job application. Take performance enhancing drugs. Curry favor even if it means going against your moral compass or what God's Word tells you is best for you.

This chapter is about winning—what the world demands, and some other ways to win. Since winning is most easily measured by scoreboards, I'm going to begin with the world of sports

WE ARE MARSHALL

Recently I watched *We Are Marshall*, a movie telling the true story of the rebuilding of a football team after a plane crash that killed all seventy-five people on board, including all of "The Thundering Herd," their coaching staff, doctors, lawyers, city councilmen, the athletic department, boosters, and leaders of the community. Mom's and dad's died in the crash and twenty-two children lost both parents. Coach Jack Lengyel from Wooster saw the need and went to see if he could help. He soon realized he had to rebuild a lot more than a football team. The whole community was shattered. Many in the town wanted to suspend the football program altogether, though no one knew for how long. All they wanted to do was grieve, and they believed the way to honor the dead was to stop living too. So this outsider came in to coach and what he had to work with were freshmen who were granted a special dispensation to play college football, and three varsity players who had not gone to the game because they were injured.

The new team, the Young Thundering Herd, didn't win much—just two games the first season, but then again, they weren't expected to win any games at all. Coach Lengyel tells them the point was not about winning; their success was they showed up week after week and played the game. He redefined the meaning of winning.

In the film, the former coach told the team, "There's only one thing they judge us on. There's only one thing they remember. And it ain't how we played the game. Winning is everything." I don't know if that's actually what he said before they boarded the plane that took all of their lives, but it certainly has been the prevailing worldview—and not just in sports. But what if you can't win?

This is what the real Coach Lengyle told the 1971 team. "We have an opportunity to exemplify what I think is one of the greatest lessons in athletics—to face adversity, get off the ground, and go on to success.

The fact that we played the game and we were back was a victory.

While we may not have many victories on the scoreboard, our victories will come in the years to come and we will share in those victories knowing that we had some small part in building the foundation for this football team."

Those first brave young men were true heroes; they drew the entire community back into willingness to live again. They played even knowing they probably couldn't win. That's a tough thing for anyone to face, especially competitive young men. But what do you think would have happened if nobody had been willing to play football at Marshall back then? How long do you think it would have taken for the community to heal enough to have football again? Maybe never? Do you think those new players knew it? And if so, what do you think it did for them inside?

In the 1970s Marshall lost more games than any other football team in the nation. But they kept on, team after new team of football players knowing they were investing in a losing proposition. In 1984, the Herd had their first winning record in twenty years. After that, they won eight conference titles, had five straight bowl wins, and two national championships. It took twenty years and a lot of heroic young men to make those accomplishments possible. What impresses me most is not those wins, but twenty years of youngsters, coaches, and communities that kept playing, as Coach Lengyle says, "till the final whistle blows."

JONI

Here's another example of someone who can't compete in normal ways:

Joni Eareckson Tada (pronounced like "Johnny," not "Joanie") was a healthy, athletic, fun-loving seventeen-year-old. A popular high school senior, she hadn't thought much about God, and says she might not have, except one day she dove into a lake and broke her neck, severing her spinal cord. She was paralyzed from the shoulders down.

Joni reflects back on her first months in the Stryker Frame—enclosed in an envelope of canvas attached to a frame of pipes that made it easy to turn her. "When I was first injured I imagined myself as kind of a human guinea pig lying there in my Stryker Frame. I was doing nothing but eating and breathing and sleeping. I was really just existing and I thought most people out beyond these hospital walls are going to college and getting married, having children, going to work, and I'm just lying here sleeping, breathing, eating. I realized, Oh my goodness! Upon my life all the truths of the human race are going to be tested. Is there a God? Does He care? What's the purpose in life? And if there is no God, then why not have my girlfriend slit my wrists? Why not take my mother's sleeping pills? Why not end it all? Who can face a life of total paralysis? And somewhere in there, in my anger and frustration, I realized life's got to be more than just getting born and growing old and dying. There's got to be a God Who cares. We're too significant. There must be meaning in all of this. I don't think I would have asked those larger-than-life questions were it not for my suffering."

Since Joni chose to seek God, she asked those profound worldview questions and concluded God had a reason for preserving her life, and in what life she had remaining, she chose to embrace that purpose. Her life has affected millions for the glory of God, and though she's heartily tired of the wheelchair, she says if it will help even one more person find hope in Christ, it's worth it.

I remember hearing about Joni when I was a new Christian. She had learned how to paint with a brush between her teeth. I remember hearing her talks about God and envying her. Yes, I, a healthy thirty year-old envied a quadriplegic. It wasn't her world-wide ministry, books, music, the movie on her life, and all the people she has led to Christ. It was her relationship with God. "Meaningless suffering is what defeats us." That's the conclusion of a rabbi who interviewed survivors of the holocaust. Joni gave her future to Jesus and has become a living example of God's ability to transform suffering and catastrophic loss into immeasurable good.

Nick Vujisic was born without arms or legs. All he has is a head, torso, and one small partial left foot. I watched him move back and forth atop a long table, addressing hardened inmates in a maximum security prison with a message of hope in Jesus. When he gave the altar call, men filled the front of the room, weeping, heads bowed, humbly repeating the words of commitment to Jesus Christ with voices that sounded surprisingly like innocent little children. There was no swagger, bravado, attempt to present themselves proud and strong. They believed Nick and they wanted what he had—hope that can make them free inside even though they might spend the rest of their years behind bars. Do you think they would have been as convinced they could have this hope had Nick been a healthy young man who got to go home after the talk to his normal free life?

I don't know Nick's story so I don't know whether he had to fight his way out of anger and depression to the place of faith and freedom he now has in Christ, but he has certainly maximized his limb-less life and made it count for the kingdom of God, and he has joy that can't be faked. Only God can give that joy, and only a life surrendered to God's purposes can transform what the world says is deformity and disability into something enviable and life-giving.

What does God say? "Seek first the Kingdom of God and His righteousness and all the rest will be added unto you." Does that sound like God is trying to make all His children unremarkable? "All the rest will be added unto you." Sounds pretty lavish to me. God is a good Father. He knows what will make a life fruitful and joyful, peaceful and fulfilled. We never lose by putting God first. It's His first commandment, and when we take Him seriously and align with Him, our lives make a difference in ways we can't imagine.

PRIORITIES

To me, the best example of a person with the right priorities is Eric Liddell (pronounced like "little" with a "D"). Eric was a man of conviction that astonished the world when he chose not to run in the 100 meter race at the 1924 Olympics, though he was favored to win. The reason? The heats for the race were on Sunday. When authorities tried to pressure him by talking about patriotism and loyalty to king and country, he refused to bow the knee to a lesser monarch than the King of kings. When one man said the difference in time zones meant Sunday at home would be over by the time the heats in Paris were to be run, Eric answered that his Sabbath lasted all day. He ended up competing in the 400 meter race, which didn't interfere with his Sabbath, and, to everyone's astonishment, he won.

Eric Liddell's eldest daughter, Patricia, said, "The gold was lovely, but it wasn't the most important thing. And I truly, truly believe that if he had run on the Sunday that he would not have won. If he had sold out his principles for the gold, he would not have won it. He wouldn't have had the fire to do that. He was running for God."

A missionary once asked Eric Liddell if he prayed that he would win the race. He said no. He prayed that in the athletics meetings God would be glorified. He wasn't trying to beat everyone; he was just trying to do his best. I love it when athletes are more concerned about improving their personal best than beating the socks off the other athletes. I know this is what Eric taught his children. His daughter Patricia said, "I remember a little race we had, father and daughter. We both ran. He ran and then he gave the baton to me so I ran, and I waited for other people to catch up. And he said, 'No, no. It must be fair. You run. You do your best. You run your fastest, but you don't knock anybody else down for it. You have to be fair. But you do your very best. Always do your best.'"

Quality of character, personal integrity, generosity, patience, kindness, a high moral standard, compassion, purity, humility, noticing the needs of others—cooperation instead of domination—these are values that will give us lives that will be a pleasure to be around. We will have internal stability because our validation is coming from the standard set by Heaven in a higher place, not this temporal world.

COACHING ON LIFE

I thought you might be interested in what some outstanding coaches have to say. If you're into sports, you'll probably recognize their names. I'm not going to list all their awards and accomplishments; I'm only mentioning that they have some because these guys have credibility. They know what it takes to win. And they understand what winning, success, and life are really about.

John Wooden, Head Basketball Coach for UCLA, said, "Never try to be better than somebody else. You have no control over that. That's something that my father gave me years before when I was in grade school. Never try to be better than somebody else. Just learn from them and never cease trying to be the best you can be. That's under your control and the other isn't."

I love that! First, it's a life-lesson John Wooden learned from his dad and he's remembered it all throughout his life, living by it, coaching by it. Second, it takes the dog-eat-dog-aspect out of life. Let's think about that a moment. What do we gain by devouring someone else? I remember something from the Book of Numbers. The Israelites were tired of manna and cried out for flesh, so God brought them quail, but while it was still between their teeth, bad news. God gave them their request, but they also got leanness of soul. (Ps 106:15) Clearly, getting what you want most doesn't necessarily lead to fulfillment or a wonderful, memorable life.

I like what Coach Lute Olson says about being a team. "The thing about basketball is it's so much of a team game. If a team's going to be successful, you can't have five stars. You have to have people that are going to be supportive type players. You're going to have some guys that are going to rebound, and be your leader in that area. What you try to do in team-building is to get everyone on that team to feel like they have a real reason for being there and they're going to make a great contribution."

George Horton, Head Baseball Coach at Cal State Fullerton, says, "It's not just about sports; it's about life application, character, and teaching players how to deal with failure. Baseball is the perfect vehicle to convey that message because of its very nature. In life, winning is not guaranteed. To have a successful and satisfied life, kids need to learn how to deal with loss and slumps, failure and adversity. The sport of baseball is a failure-based sport because the best hitters in the world fail seven out of ten times. It's not so much are you going to fail or are you going to succeed, it's how you deal with that failure that really separates the men from the boys to prepare them for the challenges in life, and for Minor League Baseball when they go out and they fail and they have a week where they go 0 for 40, I want to provide tools for them to be able to deal with that. No coach alive can prevent slumps or failure in athletics, but what a coach can do is create a series of tools for that particular young man to have a bounce back effort to overcome things, to overcome failure. The way we look at failure here in our program is it's just an opportunity to turn something around or to bounce back."

Coach Horton also teaches his players skills that will help them navigate real life effectively and efficiently, one thing at a time. He says, "Rules, guidelines, philosophy and structure in almost any arena is very valuable. We use the 3 P's, and we use this in competition and in our everyday life. The 3 P's are we want to stay present. It doesn't really matter how we got to this point—good day, bad day—and we are positive. We want to take that present mentality and have a positive outlook, with taking an exam, taking an at bat. And the third P is a big one: staying with the process. We don't just take it one inning at a time, we take it one pitch at a time."

The end justifies the means is nothing new. In the past, it was associated with the unethical Machiavellian worldview that was regarded as offensive and dishonorable. Now it's accepted as normal, even desirable. In business, in politics, in show biz, in just about every field in which there is any element of competition, the prevailing worldview and situational ethics still place this motivation at the top of their priorities: Win at any cost. Doesn't that sound like survival of the fittest? Therefore, I was impressed by Bobby Bowden, Head Football Coach of Florida State University. His teams have had lots of wins under his leadership, but his approach is not based on "kill or be killed." He prays with his team. He uses the sport to help develop their character. And he keeps things in perspective—the Big, most important one.

Coach Bobby Bowden recalls, "When I first started coaching back in the '50s, the approach that coaches took to football was to kill. Kill! Go out there and kill 'em! You've gotta be mean. You've got to physically whip 'em. And that was kind of the theme back in those days. But now our approach is love. If my players love each other they have brotherly love for each other, then they'll fight for each other. I think love is so important. If I don't like you, I ain't gonna block. You think I'm gonna block that guy just so you can make a doggone run? But if I love him and I want him to succeed, we're both gonna block for each other. We're gonna be a better team.

"Don't dwell on whether you're gonna win or lose, because you can talk yourself right out of a doggone ball game. You prepare yourself the best you can. Then we'll take our chance on what happens here.

"I try to keep football in the correct priority. I'm continually reminding my kids, 'Hey boys, you ain't gonna live forever. When you're your age, you think you're gonna be an old man before you finally die.' Last week I had to remind them we played Rice University. The next Monday one of their players dropped dead. So I have to bring that to my boys' attention, 'Men, you've got to be ready to go. You don't know when that time is gonna come.'

"Football is not *the* priority in my life. It is a priority. It's a big one—it's the way I make my living. But it ain't life and death. I ain't cutting my wrist because of a loss. I want my boys to come out of Florida State a better player, academically complete, and a very deep realization that there's more to life than just football and a job."

Coach Bowden says, "You've got to get over the bad times. If you've never had adversity, you ain't gonna be nothin'. You have got to have adversity to build your character and find out how tough you are, and find out how good your judgment is."

Dealing with adversities prepares us for things to come. I think of the test pilots who risk their lives every day deliberately looking for weaknesses in their aircraft so they can be made safe for others. Those guys know what it means to face danger. They know how to stay cool no matter what happens. They have skills and maneuvers beyond mechanics. And they're brave. No wonder NASA picked test pilots to be the first astronauts!

GOD'S VIEW OF OUR KIDS

The prevailing worldview affects the ability of our kids to see themselves as acceptable and meaningful in the unique design God has given them. It pressures them to be dissatisfied with what they have and who they are. It tells them they can be whatever they want if they just want it and work for it enough. It tells them they are what they do, and if they're really good at it, the world (and others) will fall at their feet and they'll be happy and satisfied. It tells them winning is everything; it doesn't matter how you played the game. And if you don't win, you're a loser.

The good news is no one has more influence on your kids than you do. Parents are amazingly powerful in creating a sense of personhood and worth in their children. You can help them understand their value, divinely ordained. God made them who they are. They are unique. They aren't meant to fit into the world's mold. It's too restrictive and unimaginative.

In day-to-day life as each situation comes up, we invest in our children as we teach them what God values. It makes me think of the tellers at the bank. They study a genuine $100 bill—what it looks like, smells like, feels like—not a bunch of counterfeits. That way they can immediately spot a counterfeit because they know what the real thing looks like, feels like, smells like. We teach our kids what's acceptable to God. Is this how Jesus would act? Is it something He would say? Would it please Him? We teach them not to berate or bully, and when they see bullies on the playground, or on the news, they'll know it's not right. When the world says, "This is what you do when you're a star," and it doesn't harmonize with the character of Christ, they'll know and they won't be fooled into believing counterfeits have any value.

BEYOND YOUR WILDEST DREAMS

When I started writing this chapter many months ago, I wanted to point out the world's values and expose their damaging effects on us. But now I'm realizing it's something more. It's about finding life's meanings in God's purposes for our lives. No idols. No self-seeking. No striving to make dreams come true. I told God that's very unAmerican and I really didn't want to write it. He said, "Tell them their dreams are too small."

What does that mean?

Recently a friend told me she had said something about the strange state of the world, and her fifteen-year-old grandson immediately snapped, "I'm so tired of hearing about End Times! I just want to live my life. I just want to have a normal life." I think he means he wants things comfortable, predictable, normal (meaning the way it was before). He's not alone in this. A lot of people want things to go back to Before: You choose your path. You put in your time. You make the effort. You set your goals and reach for them. Predictable. Cause and effect. Diligence, investment, and reward. You know—normal. Stable. No surprises.

There's a poignant exchange between Frodo and Gandalf In J.R.R. Tolkien's *The Lord of the Ring* when the peace-loving hobbit realizes he has a terrible task ahead.

"I wish it need not have happened in my time," said Frodo.

"So do I," said Gandalf, "and so do all who live to see such times, but that is not for them to decide. All we have to decide is what to do with the time that is given us."

Tolkien's own peaceful, scholarly life was torn apart by World War I. Most of his friends were killed. The tragic losses and horrors of the battlefield left their wounds in his sensitive, poetry-loving soul, and they shade his books with the realities of evil that encroaches even if we wish it were not so. Nevertheless, Tolkien held onto his faith in Jesus and even coined a word, "eucatastrophe," meaning a sudden reversal from disaster to astonishing good. He saw it in the cross, and he wrote it in the last battle where the destruction of the ring ends the evil that was about to destroy all the peoples of Middle Earth.

World War I also took many of C.S. Lewis' friends and helped confirm him in his atheism. But God made sure both of these men survived that brutal war and arranged for them to meet at Oxford over the love of the same kind of literature. Do you think for a moment that was coincidence? God used a man with equally brilliant intellect as Lewis to lead him to the Lord. Both of them would see the world ravaged by a second world war, but what they did with the time that was given them was to write books that would change millions of lives with insights into the heart of God and the divine reality beyond this world that triumphs over all evil no matter what the circumstances seem to be.

My friend Carol says, "It's hard to not be earthly minded. We love our life, our family and friends. Our homes, churches, etc., etc. We're attached to this world, this life, this Earth because it's the only life we've known."

It's true. We only know what we see. But then again, the Bible tells us repeatedly this is not all there is. I'm not talking about afterwards; I'm talking about things we don't see happening now. There's transformation taking place in the chrysalises of our Christian lives, and there's massive conflict going on in the invisible realm. Scripture says, "We wrestle not with flesh and blood but principalities, powers, spiritual wickedness in high places." (Eph 6:12) And "The message is true, but the struggle is hard, the conflict is long, and the war is great." (Daniel 10:1)

Let's take a look at the belief that we're entitled to a full expectation of days, none of them cut short because of End Times. Some have the idea we're entitled—to have a long and healthy life, and a chance to achieve a fulfilling and financially rewarding career. Frankly, I don't see anything in the Bible that guarantees that kind of life. It sounds like the American Dream, and we think the Constitution guarantees us at least a good shot at it? Really? What about the seventy-five folks on the plane that crashed with nearly the entire Marshall football team onboard? Those young men were in their late teens and early twenties. For them, it was their own End Times. There are no guarantees. One of my classmates at guide dog school went completely blind as he was speeding along the L.A. freeway at sixty miles per hour. Another friend went to the doctor for some swelling in her belly. It was Stage 4 ovarian cancer, and it had metastasized.

Taking another look at the "Let's go back to before" scenario—is it even possible? When the bomb hit Pearl Harbor, World War II for us began. When the atom bomb hit Hiroshima, the nuclear age began. And when God's sacrificial Love hit Earth more than two thousand years ago, even Eternity changed. Things change forever. But God always has opportunities unique to the times, available to us if we're interested. He wants to give us turn-by-turn guidance through the toxic atmospheres, and accurate forecasts so we can prepare for whatever storms are ahead. He is always calling to us— "Come let us reason together." There's something supernatural going on here, and we can have our divinely-designed part in it. It's totally up to us. God is not into forcing obedience. Jesus came to make us free. He doesn't demand our participation in His Plan; He invites.

So I would ask my friend's grandson, "Would you rather be a fisherman, a tax collector, a self-righteous Pharisee living your normal life, or heal the sick, raise the dead, change the world, and write the New Testament?" God keeps impressing upon me that it's a privilege and honor to be alive now, during these extraordinary days. Do you think Saul of Tarsus wishes he could have kept on persecuting Christians? God had a destiny for him he couldn't have imagined. And when his own end time came, he was received Home in the greatest joy of all.

Coach Bobby Bowden said, "In football, you don't get many opportunities. What is sad is when opportunities come and you ain't ready. It's sad when an opportunity comes and you did not prepare yourself to take advantage of that opportunity."

For all of us on Earth at this time, the future has already been significantly changed. God says our dreams are too small. We were each born for such a time as this. Let us never believe we are insignificant, another nameless face amidst the billions that have lived. We have been chosen for this specific time. We're designed for it. We're meant to be good at it. We have opportunities to change the world as no one has ever done before. And we have time now to do whatever course-correction is necessary to get ourselves prepared, our hearts tuned to God's voice, no longer distracted by the enticements of what the world offers.

My son John said, "It's true. We are created for this time and purpose. Would I rather just be another drudge in the endless masses of humanity that lives out his existence in anonymity and mediocrity? Or do I want this life? Yeah. It's painful now. But I'm believing the results will be worth it."

"For I know the thoughts that I think toward you, says the Lord, thoughts of peace and not of evil, to give you a future and a hope." (Jeremiah 29:11 NKJV)

I'm not saying it's easy or simple or pleasant, and it's up to us to decide if we're in or out. Jesus, Himself, had to make a choice. He really didn't want to drink that Cup. He knew what it would entail, and His humanity shivered at the prospect. He may have even wondered if He'd make it through. Why do I think that? Scripture says He was tempted in all things such as we, yet without sin. All things. Ever think you couldn't go another step? Ever cry out, "I'm done, God! I'm going to crack! I can't make it!" Yes, I think He wondered. In His humanity He wondered. But He said, "Father, what shall I say? Deliver Me from this hour? But it's for this hour I came. Thy will be done. Glorify Yourself." (John 12:27) At that moment, Jesus chose to submit Himself and then went on in perfect peace till He finished the course. Is that how it went? Scripture says He was sorely troubled and, three chapters later, we see Him in Gethsemane, so distressed He can hardly bear it.

And taking with Him Peter and the two sons of Zebedee, He began to show grief and distress of mind and was deeply depressed. Then He said to them, "My soul is very sad and deeply grieved, so that I am almost dying of sorrow. Stay here and keep awake and keep watch with Me." And going a little farther, He threw Himself upon the ground on His face and prayed saying, "My Father, if it is possible, let this cup pass away from Me; nevertheless, not what I will [not what I desire], but as You will and desire." And He came to the disciples and found them sleeping..."

I want to interrupt this familiar scene with a detail you might not know. Directly across from the garden of Gethsemane was a clear view of the temple mount. Both the garden and the temple were on hills, with a sloping valley between. In the black night, Jesus could have easily seen, coming through the temple gate, a crowd of men carrying torches. Jesus could watch them coming across the slopes, clearly visible for however long it took them to get to the garden. Jesus knew what it meant. As He implored His Father to let the cup pass from Him, His disciples slept, and the torches were coming ever nearer.

"Again a second time He went away and prayed, "My Father, if this cannot pass by unless I drink it, Your will be done." And again He came and found them sleeping... So, leaving them again, He went away and prayed for the third time, using the same words. (Matt 26:37-44 AMP)

Luke adds that Jesus sweated drops of blood. Do you think He would have been that distressed if He knew He couldn't fail? No stacked deck. No guarantees. No safety net. No plan of escape. Well, yes, He did say He could call for a bunch of angels to rescue Him, but in some ways that made it worse. Just one whisper, and 12 legions of angels (more than 80,000) rush to rescue You (Matt 26:53) I think the temptation to quit would have been the strongest when He was feeling the absence of His Father. Picture being separated from the one you love most—out of reach because of things you can't control: quarantine, deployment, imprisonment, moving away, nursing home, Alzheimer's, death. There isn't anything we suffer that He hasn't suffered at least as much. Separation can be worse than floggings and beatings. It can be worse than a spear near your heart. He came to rescue us so we would never be separated from the One Who loves us most—unless we choose not to want Him. He suffered and died to give us that option. And He made the choice four times recorded in Scripture, but probably many times more than that in His heart of hearts—to say yes to His Father, "Thy will be done."

And He received the strength to do everything required to fulfill His purpose.

Should we say, "Father, deliver us from these frightening times of madness and let me have a normal life"? In these strange days, we have opportunities no one else has ever had. It's your life, your choice. You can hang onto your hopes for a return to what was before, or say, "Your will, Father. You sent me here for this hour. Glorify Yourself," and let go and see what new opportunities arise. Would you rather be a caterpillar or a butterfly?

If you're still reading, I'm going to believe that you've already made your choice and are curious about what lies ahead. So let's look together at the time line in the Bible, we're getting toward the end of the book. Jesus told His disciples about famines, wars and rumors of wars, troubles, earthquakes in various places, but don't be afraid. The End is not yet. These are the beginnings of sorrows. (a better translation is "birth pangs) (Matt 24) Something is in the process of being birthed that no one has ever seen before—and I have the sense we have the astonishing opportunity to prove God was right when He designed beings with free will. Can you imagine that? We get to be Exhibit A. Like Job, but different because we know Jesus defeated sin, death, and the devil. But it's also the same because the invisible realm is watching to see if we'll curse God and die. Will we say, "Father, glorify Your name. In the midst of the chaos, we have a chance to put our futures firmly into His hands. He can do wonders when we humans give our lives to Him, not guessing, complaining, insisting, whining, but cooperating, trusting, leaning not on our own understanding. He promises us turn-by-turn guidance. Like the Book of Acts, Twenty-first Century-style. This could be the most exciting time of our lives. God says our dreams are too small.

Call upon Me. I will show you great and mighty things, things you have never seen. (Jeremiah 33:3)

In the coming chapters, I'll be sharing stories of people who've had the courage to live their life in Christ, God-centered, making use of their gifts to help others within whatever opportunities presented themselves in the trials they encountered. All have given me a whole different way to evaluate what makes a life a success, and they have proven to me how dim and flimsy and fleeting are the accolades of the world.

Right now you have the time to find God's purposes for you as forecast for your future from a very high place. In the meantime, know that you have a real reason for being here and you're going to make a great contribution, so keep Present, taking it pitch by pitch, balanced and able to bounce back from failure. Keep things in perspective. Help your team, be fair, always do your best, don't knock anybody down, watch for opportunities, keep your priorities straight, trust in the Lord with all your heart, and keep playing till the final whistle blows.

9

THE STRAIGHT WALL

The Lord had been trying to get the prophet Amos to deliver His message of impending judgment to His rebellious, idolatrous people, but Amos had refused twice saying, "Jacob is too small." In other words, the Lord's people were incapable of doing what He required because it was too difficult. Then the Lord showed Amos a man standing by a wall, a plumb line in his hand. The wall was perfectly straight. Without another word, Amos went out and delivered the Lord's message.

Really? Wouldn't a crooked wall have shown more graphically that the people weren't measuring up? No. A straight wall had a much more powerful message. It said some people were staying aligned with God no matter how difficult the circumstances. They are the straight walls.

PRIORITIES

My son John worked for a company whose priority was production and profit, not people. Their management style was "Power Over," a term coined by interpersonal communications specialist Patricia Evans to represent a way of dealing with others. It is characterized, not by cooperation, but by domination. The goal of Power Over is to win at any cost. The company management style included threats and intimidation and they wanted the talented employees to grow in their image. John is not like that and refused to be. He was kind to his co-workers, diligent in his own work, and his bay was consistently the top-producing one. But when it came to promotions, he was always passed over.

When my father died, I asked John to speak at the funeral. John did not hesitate. His grandpa had been a significant part of his life and he wanted to honor him. Immediately John asked his manager for the time off. John's schedule was 12 hour days, 3 days on, 3 days off, 4 days on, 4 days off. He planned his trip so he would only miss two days of work. His manager gave him a shrug and a "That will probably be okay." Though John asked him several times, his manager would not give him a more definite answer. Time was short, so John bought five non-refundable tickets for his family's flight to Southern California.

But there was a problem. During the days between John's shifts, the definitive answer finally came. John said, "The day before I was scheduled to leave, I found an email my manager had sent earlier in the week that denied my time off. When I went looking for him to find out what had happened, I was informed he was away on vacation."

Alarmed, John went to his supervisor, explained the situation, and was told the request had been denied. The supervisor said flatly, "You're expected to be at work on Friday." When John said his grandpa was important to him and he had to go, the supervisor said if he went he would no longer have a job. When John returned, he no longer had a job.

John told me his priority was his family. If it came to a choice between job and family, family would win every time. But it cost him. He was unemployed for six months.

Now the thing about that job was it was long hours and extremely stressful. With the 15 minutes it took to get into his clean suit (he worked in a clean room) and be at his station by 7:00 a.m., then the 15 minutes to change back after his shift, he was leaving the house at 6:15 and getting home after 8:30 at night, whereupon he fed the kids, cleaned the house, and fell into bed exhausted. The first day off after the shifts, he was so tired all he did was sleep. But after he lost his job, he had time at home to be with his family and work on rebuilding his health, which had begun to fail. As his mom, I was upset about this reprehensible treatment of my son, but not unhappy that they let him go. John is a conscientious hard-worker who always tries to do his best. He did the grueling days without complaint, but his spirit was being crushed by the domineering style of leadership. Knowing my son, I think that was harder on him than the physical strain of trying to meet quotas under physically exhausting conditions. Now he's a respiratory therapist and known in his office for being able to handle the most grumpy, disgruntled, and hostile of the patients under their care. John likes his job, is very good at it, and his co-workers and bosses are like a family with mutual respect and concern for one another. For John, it's no longer a matter of enduring the job so he can support his family; it's a fulfilling ministry of service to everyone he encounters in his days. It's life-giving all around.

Sometimes aligning with God will cost you something, but your heart will be whole and God knows what you need—always. God knows how to work all things together for good (Romans 8:28) even though the world, or your employer, thinks you're a fool.

John's story horrifies me. How can a company treat its employees like that? It was a kind of legalized slavery. The problem is, many Christians do the same thing to their employees, being thoroughly steeped in the materialism of this world that is well accepted, legal, usual, socially acceptable and even expected. It's not the way Jesus wants us to live.

In Mark 10, as the disciples debated yet again about who was the greatest, He told them the Gentiles lord it over one another (Gentiles being those who have not known the laws and ways of Yahweh). The Gentiles dominate, exploit, and capitalize on other human beings, "but it should not be so among you." We're to be kindly affectioned one to another in brotherly love. We are to each esteem others higher than ourselves. We are to love our neighbor as ourselves. We're even to do good to those who hate us. That's God's way. That's how He does things. We are to represent His heart on Earth. Are we doing that? We're so saturated with the mindset of the world, our culture of dominance and acquisition, our obsession with personal pleasure. How can we be straight walls in such a crooked world when our hearts are in agreement with its values?

Several Christians come to mind. DL Moody was a scoundrel. George Meuller was a playboy. Brother Andrew was a rascal. My guess is *they* didn't suddenly become great men of faith. It was a process. God is patient with process, but He also intends us to grow in our understanding of His heart, our lives revealing Him through actions that flow out of that relationship. Those "good deeds" shown to an unbelieving world that God is real and human life stops being grabbing and grubby because of His supernatural transforming Life within us. However, some of us are slower on the uptake than others.

John Newton was a slave trader who converted during a violent storm. I think he even once lightened the load to keep from swamping by throwing some of his cargo overboard— live human beings. When he wrote, "Amazing grace, how sweet the sound that saved a wretch like me," he wasn't kidding. But wait. It's worse. After he got saved, he continued being a slave trader. Somehow, it's possible that a person can be born again and continue in totally immoral, ungodly practices. Eventually the Holy Spirit made it through John Newton's worldly mindset and that's when the good stuff for him really began. That's when he wrote the hymn that reminds all of us that God can transform any life, no matter how wretched, if we'll let Him.

Several things come to mind. The first is Revelation 18— the destruction of Babylon, which represents false religion and commercialism. As she goes up in smoke, merchants from land and sea weep for the loss of the goods, money, and power they once received from their intimacies with her. Someday it's all going to burn.

In the Hebrew culture, betrothal (a formal engagement) was as binding as marriage. It was a commitment of purity and exclusivity, intimacy reserved for the spouse after the marriage. I don't expect the world to care about this, but Christians who have been bought with the blood of Jesus have claimed a relationship with Him that the Bible equates with betrothal and the eventual marriage with a special wedding feast in heaven to celebrate. I pray that we will remember we gave ourselves to Him when we accepted His payment of the Bride price for us in blood. We are betrothed to Him and He is coming back for us. Let us remember to keep ourselves pure, set aside and reserved for Him alone.

Then there are all those parables about the master going away and leaving his servants in charge. In one, he gives them talents to invest. In another, he gives them tasks to do, and makes a point of mentioning the doorkeeper. They're told to watch. For what? Maybe to make sure nobody breaks in and steals? Maybe to make sure everyone is safe. Maybe anticipating his return so they can be sure everything is in order for their master. In another, the master puts them in charge of caring for his property. There is a warning about the servant saying, "the master is delaying his coming," and then getting drunk and beating his fellow servants. Jesus said the master will return when he is not expected, and there will be a reckoning.

Another Scripture reminds us, "Be not deceived. God is not mocked, for whatever a man sows that he shall reap. He that soweth to the flesh reapeth corruption, but he that soweth to the Spirit, life everlasting." (Gal 6:7) If you keep sowing to the flesh, it's not going to be pretty. By their very nature, seeds produce a harvest many times more than what you plant. The good news is we can sow good seeds that have spiritual value and the harvest will be bountiful and result in *zoe* life for us and those around us.

Jesus said, "I am coming as a thief in the night." We won't know when. It will be sudden. This is not so we live in terror—the "left behind" syndrome that makes people worried and anxious, but so we will be mindful that we have been left in charge and we have things to do. For Him. When Jesus returns, I want to be able to present to Him an increase for His investment, because He made that investment in me. In my life. It was His gift to me, and I want to have something to give back to Him, like Mary and the spikenard. Again, it's a matter of priorities and perspective. The scoffers say He's delaying His coming. Even Christians say this. But the truth is, He *is* coming. And nobody knows when their individual end time will be. A number of dear friends and family have had COVID. Most have survived. I want to add that two of them are Christian men who have deported themselves with integrity, kindness, good morals, and hearts of service to others, but weren't deeply connected to Jesus. They both had severe cases of the disease to the point they thought they were going to die. And both have declared it the most spiritual experience of their lives. They're different now. They radiate a peace and kingdom-minded purpose that can only come from being face to face with Almighty God. And both of them have remarked how much more exciting and fulfilling their lives are now that they're walking with Jesus, close as good friends.

We know from what Jesus said that the Word can be sown in a heart, be joyfully received and even take root, but the deceitfulness of riches and the cares of this life can choke it out. However, when you're peering into the possibility of your impending departure from this world, your values can change. Suddenly The Main Thing becomes truly the main thing. Suddenly, you get crystalline clarity of what really matters.

Where your treasure is, that's where your heart is. Jesus said to seek first His kingdom and all the rest will be added to us. All the good stuff. All that satisfies and makes life worth living. All that fulfills our innermost being because we're made for a kingdom that has no limits. This world on Earth is much too small.

One more Scripture, "What does it profit a man to gain the whole world and lose his own soul?" Mark 8:36.

I know three godly Christian women, each employed as an accountant, each for a different company, and even in different states. I know this because I prayed with them as they struggled with what to do about the illegal things their bosses wanted them to do. Sadly, one of the companies was owned by Christians. I'm sharing this because those women were in agony, afraid to lose their jobs, yet knowing they were being told to do wrong. It wasn't easy for them. Eventually all three of them did quit, but one still doesn't have a job.

There's so much pressure in the world to compromise our values, both as the boss and as the employee. The Scripture Gal. 6:9, goes on to say, "Let us not grow weary in well doing, for in due season we shall reap if we faint not." What will we reap? Life everlasting—*zoe*—God life now in our Earthly life, and then in the heavenly realm. Lord, help us not be deceived by the lure of riches or the fear of loss! Let us come before you at the End unashamed. The world needs to see straight walls. It can be done, and You will enable us to do it.

LOVE YOUR NEIGHBOR AS YOURSELF

John's experience is much too commonplace in this world, bosses demanding allegiance to their company over everything else but not everyone in leadership acts like that. This story is about my son Thomas whose choices came from his alignment with Jesus, though it could have cost him plenty.

Thinking about this event, I am reminded of one of the seeds Thomas planted in his heart very early in his life. When he was still a little boy, he told me his favorite Scripture was "Thy Word have I hid in my heart that I might not sin against Thee." (Ps 119:11) I believe it's the Word, sown on good ground, that enabled him to do what he did.

After years of excellent work, Thomas had been entrusted with a huge project with a big team of programmers. A lot of money was involved, but he had faced many deadlines and had always managed to get the job done on time. Since the job included terms and technologies I don't understand, I asked Thomas to send me details to give you an accurate picture of what was involved. Here is what he sent.

"We were at the beginning of a ten-year project worth tens of millions of dollars. I knew that getting it started would be the most difficult part because we had to mimic a very complex set of integrated applications the outgoing vendor had been running for many years to a new data center. Moving applications from one environment to another always has challenges, more if you didn't write it because you don't understand why the pieces fit in a particular way, more if it's an old system because documentation tends to be missing and wrong and people who really understand it have often moved on, more if it uses outdated technologies because it is more difficult to get support or find people who know how to work with them, more if your team has not worked together before because they don't know if they can trust each other or will even be able to work together, and more if there are other complications. We had all of those "more's," particularly the complications."

One night Thomas called me on his way home from work. It was kind of late, and that always makes my mom-ears perk up. He sounded tired as he gave me a general overview of his latest assignment. I said, "Well, you're a good boss. Big as this project is, I'm sure you'll be able to handle it.

Thomas surprised me by saying he wasn't sure he was such a good boss. When I asked why, he said one of his team had learned his father was very ill, and he gave him permission to go, even though the guy had to travel overseas. Thomas reasoned the project was in good shape and others could cover for him. Then another team member approached Thomas in need. Then another. Here's his account of these new "complications." Meanwhile, the first member was still overseas.

Thomas said, "While he was gone, another member of the team mentioned that her father was going to have surgery and that she would like to be with him and be with the family. The procedure was already scheduled so it would be a quick trip, though also overseas, and she would work as much as she could while she was there. Her part was a key piece and it had a long way to go but it still felt like the right thing to let her go. I told her I appreciated any work she could do while there but that I didn't really have any expectation that she would accomplish anything and it was okay.

"Once she arrived, she found that her family had not told her everything. Her father had stage four cancer, the operation was one last attempt to cure him, and she had not been told because the family didn't think she would be allowed to go and they didn't want to make her feel bad. She emailed me, apologetic that she had not been able to work because her father was in a lot of pain and she had spent her time trying to make him more comfortable. I reminded her that I didn't expect her to get anything done while she was there, that I meant it, and that I would be praying for her father's surgery. A few days later, she emailed again. Her father had died during the surgery. She had planned to come back on Thursday but was asking permission to stay over the weekend so she could attend his funeral. Of course I said yes! She could stay however long she needed to. True to her word, she came back right after the funeral.

"A third member of the team, also with a critical, poorly understood piece, where he was the only one on the team with any real knowledge of how it worked also had a family emergency. At least his didn't require international travel. It did, however, require multiple trips over 500 miles each way to understand his parents' health issues and then move them so they lived close to him. It took weeks for him to work through the details and there were several moments when I wondered if I had doomed the project with my decisions."

In view of their human need, Thomas had given all three of his team permission to go, and now they were behind and another company that was supposed to take care of getting them live online was dealing with equipment that had suddenly, inexplicably stopped working. The company that had hired Thomas did have a Plan B, but it would be millions of dollars and have a devastating impact on Thomas' company—and career.

As soon as I got off the phone, I prayed. The Holy Spirit came with such force I was astonished. It was intense and prolonged, and I knew I must not stop. I have no idea how long it went on. I told the Lord if it took all night I would keep praying. It went on and on, and I knew He was doing a sovereign, divine intervention. At last it was over. I could tell.

I continued to pray over the next days, and I know there were others praying as well. Thomas had requested prayer, not only for the project, but also for the souls of the team members.

Then, one early evening, Thomas called. "I'm on my way home," he said cheerily. "We finished early." They made their deadline and the other company's equipment inexplicably started working again—suddenly, mysteriously. That Saturday, they went live.

I have never prayed as I did that night. I think God wanted to show me two things. First, He was honoring my son for caring more about human beings than a big project, even though it involved millions of dollars and could have severely damaged his career. I don't know how many others in Thomas' place would have made the choices he did, and I'm still amazed at how he handled it. Second, I know our intercessory prayers helped make it possible for the work to be completed on time. I have some thoughts on how that can happen, based on my own experiences with work that requires figuring out where to go, what to do, how to fit things together, and solutions that come from "thin air" where you know you received divine help. But He also does things with time, endurance, and blocking interference from the dark side. It was my first prayer of this sort, and it has become something He calls me to do from time to time. The prayers are intense, fervent, and I always know I must not stop till it's over.

We live in a world of spiritual forces and we are spiritual beings who can affect this material world powerfully as we align with the will of God. He is looking over all the earth for those whose hearts are completely His—to show Himself strong on their behalf. He shut the mouths of lions because Daniel would not stop praying to Yahweh even though it was illegal. He walked with Daniel's three friends who chose the fiery furnace rather than bowing down to the golden statue. They are straight walls. They did it though it could cost them dearly. And my two sons, under enormous corporate pressure, chose to honor human beings made in the image of God, not the systems of the world and the things that will pass away. They are straight walls in a crooked world, evidence that the values and commandments of God are not too difficult to follow. Evidence that God brings about mighty and monumental good when we do.

"And let us not lose heart and grow weary and faint in acting nobly and doing right, for in due time and at the appointed season we shall reap, if we do not loosen and relax our courage and faint." (Gal 69 AMPC)

Beloved, let us love one another, for love is (springs) from God; and he who loves [his fellowmen] is begotten (born) of God and is coming [progressively] to know and understand God [to perceive and recognize and get a better and clearer knowledge of Him]. (1 John 4:7 AMPC)

10

PLUMB LINE

Aligning with the will of God, what does it look like? Hint: It's not intuitive. Another hint: It's not easy. In fact, in some ways, it's impossible. Only when we're brand new creations born of the Spirit of the Living God does it become something we would want to do, but even then it's not easy. Here's one of the hardest things. I thought I might as well put it first.

FORGIVENESS

Forgiveness is what we've received from God. Forgiveness is what He commands us to give if we are to align with Him. A lot of Christians have trouble taking this seriously, even though it's in the Lord's prayer and quite a few other places in Jesus' own words. Maybe it will help if we look at it a different way.

First, a word on the word "love." Greek has more than one word for love, and the one Jesus used when He said, "Love your enemies" is not the one for feeling friendly and close like a brother, or passionate and crazy to be with the other like with your betrothed, but *agape*. It's God's love, and it's a matter of will, not emotion. It's a choice. It's a direction of disposition where you consider the highest good of the other, not your own comfort or convenience. It's love that's willing to forgive. Forgiveness being another act of will rather than emotion. I've met so many people who say they can't forgive because they don't want to say the words while they still hate the guts of the one who wronged them. Forgiveness is not a word of warm fuzzies where you become best buddies. It doesn't imply or guarantee reconciliation in the relationship. It is a legal releasing of debt. "You no longer owe me. I'm forgiving the debt." It's entrusting the matter to God to be the judge, not yourself, and it releases you in splendid and spectacular freedom from having to somehow get revenge or make them pay or prove they were wrong. It says, "Father, I know You know, and I trust You to handle this matter." It does two amazing things. It frees you to go on with your life, and it releases on Earth the kind of supernatural workings that reflect the glory of the cross. "Father, forgive them for they know not what they do." It saves us from bitterness and shows the heart of God.

Second, here's a surprising aspect of forgiveness. My friend Dan says sometimes we can't forgive ourselves so we don't feel forgiven. Perhaps that's the key to what Jesus said when He taught His disciples to pray—"Forgive us our debts (trespasses) as we forgive our debtors (those who trespass against us). It sounds conditional. We're only forgiven if we forgive those who have wronged us. I've wondered about that for years. Jesus paid for every sin in full. Does forgiveness get doled out only if we ask and if we deserve it because we've met the criteria? It seems like a contradiction, but I know it can't be. So what am I missing here?

The rabbis say if there's something you don't understand—some mystery—there's a treasure underneath, so keep digging. What I think I'm seeing is sometimes the one who trespassed against us—who hurt us, who damaged and defiled us most—is us. When we look back at the messes we've made, we're horrified and overwhelmed with regret, but we can't get free from the guilt even though Father God, accepting Jesus's payment for our sins, has pronounced us not guilty. It's as if we still have to atone for our sins, which is like saying, "Jesus, what You paid was not enough to cover what I did because it was so very, very bad, so I'll crawl on my face the rest of my life to show I'm really, really sorry. Really? If your kid did something wrong, even something really, really bad, would you want him to crawl on his face the rest of his life to make up for it?

Forgiving ourselves is one of the hardest things we have to do, but if we don't, we never experience the release from those sins that Jesus already paid for. Again, it's not a matter of feeling it; it's an act of will. We have to be willing to take God at His Word, accept the grace, acknowledge that we certainly don't deserve it, but embrace it fully as our own. It may take multiple exertions of will, just as it may take years to forgive another human being who has done great evil to us, but the truth is we have already been forgiven. The debt has already been paid. It takes faith to accept that truth, but when we do, once again, two amazing things happen. It frees us to go on with our life, and it releases on Earth the kind of supernatural workings that reflect the glory of the cross. "Father, forgive them for they know not what they do." Truly, when we did those things, we didn't know what we were doing. Then, receiving this forgiveness for real, we find we can more easily forgive others because they, too, really didn't know what they were doing.

Great in theory. Hard to fathom. It's a supernatural grace, a God-hearted gift that our moral minds have difficulty comprehending, let alone trusting completely. Here's something that I think will help. More than twenty years ago, my son Thomas was a new father. He began sending me letters with his thoughts from the perspective of a brand new first-time dad. This story is a good reminder of how God sees us from the perspective of the completed work on the cross, and how very precious we are to Him.

THE DIAPER ADVENTURE

"Mom,

"When we first brought Anna home, we put her crib at the foot of the bed for the convenience of it, especially as her mom had to heal from the baby-eviction surgery. Before I would go to work, I would often try to do one last thing for my wife, usually a diaper changing or feeding. One less thing for her to do.

"I don't know if you remember what poop from a newborn who has only eaten from Mom is like but it's largely odorless and comes out in little pellet-like bits. For some reason that the baby book probably explained but I have long forgotten, it also has a tendency to come out like bullets from a machine gun. One other thing to note, particularly for parents of a newborn, is that babies seem to enjoy the freedom that comes from having a diaper removed.

"One morning, I had gotten ready for work. This was at a time where you didn't have to wear a tie every day and you could remove the coat once you arrived at work. My wife was not really in any condition to iron everything for me so I did it myself even though I really hate ironing things. Nicely dressed and ready to go, it was time to see if there was one more thing I could do to be helpful. The newborn was crying so I checked her diaper and, sure enough, she was wet. Easy enough to rectify so I whipped off her diaper and promptly got machine-gunned.

"It was a rather odd situation as I realized I could not dodge the projectiles as clean-up in a carpeted area would be really difficult. In fact, I needed to lean in to make sure none of the ricocheting bits could escape. Maybe I'm a soft-touch but I find it difficult to be mad at a happy baby. I did have a mess I needed to clean up carefully and I did need to iron a new shirt so I could change.

"So here's the thing: God is fully aware that we make messes, especially when we are young Christians. You might wonder if He leans into it the way I did to minimize the damage, but I can tell you that He already did. Calvary and everything leading up to it was God leaning in. Our mess. His taking the brunt directly and, through the unimaginable pain, I think He has so much love for us, there was joy too."

MORE WAYS TO ALIGN

In 1 Thessalonians 5:16-18, the Apostle Paul says, "This is the will of God in Christ Jesus concerning you: rejoice evermore, pray without ceasing, in everything give thanks."

Let's take a short look at rejoicing and thanksgiving, then a longer, more detailed exploration of prayer.

REJOICE

Not easy to do when circumstances are grim. A reminder that in His presence is fullness of joy (Ps 16:11). If you're lacking joy, you might need to get closer to the One who is all-powerful and big enough and smart enough to get you with joy through whatever you face. "My help cometh from the Lord, which made heaven and earth." (Psalm 121:2 KJV) It helps to remember Yahweh made it all and Jesus personally is holding it all together at this very moment.

Why do we need joy? The joy of the LORD is our strength (Nehemiah: 8:10). Remember, Nehemiah rebuilt the wall around Jerusalem in spite of rotten bureaucrats and skullduggery, traitors, and treacherous attacks. God still does the miraculous, and He does it through humans who are willing and available.

James 1 says to count it all joy when you face various trials because the testing of your faith worketh patience. The word translated "patience" is *hupomeno* in Greek. It's not about waiting around for something to happen, and it's not about how we are to behave around annoying people. *Macrothumia* is the Greek for dealing patiently with people, and it means having a long fuse, slow to burn. *Hupomeno* is about enduring things. It means the ability to bear up under pressure.

Like weightlifting with multiple reps, trials build up our ability to persevere, a really good thing when hard things go on and on and on and one thing gets piled on another. God tailors each trial to provide something for your character you could not get any other way except by learning that He is faithful always. That gives you the ability to bear up under pressure and run the race with perseverance.

The Apostle Paul, who had a lot of pressure on him much of his Christian life, put it this way: "We are hard-pressed on every side, yet not crushed; we are perplexed, but not in despair; persecuted, but not forsaken; struck down, but not destroyed—Therefore we do not lose heart. Even though our outward man is perishing, yet the inward man is being renewed day by day. For our light affliction, which is but for a moment, is working for us a far more exceeding and eternal weight of glory, 18 while we do not look at the things which are seen, but at the things which are not seen. For the things which are seen are temporary, but the things which are not seen are eternal." (2 Cor 4:8, 9, 16, 17 NKJV)

THANKSGIVING

In everything give thanks. It doesn't say "*for* everything," it says "*in* everything." Why? Because Jesus entered human history, partaking of our difficult, dusty physical life, specifically to die and rescue us from the fear of death which the devil was using to enslave and torment us. In everything we face, Jesus is there with us. He's been through it Himself. He knows how bad it feels, how hopeless, how frustrating, how crushing, and He will walk through every bit of it again—by your side.

PRAYER

Now for praying without ceasing. Why do we pray? Because we *need* to. Our best example is Jesus. He thought it so essential that He stayed up very late or got up very early just to make sure He had enough time to talk to His Abba. Yes, it's true He had a lot to do—save the world and all the rest—but He also said we are to do what He did and more. In order to do that, we need to pray.

The first, most vital thing that happens in prayer is it connects us to God, the One Who made heaven and Earth and all there is therein. He created it. He is not it. He is Spirit. He is not molecules. He is not inside time. He's not limited to our universe. He's not subject to it. He calls by name each of the hundreds of trillions of stars, and He's watching out for each of us. This all-powerful sovereign Lord is the One listening when we pray.

But many of us still don't. Why not? Maybe it feels to modern Christians too much like talking to the air—an imaginary friend from childhood. My son John said he used to think of it as a nice thing to say. "I'll pray for you," was like "Have a nice day." Or like Chun Shee with her collection of various idols. They were inert, and she never expected anything else from them. Some people use the word "pray" interchangeably with the word "hope." "I pray things will get better." "I pray I'll get that job." Really? When Jesus told His disciples about the End Times, He said when they saw the abomination of desolation in the temple, take off for the hills. He told them, "pray it's not in winter." That got me thinking. I've always believed the Lord's timetable was already set, so "pray it's not in winter" was kind of the "I hope it's not in winter cuz we'll be really cold in them thar hills." I now think Jesus was revealing to them something surprising about prayer: they can affect the timing of significant events on Earth.

Prayer has power. It's part of the spiritual armor listed in Ephesians 6. Of the seven pieces, only two are offensive weapons—the sword of the Spirit, which is the Word of God, and prayer. And if we combine prayer with the Word, it's even more powerful. Jesus did that all three times in the wilderness when He was being tempted by the devil. He knew the Word and how to wield it. "It is written." Good to remember when you're being tempted in a time of great weakness and need.

I asked my friend Dan if he thought Father God and the Holy Spirit talked with Jesus in the Wilderness of Judea those 40 days and nights. He said, "Of course. I think He got a big download. They told Him what was going to happen." That's plausible. A lot of what we struggle with is our thoughts of what's happening and conjectures of what to do about it. I know I'm much more able to navigate when I have God's perspective on the issues that confound me.

One time I was asked to do a service for the residents in a skilled nursing facility. What could I tell those feeble ones, slumped in their wheelchairs? He said to tell them, "The fact that you woke up this morning means God has something for you today." I have subsequently discovered that people who are in comas and varying degrees of unconsciousness (including Alzheimer's) are perfectly aware of what's going on. Their spirit is perceiving and comprehending with clarity though it looks as if no one is home. I used to visit friends in memory care facilities. One in particular had wanted to be a nun when she was young, but she married, had kids, and the cares of this life kept her too busy to make God her top priority. Then, as her body became less responsive to the outside world, her spirit became free to fellowship richly with her Savior God. The Lord told me that, inside the quiet exterior of her mortal shell, He and she were having a wonderful time of fellowship that was delighting both of them. I never would have known any of this except for the time I spent seeking God for the sake of His beloved wheelchair-bound children.

Our God is a communicator. He wants to tell us things. He wants to help us with our worries. "What a Friend we have in Jesus/ All our sins and griefs to bear/ What a privilege to carry/ Everything to God in prayer!/ Oh, what peace we often forfeit/ Oh, what needless pain we bear/ All because we do not carry/ Everything to God in prayer." So many times I've gone into my prayer time with armloads of cares, and one by one the Holy Spirit has replaced them with solutions or assurance He was working on these cares and worries. There have also been anxieties as I face compounding problems in so many areas of what used to be normal, predictable human life. The Word of God has the antidote. While he was in prison yet again, the Apostle Paul wrote, "Be anxious for nothing, but in all things, by prayer and supplication, with thanksgiving, make your needs known to God and the peace of God which passes all understanding will guard your hearts and minds through Christ." (Phil 4:6-7)

We all need the peace of God that passes all understanding, but when it comes to prayer, One friend told me he didn't feel he could talk to God, especially when he was struggling with things, because he felt too dirty to be in the holy Presence. Let's look at that. If your little boy fell in something slimy and yucky, would you want him to run away from you and hide or come to you so you could help him get cleaned up? When they felt the slime of sin, Adam and Eve ran away and hid. Jesus came to take all the slime on Himself so nothing could ever separate us from Father God again. When we feel most defiled is when we most need our Abba. When we let our shame drive us away from Him, it breaks His heart.

Prayer is totally supernatural because it's communication with the Creator of the universe. It cost Him thirty-three years of living without sinning once in a wicked, vicious world and a torturous death so we can talk to Him directly. The veil has been torn. Nothing can separate us now from the love of God. We may talk as friend to friend, as Jesus said we are. We can talk to Him as beloved child. He is our Abba, our Papa God. In Jesus we are accepted in the Beloved, joint heirs with Christ, covered with His righteousness. That's what the Bible says. Do we believe it? When we trust that we are *that* accepted, *that* privileged, *that* beloved, we will find it easy to talk to Him all day long. That's what my son John has discovered. In the worst of the worst times, he's found that prayer is the most powerful thing he can do for himself, for others, for circumstances, for wisdom, guidance, peace, and for sheer enjoyment. John tells me Jesus is in the passenger seat right next to him as he drives to work, and close as a whisper if he needs to talk to a difficult patient. In times of his worst worries, John has found the peace of God calming him and giving him strength. It's the peace of God we're told will pass all understanding. How can John feel this calm security at such a time as this? Only in God. Only under the shadow of His wing.

Dear brothers and sisters in Christ, we *need* our Abba now more than ever. We need to be able to tell Him our sorrows, our worries, our troubles. We need to speak our anxieties, uncertainties, fears. We need to know we can unload our hearts at His feet and let Him pour His peace over us, His perfect love that casts out all fear, refreshing us and giving us His wisdom as we face each new day.

HERE ARE SOME KINDS OF PRAYERS I ESPECIALLY LIKE.

I call it "The Door Prayer." In Rev 3:7, Jesus says, "This is the solemn pronouncement of the Holy One, the True One, who holds the key of David, who opens doors no one can shut, and shuts doors no one can open" (Rev 3:7) It's simple: you're facing a dilemma where you're not sure what path to take, so you ask God to open the door He wants you to go through and shut all the other ones.

Once I was looking for a house and I found a charming, custom one right on the lake. It was a good price, a convenient location, I fell in love with it, and decided that would be my new home. Almost as an afterthought, I said The Door

Prayer. Doors slammed shut so fast I was shocked. I sort of hadn't really meant it, but God made it impossible to proceed. I was disappointed until about a week later at church when a contractor friend of mine mentioned that he had just come from working on a frustrating job—a house on the lake so poorly built that every winter the basement fills up with water. The Door Prayer is a thing of beauty.

"Love Bomb." That's what my friend Debra calls the kind of prayer that drops an explosion of the love of God on the targeted person, place, or thing to which it is sent. Ever since she coined that term, we have been love bombing neighborhoods, schools, prisons, hospitals, stores, courthouses and places where troubled people are struggling.

We've been seeing some astonishing changes. I guess we shouldn't be surprised. The Bible says the weapons of our warfare are not carnal (flesh and blood, physical) but mighty through God for the pulling down of strongholds, casting down imaginations, and every high and lofty thing that exalts itself against the knowledge of God. (2 Cor. 10:4) Ephesians 6:12 says, "We wrestle not with flesh and blood but principalities, powers, spiritual wickedness in high places, the rulers of the darkness of this world." It's not a horizontal war we're fighting. This one is on a cosmic scale, and it includes the atmospheres and dimensions of spiritual realms beyond this material existence. That's why we need to use spiritual weapons. Nothing else will have truly powerful effects on the evils of this age or the turmoil and confusion human beings are struggling with. Let me assure you, what Jesus has put into our hands in prayer is much, much more powerful than we can imagine. Here's one of my favorite examples.

A friend of mine has neighbors who are so unhappy that she finally dubbed them, "The Old Yellers" because that's what they did. Day and night they would curse each other, loudly spewing hatred at family members whether indoors or out in their yard. It was pretty distressing to my friend who knew there were two little kids living in that cacophony and wondered if she should call Child Protection Services.

Some of us got together and prayed for this family, love bombing them and praying whatever the Holy Spirit laid on our hearts to ask on their behalf. I'll give you the short version. Eventually, they were still yelling at one another, but it was words such as, "I love you." Wow! Who knew?

Along those lines, the other day I was standing out on my deck, enjoying the cooling as the sun went behind the mountain. I heard birds and some light sounds of cars and voices. A dog barking in the distance. I was thanking the Lord for this incredibly peaceful summer. The whole season had been extraordinarily tranquil, which is not how Lake County usually is during tourist season. I felt a gentle breeze as the light dimmed into magentas, pinks, and dusky grays. I was reveling in the loveliness when a Scripture and a thought came into my mind. It was instructions Jeremiah had written to the elders, priests, and prophets who were being taken to captivity in Babylon. The Lord said, "Build houses and dwell in them; plant gardens and eat their fruit. And seek the peace of the city where I have caused you to be carried away captive, and pray to the Lord for it; for in its peace you will have peace." (Jeremiah 29:5, 7 NKJV)

The Lord reminded me that I ask him every morning to bless my neighborhood with His shalom—His peace that destroys chaos. I ask Him to bless my neighbors with His love and a desire for cooperation and harmony. I had the impression He was saying, "Why are you surprised?"

For me, it's a time of captivity in Babylon, the society obsessed with pleasure, power, greed, control—regulations changing, edicts that make no sense, and heavy restrictions on meetings, gatherings, and travel. In nearly two years I have left my house only twice. Other than that, I've been home.

But in this captivity, I have been praying every day, and the blessing is this immense peace in the place where I live.

We are not trapped or helpless. We don't have to "put up with" the madness that is seemingly rampant and unstoppable. We can make a significant difference. Jesus said to do what He did. We can bring His light into darkness, speak His order into chaos, comfort those who mourn, bind up the brokenhearted, set the captives free. And we can participate in prophecies and pray for the peace where we dwell, that there might be peace for everyone because we've asked.

"Prophecy" is kind of an intimidating word. It seems so big, delivered in a thunderous voice accompanied by flashes of lightning and violently shaking earth. Really, it's not meant to be scary. It's the vehicle God uses to tell us things. He says what He's going to do or what He's doing now. It's to help us—light in the darkness, like the torch in the Dark Cave. It's a new thing to me, this idea that I can actually participate in the fulfillment of prophecy, and yet, I have been doing just that. Recently God gave me these words: facilitate, implement, expedite. In the Scriptures, God said certain things are going to happen, and here's what you do. When we do them, we facilitate, implement, and expedite His purposes in the circle of influence, in the places we have authority, in the inspirations He gives us to speak into the spiritual atmosphere. We can shift the balance of power that is being expressed, like a sweet rain clearing toxic smoke from the air.

I don't think we realize how much power we have in prayer or how strategically we're placed. We're here, each planted in a certain location with a specific circle of friends family, co-workers, neighbors. We have authority wherever we have a right to be—by ownership or renting or invitation. We have a past that is filled with experiences unique to our times and settings. A number of my friends used to be alcoholics, drug addicts, promiscuous, liars, thieves, violent, rebellious, lawless, throwing their lives away on pleasures and partying with no understanding that there could be anything more meaningful and desirable to do in life. All of them should have died from the dangerous things they did—from overdose to auto accidents from DUI. But God rescued them. One has spent her Christian life helping others in rehab programs such as Celebrate Recovery. Another is persistently loving his extended family into sobriety with his own example and extraordinary efforts he makes to help them clean up their houses as well as their acts. Some are helping the homeless, having been homeless themselves. They can reach people I can't. They know how to pray for them in depths that are much more effective than anything I could say. One of them delivers hard-hitting words to addicts, telling them they need Jesus in an amazing combination of Holy Spirit power that is non-judgmental, compassionate, loving, and without compromise. I remember how lost I felt when I was controlled by demons, but I never took drugs. I don't understand what it's like to be addicted, to feel so desperate that you would steal from your best friend. But they know. And they can use their view from inside the insanity of those times to pray with insight, compassion, and power on behalf of those still trapped in what is destroying their beautiful lives.

Then there are those prayer requests that come in from people in horrible situations. I'm connected through emails to a small group of seriously earnest praying people with whom I share requests. Today I received the following message, which I think is particularly helpful because it applies insights from Jesus' teachings to the present disasters. When we aim our weapons at the source of the problem, those sharpshooter prayers are powerfully effective in dealing with the true issues in the context of the cosmic war.

"Good Morning, Carolyn, I was reading your friend's prayer request and it sounds so much like what my brother is going thru. The enemy is on a roll. God showed me thru a vision my son had about it. He has the gift of prophecy thru pictures. He said he saw the Seed that's planted in my brother's heart taking root, and the enemy is trying to uproot the seed with the worries of the world and money as in Matthew 13:21-22. The enemy is trying to push the Word out because of trouble and worries of the world. It was so powerful, I could see the battle. Also, reading, "you will be ever hearing but never understanding, you will be ever seeing but never perceiving." My prayer for your friend and her husband is that God would protect their faith, and open their eyes of understanding. I know the season we are in is hard, but necessary for good root growth.

"Please continue to pray for my brother and his wife and family."

We need each other. It's called "The Body of Christ" because we are members together. When you have a paper cut on your finger, your whole body winces when you smack it on something. And most people these days are feeling more than paper cuts. There are so many serious needs in addition to the circumstances. As in the prayer requests above, there is verbal domestic violence happening where those who should love each other are ripping one another to bloody shreds. Guess who is applauding? The real enemy, not the one who used to be their best friend.

Praying has another important purpose. It helps us hold each other up. It lets us know we're not alone. Things are much, much worse when we feel overwhelmed and isolated. Here's a recent email from the friend who made the original cry for help addressed above.

"It definitely does help to know we're helping each other. It can feel so lonely otherwise. The evil that's flying around is just exhausting. That I have the support of you and the other praying friends means the world to me. I can't possibly go it alone, and God is using this situation to remind me of that."

The one under attack is a front-line person who has spent decades waging war in dangerous battles. She has been stalwart and faithful through the most horrendous conflicts, a person who has been able to keep going on when other people would be dropping in their tracks. She has so many gifts and talents and such a strong core that she has been able to continue for many years, but now the battles are infused with spiritual poisons and her own self-reliance is proving insufficient. Makes me think of the disciples in the storm. "Jesus! Don't You care we're perishing?" He asks why they're afraid. He asks where's their faith. He has let them see they can't rely on what they know, their experience, their expertise. He's proven to them they need supernatural help—and they have it if they will only stop and ask. That's what I see happening for my friend today. God is showing her the weakness in her armor so He can heal her. He's also letting her know she is loved, supported, valued, and accepted even when she's not able to have everything under control. It's a good thing. Days are upon us where we really can't be in control. Birth pangs. God wants us to switch from self-reliance to God-reliance. And then He will take us places we could never otherwise go. To get there, we can't be a caterpillar. We must be able to fly.

Oh, I forgot to mention the update on the "Old Yellers." My friend is now calling them "The Singers" because the other day she heard one of them out in the backyard doing just that—singing. Happy singing. The weapons of our warfare are not confined to human reasoning and resources, but mighty through God, who has already defeated death, hell, and the grave.

Some other things. October is Fire Season in Lake County. We've had six or seven years of hot, dry, smoke-filled, frightening months. All of California has been in terrible drought. Finally a local pastor put out the call for fasting, prayer, and repentance for our own sins and the wickedness of our state. On the evening of the last day of the time of repentance, it began to rain. It was a big surprise. Rain wasn't even mentioned in the daily forecast. It was like a whisper, a promise, and I, who had been praying, took it as a sign from God that He had heard our prayers and was letting us know they mattered.

That was September. But Fire Season still loomed ahead. October. And then the rains came, gentle, but steady, water falling seriously, not wimpy little sprinkles that barely settled the dust. We had a week of rain. Then a few days to give the land time to soak it in. Then more rain. The pattern continued through the weeks. Word came that Fire Season was officially over. This October, no one was terrorized, threatened, evacuated, or burned to the ground. And all those power shutoffs that had caused such suffering and losses—here and in most of the county we didn't have any.

Not long ago, my friend Jill sent an email asking for prayer. She wrote, "I had just had a routine mammogram…they had always been clear…and got a call from my doctor that afternoon telling me that they'd seen something on the mammo and wanted me to go in for an ultrasound…so, of course I did that, and that's when they confirmed a 9 mm 'something' and scheduled a biopsy. It was too little for me to feel anything. Boy, oh boy, it was hard to control my thought processes, but I understood that the enemy wanted me to worry…I kept 'flipping' the switch and remembering to trust in the Lord."

Jill sent out her request, asking us to pray for the 9 mm "something." Today I received this email from her.

"Dear Carolyn and Sarah,

I went in for the biopsy this morning. The tech ultra-sounded me, then went and talked to the doctor, who came in and ultrasounded me, then another tech came in and looked at the screen while the first one ultrasounded me again, then they compared the screen to the previous ultrasound, then the doctor came in and said that they couldn't find what they saw before.

"I'll go back in six months for another look, but for today, and until then, no lumps!

Love you both to the moon and back,
Jill"

Jesus told His disciples to ask in His name, as His representative, so Father could be glorified (His image and character could be revealed) and their joy might be full. When I read Jill's email you can bet I was doing some significant rejoicing—in thankfulness and tears. I immediately asked Jill if I could include her story in this book and she wrote back, "Of course."

I love stories that are so fresh they're just hours old! It's not like reading about some miracle from when Jesus walked the earth. This is here and now, and WOW!

WHAT ELSE WE CAN DO

Zachariah 1 says the Lord sent craftsmen to terrify the horns of power and authority that were scattering His people, beating them down to the point they couldn't even raise their heads. Why craftsmen? When something is done beautifully, it has a way of lifting the heart.

I think of Elizabeth who writes articles day after day for local readers, each piece thoroughly researched, fair, clear, and beautifully written. I think of Kimberly taking meals to a family struggling with COVID, and Heather and Amber dealing with a difficult, strong-minded puppy, giving up 18 months of peace and quiet to prepare Hedy for her purpose in life. I remember Nancy, who brought a feast to my father's house after my mother died. She had wrapped and carefully labeled each item, ending with a beautiful, moist, richly chocolate cake. I had no idea food could be such a powerful ministry of love and comfort, and it made me weep. All of these are busy people who gave up their own time and energy for the sake of someone else, and they did it willingly and with grace that lifted the downcast or helpless or grieving or needy and it destroyed the power that would beat them into the ground.

When we apply our skills in whatever life we're living, when it's elevated past the mere physical need into something that shows the expertise of an artisan, it reveals the image and character of God Himself, Whose own workmanship is always something of breathtaking beauty. And it terrifies the powers that have amassed to beat down the people of God—and everyone else these days.

My friend Marc repairs boat engines with such care they look new. His workmanship is so excellent he never has to advertise. Customers return year after year for decades, and they tell their friends. But Marc doesn't just do excellent work. He's concerned about their souls. When water levels in the lake were so low boaters were complaining and worrying, Marc didn't join in, adding to the dismay. He told them to pray for rain. A lot of them aren't Christians or even interested in God. Nevertheless, I wonder how many of them decided to give it a try, just in case. I have the sense that some did, and the early and plentiful October rains were, to them, a little fond kiss from the Lord of the Universe Who wants them to know He hears them even though they might not quite believe He's there. Marc, who is trusted and respected for his integrity and beautiful workmanship, told his customers to pray, and some did. They asked God to give Lake County rain. And, you know what? He did.

Live your life as a work of art. It will bring glory to God because you will be revealing Him in Whose image and character you have been reborn. Light in the darkness. Hope that does not disappoint. It terrifies the darkness, which can never overcome that which flows from a heart full of God.

A REVELATION FROM THE THRONE ROOM OF GOD

In Revelation 5:8, Jesus takes the title deed of Earth from the One Who sits on the throne. "Now when He had taken the scroll, the four living creatures and the twenty-four elders fell down before the Lamb, each having a harp, and golden bowls full of incense, which are the prayers of the saints."

Who are those elders? Verse 9 tells us. "And they sang a new song, saying: 'You are worthy to take the scroll, and to open its seals; for You were slain, and have redeemed us to God by Your blood out of every tribe and tongue and people and nation,'" (Rev 5:9 NKJV) They represent us! We're the redeemed out of everywhere on the earth. We're the ones washed in the blood of the Lamb. And we're there *before* He begins to open the seals that release the four horsemen who start the outpouring of God's judgments during the seven last years of Earth.

I'm bringing this up because it's such an amazing revelation of our part of God's Plan. Look again at the elders. What are they holding in their hands? A stringed instrument and a golden bowl full of incense which are the prayers of the saints. First, unless the atmosphere of heaven brings about the sprouting of new appendages, those elders have only two hands. Everyone knows, in order to play a stringed instrument, you need to use both hands. So obviously they represent something; it's not something they're doing. Second, in the other hand, they're holding a golden bowl full of prayers. They aren't praying; they're representing something they are holding before the throne of God.

When I thought about this, I realized I was seeing a beautiful truth: we, the redeemed of the Lamb, hold the prayers of our brothers and sisters before the Lord in the throne room of heaven. It's what we do. Even on Earth, we hold each other up before Almighty God. It's an astonishing thought—that we will someday be there where our calls for help, our songs of praise, our prayers on behalf of others, and our cries for justice in a wicked world are still being presented to God in golden bowls.

I have sometimes felt the heavens were brass and my prayers didn't get any higher than my head. I have prayed fervently against the evil that is going on seemingly unchecked with no way to stop the overwhelming flood. In the throne room, John sees martyrs under the altar crying out, "How long before You avenge our blood?" The Lord tells them to be patient. It's going to happen. He hasn't forgotten them. There's an order to His Plan, a sequence to the wrap up of all evil and the establishment of righteousness on Earth. There will be justice. All wrongs will be made right.

You may be feeling like that—under the altar, having been murdered in a number of legalized and thoroughly immoral, unethical, and even indecent ways. God said Mystery Babylon is drunk on the blood of the martyrs who are crushed by false religion and the greed and wanton lusts of the world. No, we can't stop it, but we can make a difference. God hears us and He has not forgotten. He tells us to call upon Him and He will show us great and mighty things we have never seen (Jeremiah 33:3) When we pray, things in the invisible realm are initiated, facilitated, implemented. Recently He said to me, and now He's saying to you, "I have kept your every tear and every prayer." So let's keep praying fervently, faithfully. The Lord is listening.

Now to Him Who, by (in consequence of) the [action of His] power that is at work within us, is able to [carry out His purpose and] do superabundantly, far over and above all that we [dare] ask or think [infinitely beyond our highest prayers, desires, thoughts, hopes, or dreams]—To Him be glory in the church and in Christ Jesus throughout all generations forever and ever. Amen (Ephesians 3:20, 21 AMPC)

11

WALKING HUMBLY WITH OUR GOD

The eyes of the Lord go to and fro looking over all the earth seeking those whose hearts are completely His to show Himself strong on their behalf. (2 Chron 16:9)

"Surrender" used to make me think of a tattered white flag feebly waved before the enemy as a sign of total defeat. "I give up. You win. Do what you will." I don't think that's it anymore. It's the total abandonment that comes from vibrant First Love where your focus is on the Beloved and you joyfully give yourself to Him. We are called the Bride of Christ. Our Bridegroom King has gone to extremes to pay the price of a bride, and we have the awesome privilege of being His beloved. Really? A dear friend of mine just got married. She is head-over-heels, over the moon, walking on air... You name it, she's living it. She's crazy about her bridegroom, the love of her life.

But there's more to this surrender-thing, and you might not like it. In his letters, the Apostle Paul calls himself His *doulos*—His slave. In this country, we aren't used to terms such as Master, Lord, or King, and we shy away from "servant" or (worse yet) "slave." But didn't Jesus pay for us? "It is finished!" means, "Paid in full!" It's a glorious freedom to know there is not one sin, rebellion, iniquity, transgression, violation, or defilement that is counted against us anymore. All has been wiped clean. That price, acknowledged as valid, accepted as our own—that's what makes us Christians.

In Chinese, the word "righteousness" is comprised of "sheep," and "me." "Me" is, interestingly enough, a combination of the words "hand" and "spear." *My* hand. I'm the one holding the spear. Those ragged wounds on His body and face are the effects of *my* sins, and He loved me enough to endure the cross, so I could have His righteousness and be dressed in spotless white. All of that for me. For you. But not so I have to spend the rest of my life doggedly paying off the price He paid for me. Once He told me, and now He's telling you, "I didn't do it so you'd owe Me. I did it because I love you." Wow! You mean I'm not a forever debtor? I've been set free? You love me so much You're not even insisting on Your rights to me? Yep. Bought with a price, with no strings attached. He gave us free will. We can choose to go our merry way or fall at His feet and surrender our life to Him because He's so wonderful and we never want to be apart from Him.

But wait! The One to Whom we belong is no longer the Suffering Servant sacrificed for us; He's Himself, YHWH, the Great I AM in all His majesty, having taken back to Himself the glory He had from eternities past, before He emptied Himself, deliberately humbling Himself in order to be able to die for us—as a human being. But just take a look at Him now, not as a few disciples saw Him on the Mount of Transfiguration, all dazzling, radiant and bright, but as John saw Him preparing for His final return to Earth. He's coming on a gorgeous white horse (I picture an Andalusian stallion), wearing a robe dipped in blood, with many crowns on His head (signifying many authorities), His Name upon Him: KING OF KINGS AND LORD OF LORDS. His eyes are intense as flames of fire, His skin is radiant and glowing, The Word of God, Maker of Heaven and Earth and everything else. And with Him, also on beautiful white horses and dressed in white linen, are those who love to be with Him—us. That's our Bridegroom King, regal, triumphant, glorious. It's not hard for me to surrender to One like that! Wow! I can have confidence and trust in Him, accepting from His hand new possibilities in each turn of circumstances, delay, closed door, dying dream. With a clear view of Him, I can do so without rancor because I trust the heart of God in whatever comes. I think surrender and humility go together well. Humility used to mean weakness, the doormat syndrome. But now I know it simply means "You're God; I'm not." God told me, "Humility is a relief." I want to clarify those two terms because, in today's society, they still have overtones of weakness and defeat. There's an overwhelming message in the media (especially movies and books and video games) that having the power and being in control is not only preferable for survival, it's necessary. Sound familiar? Eat or be eaten. Control or be controlled. Spear and live or be speared and die. Who wants to be under the boot of an oppressive dictator? Jesus lived under the oppressive rule of Rome. Did He tell His disciples His Kingdom was more powerful than any other on Earth, so rise up and kill and eat anyone lower on the food chain? No. Jesus said His Kingdom is not of Earth. He came to model and establish an entirely new way of relating to one another and to God. And it would involve humility and surrender. Very different from our Power Over ways of thinking. It's possible only when we decide to trust His wisdom instead of our own. Otherwise, we can be so disappointed we become offended, begin to distrust, and then desert Him and fall away as the disciples did when Jesus didn't crush Rome as they expected. Instead, He let soldiers bind Him and take Him away. More than once He had told His disciples in detail exactly what was going to happen, but they were so convinced they knew what He was supposed to do that, when it didn't happen according to their plans, they all ran away.

Disappointed with God is such a dangerous place to be. In this, let me give you one of the greatest treasures He's ever given me. At the moment I was most horribly disappointed in my circumstances, He said, "When you know why, you'll be glad." The next night, I found out why, and boy! Was I glad! Other times it has taken years, but always, when I know why,

I'm glad. It's never a casual glad; it's always overwhelming astonishment at how glad I am that God did what He did and I didn't get what I thought would have been the best outcome according to my brilliant assessment of the situation. Please carry that in your heart and let your spirit speak it to you when you are tempted to decide He's not good, trustworthy, or loving after all. He always has good reasons, and they're always better than we can imagine.

This trust in God is a crucial area in which to realign with Him. Humility and surrender. It's a much higher perspective, and it brings freedom of the mind and heart because it releases supernatural Kingdom power on Earth.

My Dad and Cal Trans

This story exemplifies what surrender and humility look like in action, and what blessings come from being able to accept what you can't change, finding new possibilities in the midst of devastating destruction. My dad surrendered to the inevitable even though he and mom had planned ahead to avoid any loss. The choices of others messed that up, but his humility opened his bright mind to other ways to go on with hope and provision for new life. In these days of so much that shifts and changes without our permission or even knowledge, God still knows how to work every bit of it together for our good.

I was totally horrified when I saw the big earth movers toppling the beautiful trees in my parents' spacious front yard. Cal Trans was widening Baseline Road to use as an alternative route for traffic while part of the 210 freeway would be shut down for a couple of years. For twenty years my parents had known it was coming, obtained the official coordinates, and planted their yard accordingly. One of their prize trees was a tall flowering magnolia with white blossoms as big as your hand. They planted well beyond the outer limit of the proposed road and it had flourished, gracious and lovely, but the big metal scoop was being positioned at its roots and, in one push, it was down, its white blossoms soon to shrivel dry and brown. My mother was in tears. As the stately Italian cypress trees fell, she whispered, "I don't have fifty years to grow another garden."

But why were they taking so much? And why that magnolia tree? The neighbors across the street had convinced the city their trellis was a national treasure and the historical society had granted them another six feet of front yard to protect it, six feet that now had to be taken from my parents' front yard. I would have cried and run inside except for my father. He was rushing here and there, signaling to the workmen who were operating the big machines. Early that morning he had gone out and made friends with them. He loved machinery of all sorts, and they were happy to cooperate with the skinny elderly man who had asked them to dig up certain plants with care so he could transplant them.

I watched as a young operator carefully scooped out a little kumquat tree, its tiny orange fruit dangling sideways. As soon as it was uprooted, my dad was on it, dragging the little tree, towards a barrel he had filled with water. Then it was the huge jade plant. Then a little dwarf peach tree. For each one he had prepared a container in the hopes of replanting it inside the new limits of their front yard. As far as I know, neither tree survived.

When it was time for me to go home, my dad handed me a shoebox full of pieces of the big jade plant. He told me to plant them because every piece would grow. So I took them and planted each one in a pot. Each one grew. I still have them, flourishing and shapely and lovely. They remind me of my father's ability to adjust to whatever comes without bitterness or even bewilderment. I have given pieces of those plants to many friends over the years. My hope is that those offspring of the one from my parents' beloved garden would remind them of my dauntless father and give them hope that they, too, may find in every situation new places to grow.

My dad had made a lifetime of adjusting to extremely difficult circumstances, and he felt it was a waste of time to try to reopen doors that were already shut, or revive what was dying because of someone else's choices. When the FDA shut him down three times, saying his new electronic acupuncture machine was not considered proven safe and effective, he went a different direction, eventually coming up with a machine that would go to the Olympics multiple times because of its effectiveness on sports injuries. A closed door to him was a chance to go a different way, one he always trusted would be better. That was my dad's confidence in the Divine Guidance he never told me about till many years later. He said he felt God wanted him to bring microcurrent to the world and it didn't matter what they did to try to stop it. God always made a way. I believe the reason my dad was able to invent so many world-changing things is his refusal to be bitter, resentful, or dismayed. Even when microcurrent became a multi-million dollar business worldwide and people ripped him off with clones they claimed to have invented, units they then sold at twice his price, he shrugged and said, "They didn't invent it so they can't go any further with it. I'll just invent something else." And he did. And it was always even better.

HORATIO SPAFFORD

Here's another example of surrender and humility. Horatio Spafford was a respected lawyer, a wealthy investor in Chicago real estate, a close friend of evangelist D.L. Moody, devout Christian, and loving husband and father. He and his wife Anna had five children—a son and four daughters, and they seemed to have the perfect life. They often hosted people at their spacious home, and were generous to ministries and to those in need. By today's standards, Horatio Spafford wouldn't have had to be humble or struggle to surrender to the will of

God in anything. He was on top of the world. Then their only son died at age four, and a year later in 1871, the Chicago fire left every one of their land investments in ashes. Two years after that, Horatio arranged for a trip to Europe for the family, but at the last minute, he was detained by business. Anna, the girls, and a group of friends set sail on the Ville du Havre, a luxury liner to Paris with Horatio's promise to meet them as soon as he could.

On November 2nd 1873, the Ville de Havre was rammed by a British vessel and sank in minutes. Two hundred twenty-six people lost their lives. Annie, Maggie, Bessie, and Tanetta, the Spafford's four young daughters, one of them just a baby, drowned. Anna was picked up unconscious, floating on a plank of wood. In her despair, Anna Spafford heard a voice speak to her, "You were spared for a purpose." And she immediately remembered something a friend had said, "It's easy to be grateful and good when you have so much, but take care that you are not a fair-weather friend to God."

Horatio immediately boarded the next ship to England to bring back his grieving wife. On the way, the captain of the ship called him to the bridge to tell him they were now passing over the place where the Ville de Havre went down. Horatio returned to his cabin and wrote the words to his hymn.

In a letter to his wife's half-sister, Horatio wrote, "On Thursday last we passed over the spot where she went down, in mid-ocean, the waters three miles deep. But I do not think of our dear ones there. They are safe, folded, the dear lambs." In humility and surrender, Horatio did not blame God or question His character.

You probably know this story, the tragedy that caused Horatio Spafford to write,

When peace like a river attendeth my way,
When sorrows like sea billows roll,
Whatever my lot, Thou hast taught me to say
It is well, it is well with my soul.

Shattered and grieving, Horatio and Anna returned to Chicago and God gave them a daughter, Bertha. Then a son, Horatio. But this son, too, died as a young child. The Spaffords had now lost six children, including their only sons. After the birth of Grace, another daughter, the Spaffords moved to Jerusalem with a group of friends—thirteen adults and three children. There they founded a Christian community that became known as the American Colony. An article reported, "Their goal was to ease the suffering of the needy there, and they carried out their philanthropic work to all, regardless of religious affiliation, thus gaining the acceptance of the Jewish, Muslim, and Christian communities." During and after World War 1, they opened soup kitchens, hospitals, orphanages, and other places for those suffering and in need.

I think God has ways of "making it up" to those who have suffered greatly. Sometimes it's afterwards, when eternity is the landscape of existence. Sometimes there's a surprise during the lifetime on Earth for one who loved the Bible, loved and served all peoples, and refused to curse God and die in the extremes of his losses, but would write instead, "It is well, it is well with my soul!"

In Jerusalem, Horatio and Anna adopted a teenager, Jacob Eliahu, who was born in Ramallah into a Turkish Jewish family. One day Jacob, playing hooky from school, slid down a tunnel, and found, chiseled into the rock wall about twenty feet from the end, an inscription in an ancient language.

Jacob Eliahu Spafford loved teaching his students about Hezekiah and the famous tunnel you read about in chapter 2. He never told them he was the boy who discovered what some have called one of the greatest archaeological finds of all time.

12

WALKING IN THE LIGHT

I've been thinking about the torchlight that I followed in the blackness of The Dark Cave. As the bright fire glanced off the looming walls, what had been invisible startled me with wonder. It was a forty-five minute walk for more than a mile deep in the earth across ancient, uneven stone, an immersion experience that so soaked into my senses that I can still smell, see, hear, and feel it though it was fifty-five years ago. There's something about taking time to absorb and gather meaning we miss if we are in a hurry. It's easy to be impatient in a society that specializes in speed. In these chapters, I am sharing some accounts of people who lived letting their lights shine in difficult, unfamiliar places. To absorb this beauty, you need more than a synopsis of the plot. May you receive insight and enrichment as you hear their voices and thoughts, and see what their choices brought about over time for the glory of God.

LILIAS TROTTER

Lilias Trotter was an artist and writer whose watercolors caught the attention of John Ruskin, the chief arbitrator of art at the time. He was a philosopher, writer, painter, and is considered by some to be the most influential man of the 19th century. He began to mentor Lilias, increasingly impressed with this young woman who had such capacity both to absorb and to communicate beauty. They developed a deep friendship and he invited her numerous times to stay at his retreat home where she was surrounded by the top artists and thinkers of the day. It must have been very heady for a woman in her early twenties. Ruskin saw great potential in this gracious

163

young woman, and let her know what her future could be as a significant artist at that time.

In one of her letters, Lilias wrote, "Ruskin says I could be England's greatest living painter, that I could do things that would be immortal. Please understand that it is not from vanity that I tell you, at least I think not, because I have no more to do with my gifts than with the color of my hair, but because I need prayer to seek God's way more clearly."

Lilias understood what Ruskin was offering her, and he was powerful enough to make it happen. It created in her an enormous crisis of faith that her biographer, Miriam Huffman Rockness, said almost broke her. Lilias loved art, and she was intrigued by what Ruskin had presented for her future, but in the end, after much intense, agonized prayer, she made her decision. In her diary, she wrote, "I cannot give myself to painting in the way that he means and continue to seek first the Kingdom of God."

At that time there was a spiritual movement happening in London. It involved reaching out to the poor and needy. Lilias had been born into a distinguished family, cultured, educated, and well-off, but she insisted on going alone down to Victoria Station, ministering to the prostitutes, getting them into safe places where they could have something to eat and learn skills that would make it possible for them to earn a living a different way. She also noticed the working women on the streets eating their lunches out of paper bags. That was not acceptable to Lilias. She helped establish the first restaurant for women in London.

Though Ruskin approved of Lilias' good works for the poor, he also thought others could do the same things and she was neglecting her God-given talent. Yet, he couldn't convince her, change her, or bend her to his will. She had an internal strength to turn her back on fame and choose obscurity. It wasn't something he understood.

One day, when a speaker at a mission meeting asked if anyone there was sensing God's call to go to North Africa, Lilias found herself standing, saying, "He's calling me."

Ruskin thought Lilias was foolish to throw away fame, fortune, and even a kind of immortality, to go to Algeria. Though she continued to correspond with Ruskin after leaving England, her heart was no longer on her art. Except for producing a few small books and pamphlets, Lilias wrote her thoughts and painted her small watercolors only in her diaries, and only for herself.

In Algeria, Lilias found a way to make contact with the people. She reached out to the children and held classes for them. Women told her their sorrows. In that culture, girls lived in their father's house until they were married at age ten or twelve. Then they were in their husband's harem until he discarded them for younger wives. They were left destitute—used, rejected with no options and no means of support. Lilias hired someone to come teach them marketable skills. She poured the love of Jesus on them and they responded. One Arab lady said to another, "Nobody ever loved us like this!"

Rockness wondered if Lilias had made the worst decision of her life, but as she researched diaries and letters, she recognized that Lilias had been faithful to what she believed God wanted her to do. She wasn't concerned about the results. Rockness said, "The adding up is not really ours to see. Who's to measure what is greatness?"

The adding up is not really ours to see. No, but we can catch a glimpse of the consequences of the choices each one makes. Lilias continued to correspond with John Ruskin until his death in 1900. In his letters to her, sometimes he scolded her, mercilessly criticized her, and complained that she was neglecting him. His fame and influence continued, but it didn't seem to bring him satisfaction or comfort. In one of his last letters to Lilias, he wrote, "You are probably at present the only person likely to help me in my chief difficulties and lost ways, so please think much of what I told you, and follow on your own path happily the Light I cannot find. Ever affectionately—J.R."

Rockness said Lilias, to the end, "felt the joy of her life." Many others have chosen the other path, enjoyed the pinnacle of success by the world's standard, and then what?

As he neared his final days, John Ruskin implored Lilias to come back and see him. Though he was a Christian, even having some acceptance as a church leader, he said he could not find the Light that she had found. His books, his art, his lectures, his influence on the culture and philosophy of life would put him in history as a great artist and thinker of the 19th century, and give him his own immortality, but there was an emptiness that I believe Lilias would have shared had she not chosen to follow her Lord.

This is not to say that she didn't have times—even long periods of times—of discouragement, ill-health, doubts, griefs, unthankful people whom she had expended great energy to help. Even so, Lilias wrote often about the blessing of a life poured out for God to bring life to others, and, as Rockness said, she felt the joy of her life to the end.

Lilias' mother was disappointed that her talented daughter had turned down Ruskin's offers, whose letters might have included a proposal of marriage. It's interesting that Lilias did not go to North Africa until after her mother's death. In the meantime, she gave one of her pamphlets to her friend, a singer and songwriter named Helen Howarth Lemmel. In *Focused,* Lilias had written, "So then, turn your eyes upon Him, look full into His face and you will find that the things of earth will acquire a strange new dimness." It inspired her friend to write the hymn, *Turn Your Eyes Upon Jesus,* which has been recorded by numerous groups and individuals, appears in many hymnals, and has been translated into languages all around the world.

As Lilias lay dying, friends surrounding her bed, they sang her favorite hymn, *Jesus, Lover of My Soul,* and then she looked out the window and said, "A chariot with six horses!" One friend asked, "Are you seeing beautiful things? "She answered, "Yes, many beautiful things."

Many Beautiful Things became the name of a documentary on Lilias' life that would never have come about were it not for Miriam Huffman Rockness. A small book of Lilias' words and watercolors came to Miriam at a period in her life when she was looking for something beautiful with which to fill her limited private time as a pastor's wife with small children. Miriam spent the next thirty years tracking down everything she could about this unknown artist, and she ended up bringing her story to people a century later who would be inspired to see her remarkable choices and the fruit of her life in the context of years.

Two of Lilias' small books, *Parables of the Cross* and *Parables of the Christian Life,* made their way into the hands of Elisabeth Eliot, Jim Eliot's widow. At the start of each chapter in her book, *A Path Through Suffering,* Elisabeth included an illustration and a quote from one of Lilias' books. I read *A Path Through Suffering* when I was in a devastated place in my life and the words of both of these godly women helped me see the truth of what Jesus meant when He said, "Unless a grain of wheat falls to earth and dies…" Life is like a seed. One apple seed can bring forth a tree with many apples for many years, each apple bearing a number of seeds, each one with the same vital energy and the potential to bring forth much more life, but it happens only if the seed, in its present condition, gives up its insular, small, limited form.

Who knows what a life can do? I'm sure Lilias would be surprised to know about her friend's song, Elizabeth's book, Miriam's documentary, and the ways their individual lives, and the lives of so many others, have been significantly changed because of her. I think Lilias had a hint, not about her own contributions to God's kingdom, but what is latent in any life that will yield itself to the purposes of God. She wrote, "God only knows the possibilities that lie folded in each one of us." The adding up is not ours to see," but what we do for the love of God and His people has a way of growing, seed by seed, into an exponential harvest of blessing far beyond the span of years for each individual life.

LOVE YOUR ENEMIES

God has ways of making sure we get the input we need for what lies ahead. Sometimes there's a "chance" meeting that changes our lives forever. In this case, what began as a result of this encounter would give Eric Liddell wisdom, strength and peace through some of the hardest years of his life. Around the time Eric was completing his education at Edinborough University, he went to a track meet where he met a young man who was involved with a group of people who were very serious about their Christian faith. This encounter at a track meet was obviously a divine appointment, one that happened because Eric was a runner and track meets were an important part of his life. I love the way God weaves significant influences into our lives through things we happen to love. This group of Christians emphasized a relationship with Jesus Christ, knowing Him and talking to Him just as you would talk to a friend. Eric's biographer, David McCasland, said, "They were very keen on studying the Bible and applying it to their lives, and following the discipline of the Four Absolutes: Absolute Purity, Absolute Unselfishness, Absolute Honesty, and Absolute Love. They also emphasized having a quiet time to be alone with God. During that time, a person would read a portion from the Bible, talk to the Lord in prayer, and then be silent, seeking to listen to what the Lord would say to them and how He would direct them for that particular day. This became Eric's lifelong practice."

Eric was particularly focused on knowing God's will for his life. He very much wanted to serve God, but he said the only abilities he had were in athletics. He was reserved, shy, and quiet. Nonetheless, he was willing to go through any door he felt God was opening for the Kingdom, so he accepted invitations to speak at evangelistic meetings, though it was not a comfortable thing for him to do. He wasn't a great speaker, but after the Olympics, he was celebrated lavishly and lots more people came to hear him than before. Crowds of nonbelievers wanted to hear what this Olympic gold medalist had to say about his Christian faith.

Doubtless it was during some soul-searching quiet times that Eric came to believe God wanted him to go to China. Some thought he could do more good there in Scotland and leave the work in China to missionaries who were already there, but after a banquet one night, Eric announced his decision to go to China. Many people were shocked, but to those who knew him well, it wasn't a surprise. He felt strongly that the missionaries had done so much more than he had.

So he left. Eventually he married Florence, the daughter of another missionary couple, but only after she completed four more years of education and became a nurse. Her father insisted upon it before he allowed the marriage. There in the land of Eric's birth, he and Florence had two daughters and Eric enjoyed the family life he had missed when he was a child. But increasing turmoil in China caused Eric and Florence to make the hard decision to separate. Florence and the girls sailed to Canada where they would be safe till things settled down. Eric remained in China because he said he couldn't rush to safety for himself and abandon his people.

When Pearl Harbor happened, the Japanese rounded up all the "enemy nationals" in China and confined them in internment camps. The largest of these was Weihsien, housing 1800 people, a very diverse group including businessmen, tourists, entertainers, travelers, families, missionaries, the elderly, babies, executives from multi-national corporations, opium addicts, Catholic priests, 300 children and teenagers from the China Inland Mission School, and Eric Liddell.

The prisoners were kept in what had been an American Presbyterian middle school, a large compound with a hospital, a large church, and many rooms. Families were put into small rooms (9'x12') and large classrooms were turned into dormitories where others were all bedded together. Before the prisoners arrived, Japanese soldiers had used it as an army barracks, and they had trashed the place, including most of the furniture and cooking equipment. Joe Coterill was a teenager at that time. He recalled, "The sewers had all become blocked up and within two or three days of our arrival there, they overflowed suddenly. Instead of just a few hundred troops there were 1800 people, so ways had to be found of dealing with it. The people who set about dealing with it in a very practical way without asking for any decision on the part of any kind of authority were a group of Roman Catholic priests who had been taken out of their monasteries and sent to camp. They set about digging trenches and doing all that was necessary to make the sewer system work.

Another Weihsien teenager, Norman Cliff, said there was a labor department that assigned them jobs. "I was working in a kitchen feeding 700 people," he said. "There were three kitchens and I had to stir a big cauldron with bread porridge, bread soup, bread everything."

Joyce Strenk, another teenager, added, "You thought about food all the time. You were hungry a lot of the time. Every one of my teeth was loose at the end. But at the same time we accepted it as just part of life.

In the midst of this misery, there was also a surprise in the camp. Norman Cliff remembered, "About the second day in camp somebody pointed this man out to me and said, "He ran for the Olympics. This is the man who wouldn't run on a Sunday." Then we knew who he was. He was very friendly. He was all over the camp, cheering people up and asking questions and he was particularly good to the Chifoo scholars whom he knew were separated from their parents by many provinces. He himself was missing his family, so he was very, very good to the Chifoo children. I was one."

Joe Coterill recalled, "I had heard of someone being afar off, kind of a star somewhere up there, one I would never meet, just a name to conjure with. Suddenly I found I was living alongside him, and later, very shortly after, living in the same dormitory with him. It took some getting used to."

Joyce said, "He was very good with teenage Bible studies. I remember Stephen Metcalf talking about that. He had Bible studies on the Sermon on the Mount and how he brought that out so clearly to be applicable to now as teenagers in a Japanese internment camp."

It could have been much worse. According to David Mc-Casland, The Weihsien internees were not tortured, but they were given the barest necessities and left to organize themselves. Out of the turmoil and confusion, they would have to figure out how to make it work. Eric had been brought up in a missionary boarding school himself, so he understood what it was like to be without parents for years. He quickly took the children under his wing. Since there was not room for classrooms, he tutored them individually and in small groups. People were found in the camp who could teach, and school went on. Eric had taught chemistry, and wrote a book with illustrations and principles and experiments that they could use to learn that subject. Teenagers would come to him for advice, and he was a stabilizing influence for them and everyone else. Adults who were in awe of the man who would not run on Sunday soon found him accessible, helpful, and non-judgmental. He did his chores and helped with theirs, organized and refereed sports games and athletic activities, and in the evenings was always repairing the equipment that had been broken during the games of the day. He gave talks to the group, had Bible studies, carried coal for those who weren't strong enough to do their assigned tasks, pumped water from a well (3 hours at a time), and went around encouraging them. He even managed to bridge the gap between the businessmen, who thought the missionaries were separate and judgmental, and the missionaries, who thought the business people were taking advantage of the Chinese. But Eric got along with both groups.

The story goes that there was a game one Sunday, and it had disintegrated into an argument because there was no referee. Eric chose to help them. Joyce said, "He came to the feeling that it was the Christ-like thing to do, to let them play with the equipment and to be with them the times he could (not during church-time of course) because it was more Christ-like to do it than to do the letter of the law and let them run amuck by themselves. So he did change on that, and for me that was very interesting because it was the one thing of course everyone remembers about Eric, but his Christian faith was very pertinent to the time and place and now—How do we live Christ now in our situation?"

Eric's Christianity was practical. He didn't waste energy fretting about the lack of food, absence of privacy, injustice of internment, or uncertainties of the future. He kept connected to God and applied the biblical perspective to daily life. He didn't try to be a holy man dropping pearls of wisdom, floating over troubles with Bible verses and positive thinking. He was ordinary and shared his struggles in a plain way. And because it was down-to-earth faith, people were able to believe him. Norman Cliff said, "I think our main problem was how long are we going to be here? This is going to go on for a long time. And he would come around and assure us that God had everything under control."

Was it God's will that Eric go to China? If he had stayed in Scotland, would he have missed God's purpose for his life? I don't think so. We can serve God in any number of scenarios. Eric would have poured out his life wherever he was. On the other hand, God being in the Eternal Now, He knows what's needed in every life and He designs each one of us with gifts to meet those needs—things no one else can do as well.

There were other missionaries in China, but Eric was gifted in just the right ways to give those 1,799 other prisoners of war the hope, encouragement, and coherent and cooperative community that would enable them to come out of that difficult time whole and inspired. Here are a few of his unique qualifications.

He had grown up in boarding school with the children of other missionaries. In those days, parents saw their children every seven years when they came home on furlough. Eric understood the challenges missionary children had, especially when they were removed from school and put in a prison camp.

He had Olympic gold, which gave him mystique with the adults who were at first in awe, and then delighted to find a man of strict principles and faith so accessible and helpful to everyone.

He was very strong. That athleticism helped him carry out extra duties on behalf of others, another way of living a servant life in a difficult circumstance.

He had years of quiet time with the Lord, rising before dawn, lighting a small peanut oil lamp, reading his Bible and waiting to hear what the Lord would say to him about the day ahead. This abiding in Christ, this alignment every early morning, gave Eric fresh light and life to share with others.

He wasn't a good preacher.

Joe Coterill said, "Eric's talks were as though he were talking to you individually, just talking about problems he met with and how he approached God in prayer in his life and in his Bible reading to come through the situations. In all situations he was seeking to bring the Gospel of God's love to all people. It was a talk rather than a sermon. In technical terms he was not a good preacher, but everyone loved to listen to him because he was speaking to people at the level they could understand with an authority, one felt, that came from a life lived in contact with God."

My personal feeling is this homey, ordinary way of talking to them was a hundred times more effective than it would have been had he been a flashy, polished public speaker with a three-point outline and a resounding conclusion at the end. Sometimes the gift God gives a person is a plain way of speaking, a plain face that does not draw attention to itself, an ordinary voice that feels comfortable and inviting. Eric was quiet, shy, reserved, and had none of the skills evangelists use to capture the attention of a crowd—and I think those were gifts God gave him that made him particularly well-suited for the work of representing the character and heart of God to his fellow prisoners.

Do you think Eric suffered in prison camp? I bet he did. Though McCasland's four years of interviews with internees, family, and others who knew Eric revealed not one negative word about him, we know he missed his own family terribly. When he and Florence agreed to separate, they thought it would be at most a year before they would be reunited. Instead, they never saw each other again, and his third daughter, who went to Canada in her mother's womb, never met her father. It was their free will that decided what they would do, and their free will to decide what they would do with what happened afterwards. Eric's oldest daughter Patricia was six when they parted, and she says her mother never blamed the Japanese for her husband's death or expressed any anger or hatred for the people and circumstances that kept them apart. Florence told the girls they had to forgive because that's what Jesus did. And Eric used his free will to serve others as much as he could, also without complaining or bitterness. He wrote a little book with some lessons in it. One part was on a subject that was very much on his heart: surrender. Three hundred children and teenagers were profoundly influenced by Eric Liddell, but so were the other internees. His life affected everyone. We can do that too. We have free will to bless or curse. It's our choice, and what we decide will set an example for everyone around us.

There's nothing like being imprisoned with 1799 other internees of diverse backgrounds, ages, and agendas in crowded, comfortless conditions with mostly bread and water to eat, and not much of that either—with an unknown future or end-point, and hostile guards making sure you don't try to escape. In those years, who you are, your phobias, fears, and character flaws can start to leak out of the cracks in your facade, if you have one. In the camp, there were a number of teenagers who hung around with Eric, and if anyone can spot a phony, it's a teenager. The following are comments from some of those teens who knew Eric best, along with comments from biographers who studied his life.

Joyce Strenk said, "To me it was the biggest awakening, the one that guided my life most because he made Christ's life so relevant. He made it feel like we who follow Christ must do what He asked us to do where we are in the situation we're in. You don't get a dispensation because you're in the camp."

One of Eric's roommates was Joe Cotterill, who also had a practice of waiting on the Lord in the morning. They became silent quiet time partners. Joe said, "It was that experience that I look back upon as being one that kept me on an even keel during the days of internment. Eric's attitude was that the ultimate aim of preaching, of reading the Bible, of prayer, was to bring about a change in one's self, an internal change, a change in one's attitude to God, in one's attitude to other people. The one word that came over time again and again is that simple Christian word 'love.' He was the most Christlike person I ever knew…He loved everyone and sought to show the love of God to everyone."

Norman Cliff said, "On my nineteenth birthday a year before the end of the war, I had a time of prayer. I said to God, "If You'll save my life, I'll serve you all my life in the ministry." I don't think Eric tried to talk the teenagers into becoming missionaries or evangelists, but I know his example of selfless love and service showed them what life looks like even in truly difficult circumstances. It was admirable, and it inspired them. Norman chose to make that commitment, one he kept, serving in Africa, Zimbabwe, and South Africa.

Bob Rendall, Director of the Eric Liddell Centre, said, "I know through talking to individuals who knew him that that commitment to them ran very very deep and had a tremendous impact on them. I remember hearing Stephen Metcalf speaking about his encounters with Eric Liddell. They were long-time encounters. When he was a young lad with no parents in the internment camp he sought guidance from Eric. He spoke of his struggles with hatred for the Japanese who were imprisoning them and of Eric's unfailing commitment to believing that we should love our enemy. And out of that, the wonder of Stephen Metcalf's call to minister to the Japanese as a missionary after the war. There's something totally wonderful about the level and the depth of care that Stephen Metcalf received from Eric Liddell that would allow that kind of influence to be there."

In camp, Eric kept up a hefty pace and seemed to have limitless stamina, but people who knew Eric well began to notice a change—weakness in his walk, an unsteadiness on his feet He was hospitalized for exhaustion, but it was a brain tumor. Joyce Strenk visited him every day, bringing him news of the camp, talking with him about God. One morning after her quiet time, she sat by his bedside, the book he'd written in her hand. They were talking about his chapter on surrender when he said, "Surren... surr." and then his head went back. In a panic, Joyce ran out and found the nurse. Annie Bucken drew the curtain around his bed and said, "What did he say?"

Joyce answered, "He said 'surrender.'

Later Joyce recalled, "My dad and Annie Bucken took me to this little shed where Annie had laid him out very lovingly, I remember seeing him there very peaceful and I remember thinking He's not here. He's just not here. It was comforting in a way because I knew he had gone to be with the Lord he loved so well."

"The day that he died," Joe Coterill said, "one found grown men who I don't think they'd shed a tear for the last fifty years were in tears at his death because he was known, not because of his Olympic prowess, but because he was Eric. He was the kind of person who was a friend to everyone. His funeral bore that out. The church wouldn't hold all the people. The church was full, and the route from the church to the graveyard was lined with the camp and the whole camp closed down. It was a very, very moving occasion."

"It was a cold day. It had been snowing," Norman Cliff said, "I was at the door when I was given the job of helping to carry the coffin down to the cemetery. The church had been crowded with people of all kinds—Christian and non-Christian."

Stephen Metcalf said, "I remember walking out absolutely shattered. It was nothing expected. And there he was, only forty-three years old and he was gone. I was pretty depressed about the whole thing. It was after that I told God that if I survived in the prison camp I'd go to Japan as a missionary.

Eric's daughter Patricia had wondered why God would separate her daddy from his family when they needed him so badly. She said, "It wasn't until years later that I found out there maybe was a reason that he stayed in that camp. I have met a lot of children that were in that camp. Same age as we were. And they were put in the camp without their parents. We were safe, and these children did not have parents. Most of them have done very well. He made a great influence in the steadiness of their lives. So, in that sense, God's hand was there."

I think of Eric, quietly rising before dawn every day, lighting the peanut oil lamp and reading his Bible, waiting in silence before the Lord in that crowded internment camp, carrying the life of God into the day. He brought the will of God to Earth.

I think of the comments made by former internees, thinking always of food, their teeth loosening from years of eating only bread and water, their hearts full of worry and fear, finding the life of God poured out to them in tasks and talks and the presence of one whose words carried the gracious love of a man deeply connected to God. It brought order into the chaos, hope in the uncertainty, light in the darkness.

The internment camps were a reality. The deprivations were real. But God gave 1799 people an extraordinary experience with one man who let Jesus live through him. I have wondered if any of those teenagers—Joyce, Joe, Norman, Stephen, or the others, would trade a day of that time with their friend. What do you think?

Patricia said, "We lived in Toronto at the time. I was just a little girl. We were in the kitchen. I said, 'Mother, you look so beautiful today.' She was just glowing. 'But you look so different.'"

"She said, 'You know what, Patricia? I think your father's coming home. Because I can feel him. I've felt him for about a week. I can feel him right here and if I turn my head a little quicker I will see him. And he's saying to me, 'It's all right, Flo. It's all right.' That was just about a week before she got the letter to say he was dead. She just couldn't believe it, but she said, 'You know, he was there. He was telling me it's all right.'"

"We were so fortunate to have the parents we had. Those were war years and my father died in a prisoner of war camp, and it would have been very easy for lots of widows to blame the country, and so the hatred goes on. It doesn't dissipate. But we never felt any anger against the Japanese at all. That was a great gift that she gave us. It was the times. It was war. And you had to forgive. You just had to forgive and get on with it. So we did.

"At the end of the war there were lots of children who didn't have their fathers. My mother went back into nursing and we had to pull together. And we did pull together very well. Even when we were little you always felt that God was walking with you. He wasn't up there far away. He was right there with you and life is easier that way. I'm not saying you get any fewer problems, because you do get problems and you get some horrible things tossed at you, but you had grounded in you that you had something stronger inside that will help you through the times."

When Eric died, even hard-bitten men were in tears. One man who was not a Christian said, "Jesus Christ used to live in our camp."

We become like the God we worship. Eric's was Jesus.

I have such a strong sense that God wants us to be like that in these days where, in significant ways, we feel imprisoned in chaos, hostility, and uncertainty. In humility and surrender, we can walk through the shaking, working out the details with Almighty God, carrying Kingdom stability, Light and *zoe* life to all those around us. In the meantime, Scripture assures us everything matters. Not a sparrow falls without the knowledge of God. Every tear is kept. Every prayer is heard. We may not see it, but we can trust Him, and someday, when we know why, we'll be glad.

13

WHAT DO YOU WANT TO KEEP?

It began with a phone call, the official-sounding pre-recorded voice saying there was an evacuation advisory for our area. In other words, get ready, but you don't have to go just yet. Over the next five years of fire seasons, there were more advisories, some escalating to mandatory. We could hear the chop of helicopter blades thumping the air, carrying buckets of water or pink fire retardant to dump on spot fires. We saw a splotch of pink right next to the only way in and out of our little mountain-side community. We spent the hottest weeks of summer watching worried as columns of smoke spread into gray blankets covering the sun. One time sheriff deputies were going house to house telling people to leave. When the fire jumped suddenly closer, a neighbor drove up and down our streets with his horn blaring. The message was clear: "Get out! Get out NOW!"

There's one thing we learned about fire: it can be fast and final. Some people had no warning at all. One friend fled from her home, cats, dogs, and one chicken crowded into her little car, fire chasing her just inches away. Another friend followed a police escort out of her neighborhood. She told me everything on both sides of the road was in flames. Many places burned to the ground.

Year after year we had to decide what mattered to us. What would we pack? What could not be replaced? A strange thing happened to some of us. Over the years we'd collected a lot of stuff, and when it came down to it, there was an awful lot we realized we could live without.

Priorities. When you have only so much time and only so much space, what really matters to you? As each year brought the same watchful preparations to flee, my list of necessities dwindled. By the fifth year, I was down to my guitar, my hard drives, and my guide dog Hedy.

The Apostle Peter tells us fires are coming. Things are going to burn. What matters most to us? What are our priorities? There's only so much time. There's only so much room in a life. What will we decide we need to keep?

A LESSON FROM CHESS

My son, Thomas, has been playing chess since he was a child. When he was in high school, his mentor told him he could be a Grand Master if he worked at it. Thomas loved chess, but decided it wasn't what God had called him to do. He told me he knew the amount of memorization and focus that would be needed to reach that level and it wasn't the right fit. He turned his back on that road and chose to follow Jesus wherever He led. God called him to be a software engineer. Thomas said it still required lots of focus and significant memorization but that work seemed more natural, more comfortable. It suits his design and satisfies him because he knows he's right where God has gifted him to be.

I think this chess story, which I asked Thomas to recount to me, exemplifies how to follow Jesus with nothing to distract us from what really matters.

"Mom, you once asked me which chess piece was my favorite. My answer was, "Whichever one my opponent can't live without." Chess is a game where you have to look at the board dispassionately and weigh the pros and cons of whatever you do next. Preferably, you look at the next several moves, doing your utmost to identify the best move for your opponent as well. If you have an emotional attachment to any piece (the queen is the most common), you will do anything to protect that piece. The second I realize that about you, I will torment that piece because I realize you are no longer able to make good decisions. You are already convinced that losing that piece means you have lost the game even though this is untrue. This means I will either eventually take the piece and you will effectively forfeit the game or you will successfully protect that piece at the cost of position and other pieces, at which time I can easily defeat you.

"In our lives as Christians, the same dynamic holds. If I have something in my life that means more to me than God, it can be used to pull me away from Him. God does not always allow those tests but He sees our hearts very clearly.

"Look at Job. Satan wanted to take all his stuff as a test and God let him but none of those were more important to Job than God. Next, Satan went after his mind and his body. If you read Job's descriptions, you realize that even his sleep is full of nightmares. His friends all refused to give him the benefit of the doubt and even his wife told him to curse God and die. To be fair, she had also just lost everything she owned and all her children in a single day, and the next day, her husband became a wreck physically and was suffering terribly. I think she just wanted him to be out of his misery. Anyway, the point is that none of these things were more important to Job than God. Not his stuff, not his relationships, not even his own health and well-being."

What in the world can't we lose? Honor? Dignity? Reputation? If we feel disrespected, do we come unglued? In the movies (and now on YouTube and the news), you see a lot of rage when someone belittles someone else. What is the piece we feel we can't live without, the one that, if lost, makes us feel defeated even when we haven't actually lost the game? Most of us react really badly when we feel berated, demeaned, disregarded, ignored. I certainly do. It's as if I have to prove I'm worth something.

But every human being is worth something. In fact, we're all worth a lot. How do I know? A diamond is worth whatever price a buyer will pay. In my case, the price Jesus paid for me is my sins. He didn't pay the group rate, and there were no discounts for quantity lots. We don't need the world's validation. We are made in the image of God, and that automatically comes with a dignity intrinsic to being a human being. We need to be grounded in this truth. We have to know we won't ever be less, no matter what the world says. In Christ we have nothing to prove. Don't need to. He already established our value by what He did for us. "For the glory set before Him, He endured the cross." The glory was not only His returning to His Father with the keys to death, hell, and the grave, He had paid the full price for everyone who had ever lived or ever would live. That's glorious.

Most of us grew up in a prevailing worldview of scientific materialism, existentialism, situational ethics. Takes a lot of effort to examine those tenets in the Light of the Word and replace them with God's Truth. Nevertheless, it's worth doing. It changes everything, down to the foundations of our identities.

Jesus said if we're to be His disciple, we have to hate our life (think in terms of rejecting a life given over to worldly values), be willing to die to it, and deny ourselves and follow Him. He said to count the cost. It will cost us everything. Jim Elliot said it this way, "He is no fool who gives what he can't keep to keep what he cannot lose." Elliot gave his life in Ecuador for the Waodani Indians. Jesus said take an inventory. What part of your life can't you give up? What's so precious to you that you will put everything else at risk in order to protect it? Whatever that is will keep you from whole-heartedly following Jesus, and finding the amazing adventure that comes only when we've let go of lesser things

By the way, it's important for you to remember your commitment to Jesus won't necessarily bring you praise, honor, or respect from the world. In fact, Scripture says the opposite. If you love the world, the world will love you, promote you, approve and honor you. But if you follow Jesus, the world will hate you because it hated Him. You are not above your Master. This is not pretty, but I think we are able to take hard truth if we understand the issues. If we're secure in our intelligence, we won't be flattened if someone says we're stupid. If we know we are valued by Jesus because He loves us, we won't need to be validated by the world. If we know Jesus said the world would oppose our values, we won't be surprised; we'll be prepared, and we'll be able to maintain our equilibrium because we've been taught how to survive the waves. Jesus is in the boat. We will be free to be fully who God created us to be. Jesus said, "If you continue in My Word, you are my disciples, and you shall know the truth and the truth shall make you free." Disciples follow the Master. They copy His example, and Jesus was humble. "Take My yoke upon you and learn of Me for I am gentle and humble in heart and you will find rest for your souls." (Matt 11:29)

Jesus didn't consider anything more important than His relationship with God—not His divinity, not His health, not His reputation, dignity, or validation. The price He paid for us was not only our sins on the cross, it was the sinless life He lived every day of those thirty-three years, not holding onto any one thing as more precious to Him than staying connected to His Father and living His will.

Jesus was humble, and He, above all others, had a right not to be. He could have cast the first stone at the adulterous woman. He could have called a lot of angels to bear Him up from the cross. He trusted Abba with His reputation, His future, His destiny. His safety, His ability to do all that was required to pay for all of us for all time. He didn't rely on His God-abilities. He trusted totally in His humanhood enabled by the Holy Spirit and Papa God, the way we're supposed to. He did none of it as God, except not being born into sin, but He had to maintain that all His life and death.

But didn't Jesus dip into His divinity here and there? He knew what people were thinking. He did miracles of healing and even raising people from the dead. Yes, but haven't you ever known what people were thinking in a way that can only be divine insight? The Holy Spirit lives inside you. And, as I said before, people have been praying since the Gospel time, and the Book of Acts, for healing and raising the dead. He said we would. We don't have to be God to do that; we only need to let Him be God through us to bring His will about on this Earth in His name. "In Jesus' name" is not a magic phrase we tack onto the ends of our prayers to guarantee their success. It means "as presenting all He is." When we pray as presenting all He is, there's power that flows because we're praying in His very nature, expressing His heart, aligned with His values. We invite His will to be done on Earth, and it shifts the spiritual terrain in supernatural ways. He said we would. He wants us to. It's part of humility before God—that availability to let Him express His heart through us to a world that needs to know miracles happen because He is God and there is no other.

BUT WILL HE SEND ME TO AFRICA?

Obviously, it's not God's will for all of His children to go to Africa or we would all be over there. Actually, when I became a Christian seeking God's will for my life, I was terrified that He'd send me back to South Central L.A., the place I failed as a new teacher in my first public school assignment. I was horrible at it, and I had nightmares for years. But God did not send me to the inner city, to Africa, or even to China; He sent me to the artistic community to become friends with people from diverse backgrounds and very little exposure to Christ. It is a community with whom I can communicate in ways He's equipped me to do well. And I enjoy them. We don't have to be afraid of the will of God. Here are four quotes that help me surrender in humility as I consider living my life aligned with the will of God. Bryan Duncan says God has three answers to prayer: "Yes," "Not yet, and "I have something better." Bob Cull says "No" is as good an answer as "Yes" if you know His heart." Chuck Missler says the worst thing we can do is choose our will over His. And someone else (whose name I can't remember) says, "The will of God is what we would always choose if we knew all the facts." The will of God isn't always what we hope it will be, but it's always much, much better, one way or another.

I want to mention here that sometimes God's will is not an either/or situation. Gayle Erwin tells of the time he was in turmoil wondering which of the churches for which he had been offered the pastoral position he should choose. He was afraid to make a mistake and miss God's will for him. One day when he was agonizing over this matter before the Lord, God said, "Pick one. I'll bless you at either church. The blessings will be different, but either one will be fine. Just pick one"

GOD'S PLAN

I've been talking about God having purpose for each life. He also has a Plan that includes the redemption of creation and the final destruction of all evil. Most people think God's Plan has to do with something they are meant to do. I think that's part of it, but we get snared in the mechanics instead of looking for the overarching theme. Recently I had a dream in which I was going around encouraging students in different classrooms. When I woke up, I thought, "I'm a teacher and encourager." But I think even that is too specific. That means if I can't teach then I'm not fulfilling His Plan. So it has to be something else. C.S. Lewis says the reason we don't see a Plan is because it's all a Plan.

What am I here to do? This may seem too general for you, but I'll explain in a minute.

I think God's Plan for every human being is to live His life in whatever circumstances come. Does this mean we will be cookie-cutter Christians with elder-approved clothing and hairdos? Not at all. Look at the Book of Acts. You can't find a more disparate group of human beings than the early Church. No, rather than making us all alike, it frees us to be fully realized original designed authentic us, unique and as specifically created as one type of butterfly from another. There's a big difference between a tiny yellow skipper and a tiger swallowtail. And what about the Monarch butterflies? Monarch adults usually live about two and a half weeks, but every fourth generation lives nine months and flies 2,500 miles from Canada to Mexico averaging 50 miles a day, often sailing along at 10,000 feet. God is into unique, even in snowflakes, and we are of much more value than skippers, snowflakes, sparrows or Methuselah Generation Monarch butterflies, astounding as they may be. By the way, there's no older, experienced adult to lead the Monarchs to Mexico. Somehow they get to the exact spot as their ancestors with nothing but God-ordained navigational powers to go unerringly to their destination. I mention these butterflies because the same God Who created them knows how to get us to our destination and He will take the flight with us. He promised.

POURING OUT

Aligning with the God of the Universe: it's a pouring out of life for His purposes that manifests in an infinite variety of ways. My friend Stephanie says she's determined to be the best wife, mother, human being she can be. She's pouring out her life for God in that ministry to her family, and she also teaches at a local high school and is a professional artist. I have friends who pour out their lives in intercessory prayers that have changed their neighborhoods and shaken the nation.

They remind me of Martha's sister Mary who poured out her entire fortune on Jesus—pure spikenard, costly and precious and rare—because she was overwhelmed with love for the One Who transformed her life. And that was even before His resurrection! I wonder if Mary was around on Pentecost when the Holy Spirit was poured out and human beings received power from a different Reality.

In the Bible, we see quite a lot of pouring out—Him on us with Living Water, power, visions, dreams, and supernatural things, and from us to Him, such as what Paul talks about in his letters. And of course Jesus poured out everything for us when he walked the Earth. But what always blesses me when I think of Mary pouring out her dowry (the equivalent of her future) on Jesus, is that it got all over her. That distinctive fragrance not only refreshed the Lord and filled the room, it left with Mary, on her face, on her clothes, in her hair.

Lilias Trotter admired the dandelion that gave and gave until there was nothing left. She chose to do the same, an unmarried Victorian woman in Algeria who arrived without a plan, spoke not a word of Arabic, and knew nothing of the culture. Yet, she felt sure God had called her to go to a Muslim country hostile to Christians, and she found her own gentle way into lives that desperately needed to know God loves them. Eric Liddell thought he'd be pouring out his life as a missionary to the Chinese. Instead, he spent the rest of his life ministering to prisoners in a Japanese internment camp. I think of Lilias and Eric like water. No matter what the size, shape, and condition of the container, they filled it to overflowing with the love of God. To me, that's how we can live God's Plan for us, pouring out wherever we are in our own, unique way.

Lilias Trotter and Eric Liddell lived in difficult situations at difficult times, but they lived them in alignment with God with Jesus at the center of their hearts. I admire them both.

You don't see many examples of people so given to God, or how that purity affects others.

A bit about purity. It makes me think of something more valuable because it is not adulterated or diluted in any way. Pure gold, pure spikenard. Nothing gets in the way of the expression of the original creation in the fulness of its exquisite integrity. Yet "purity" has an old-fashioned prude sound to our modern ears. And "righteousness"? It immediately conjures up prune-faced Pharisees feeling qualified to cast stones at people living lesser lives. But that's not what it means. Righteousness is right-standing with God, conferred by the blood of the Lamb. And there's More. The Amplified Bible expands the word "righteousness" this way: "the pure, spiritual, heaven-born possibilities that have their foundation in the holy Being of God." Wow! You mean that's what God has waiting for all of us who align ourselves with Jesus? Yes, and those possibilities will open up as paths for our feet to bring *zoe*-life into whatever circumstances we find ourselves—possibilities that have their foundation in the holy Being of God. And I wonder if any of that pouring out along the way will have the fragrance of spikenard...

I remember standing in front of a wall of toys for cats, considering shape, texture, sound, and entertainment value. It took an hour, but I finally settled on three, the *piece de resistance* was an upright cylinder covered with pink-colored carpet, topped with a small pompom on a spring. I took these treasures home, excited to see what my two newly-adopted kittens would do when they saw them.

Now I was standing just outside their view, the toys behind my back, a smile of anticipation in my heart. At that moment, the Holy Spirit said, "That's what it's like for Me. I have treasures and surprises you can't even imagine, chosen specially for you, and I can hardly wait to give them to you."

We get tired. We get discouraged. We get bewildered and confused. That's why the Holy Spirit desires earnestly to open our spiritual eyes so we become aware of how to walk in the light of His divine different reality. If your idea of life ends at the grave and you make your choices based on that brief span of years, your life will be too small and your treasures will be buried with your heart. Heaven is real. Read the last chapter in God's Book for a preview. Believe me; we won't be bored. Scripture says eye has not seen, ear has not heard, nor has entered into the heart of man what God has prepared for those who love Him. Jesus says, "Don't be afraid. Don't lose heart! I'm preparing a place for you, that where I am, you may also be. Don't let your heart be troubled. In this world you will have tribulation, but take heart. I have overcome the world. I am coming back and my reward is with Me."

C.S. Lewis said, "If we consider the unblushing promises of reward and the staggering nature of the rewards promised in the Gospels, it would seem that our Lord finds our desires not too strong but too weak. We're half-hearted creatures fooling about with drink and sex and ambition when infinite joy is offered us—like an ignorant child who wants to go on making mud pies in the slum because he cannot imagine what's meant by the offer of a holiday at the sea. We are far too easily pleased.

This world has a lot of stuff, and over the years we collect a lot of it, but, when you get down to it, what really matters? What do you really want? Paul shows us two things: strip off anything that will weigh you down, forge ahead with the goal in mind. It's a big Plan God has, and we get to be part of it. We cannot understand it now, but someday we'll see how He fit it all together and we'll be amazed. Meanwhile, he urges us to run with endurance the race set before us, keeping our eyes on Jesus, Who is waiting for us at the finish line.

I think John Lennox speaks for a lot of us when he says, "What will I say when Eternity dawns? If I had known it was going to be like this, I would have invested far more in it. And then I think I'll fall at His feet and say, 'Thank You!'"

14

BEING THE LIGHT OF THE WORLD

Jesus said, "You are the light of the world....Let your light so shine before men, that they may see your good works and glorify your Father in heaven." (Matt 5:16 NKJV)

This chapter is about making a difference—what it costs and what it brings into being. The people in these two stories transformed violence by carrying into the darkest places the Light of God and His Love.

WOODLAWN

In the 1960s, efforts to integrate the South began. There was violent push back, and the police went in with dogs and fire hoses and it was ugly. Ten years later, it was still ugly, especially in Birmingham, Alabama, one of the most racially prejudiced places in the United States. There were protests, walkouts, fights, and racial tensions in schools and communities. To make matters worse, Governor George Wallace proudly and publicly declared that his state would never be integrated.

Woodlawn's football team had formerly been a powerhouse, but they had been going downhill and, in 1973, their team had reached the bottom. Coach Gerald Tandy was faced with trying to integrate his football team, while hostilities between white and black players made it clear it just wasn't going to happen. Then, out of the blue, an evangelist named Wales Goebel knocked on Tandy's door and asked if he could talk to the team about Jesus. Even though it was a public high school, Tandy agreed. For an hour and a half, Goebel preached the Gospel to the young men. Then he gave an invitation, asking them to come and stand with him and give their hearts to

God. Out of forty-four players, forty-one went forward, knelt on the floor, and with tears and smiles, gave their hearts to Jesus. One of them was a shy, quiet, black running back named Tony Nathan. I think it's significant that, until that day, he hadn't yet surrendered his heart to Christ even though he had been brought up in a loving, close-knit Christian home. It reminds me that God has no grandchildren.

Goebel sent Hank Erwin to Woodlawn to be their team chaplain. Erwin said he had always wondered what would happen if a whole football team came to Christ, and Jesus said, "Here's your chance to find out." Erwin said, "I dared them: Why don't you give your season to Christ and play for His glory and see what can happen?" Because of Christ, the black athletes and the white athletes on the team began to bond into a brotherhood.

One of the biggest surprises was what happened to Tony Nathan. His gifting for the game of football, as impressive as it had been, began to grow. Tony said, "As time went on and practices went on, I was doing things I didn't know I could do."

Reginald Greene, Woodlawn's offensive tackle, recounted, "We couldn't play football anymore the way we used to. We wore the name of Jesus and we had to recommit ourselves to a level of excellence. It started a whole thing about caring for one another to accomplish a common goal of being the best at that point in time. It was a team of brothers. Black and white, it just didn't seem to make any difference. Suddenly this wasn't just about Woodlawn High School. It wasn't just about Tony Nathan. It was about something bigger than all of us. We felt a part of it."

Some players would write with a marker on a piece of athletic tape "One," then a cross, "Way" and attach it to the back of their helmet. Whenever someone scored, the team would lift their right index finger high, pointing to Heaven. Cheerleaders started writing Bible verses on the banners for the team to run through. Erwin said, "Every week there were Bible verses popping up everywhere. All of that began to have an impact on the field. They won a game, then another, then another.

At the school, and in his students, Coach Tandy began to see the transformation that was taking place. He knew it was something he didn't have. He said, "God, I don't know that You're there but I think You are and I want what they've got." After that, he changed. His players knew he truly loved them and he got more out of them than ever before. The team was on fire. They had gone from the bottom of the ratings to this powerful team that couldn't be defeated. The media noticed. College coaches noticed. People were wondering, "What's going on at Woodlawn?"

One day the Woodlawn captains went to Erwin and said they felt they needed to go over to Banks and tell them what the secret was to their season. This was remarkable because Banks and Woodlawn were arch rivals. They hated each other. Banks' Star Quarterback Jeff Rutledge asked Goebel to come speak to their team. He went, and the entire team and coaching staff showed up, including Head Coach Shorty White, who was ruthless when it came to winning games. Goebel gave the invitation and guess who was one of the first to come forward. Shorty White. The Banks team embraced Christ and dedicated their next season to the glory of God.

In 1974, both Woodlawn and Banks mowed down all the other teams and entered the city championship undefeated. There was so much excitement about this game that they had to move it to Legion Field where it became the most highly attended high school football game in history, with 42,000 in the stands and more than 20,000 turned away. The entire crowd sat together, united by their interest in these two teams regardless of the color of their fellow football fans sitting nearby or the players on the field they had come to see. The teams came rushing through banners with the Bible verses that the cheerleaders had made and, at the request of both teams, Wales Goebel gave the invocation, which meant he preached the Gospel to a stadium full of football fans.

Goebel said after that he began to get calls from Georgia, Mississippi, Alabama, Louisiana, to come to their high schools, "All because somebody heard of what happened at Woodlawn High School."

Erwin said, "I carry those fond memories of great days when I was able to see how Jesus could change an entire fabric of a community through a few young men dedicated to use the simple game of football to honor His name. All He's looking for is a few good men and people who will take Him at His word. Remarkable things can happen. Magic can occur. Glory can come down. And it can be the greatest days of your life."

And Tandy? He lost his job.

Later he had a successful career coaching at another high school, but between those two times of doing what he knew and loved best, he sold insurance. Sometimes it costs you. He knew it would, but he decided it was worth it.

I wanted to tell the Woodlawn story because these were teenagers in a horrific situation that some authorities were condoning. They stopped the violence, changed history, and showed what God can do with lives, no matter how young, who give their will to Him for His purposes. Do you think any of them regretted their decision?

I love pointing out to kids what can happen through the lives of young people. Their lives matter, even though they aren't grown up. In fact, some significant things *require* young people to bring them about. What happened at Woodlawn High School is a powerful historical transformation of a place known for hatred and violence. Through a couple of football teams, a spectacular expression of God's love brought the will of God to Earth. And they knew it. As Reginald Greene said,

"It was about something bigger than all of us. We felt a part of it."

WHAT DO YOU WANT MOST?

What is it young people really want? In their heart of hearts, all the noise of the world hushed for a moment, what do their innermost beings truly long for? I remember going to the first Jesus West Coast festival before gatherings of speakers and musicians were a big commercial endeavor. We sat on the hard, dry ground, the scraggly weeds sticking to our clothes. We had taken our church youth group to hear representatives from ministries such as YWAM (Youth With a Mission), musicians with a message such as Keith Green and Silverwind. We heard from Wycliffe Bible translators, missionaries to places we'd never heard of, and learned that Christians were being martyred all over the world. Silverwind, led by Georgian Banov who grew up under communist rule in Eastern Europe, made us aware of what life is like for Believers there who are persecuted for Jesus. Till then, as Americans with freedom of religion, we thought all Christians had the same liberty to worship God. Speakers challenged us to deeper commitment to Jesus. I remember being astonished by one who gave the message of denying self, taking up our cross, dying to our own aspirations. It was harsh, demanding, and not inviting with any sense of reward on the other end of all that sacrifice. Then he gave the altar call: "Come down here if you want to commit your life to the purposes of God." Hundreds of teenagers and young adults rushed to the front, their eyes alight with fire and fierce joy. I was shocked. I thought no one would be interested.

What was that about? Surrender. I believe the hearts of human beings long to give themselves totally to something bigger than themselves—Someone vaster than the universe Who demands all you are for a purpose that will take you farther than you thought possible. Why do young people commit to the rigorous training required to be a Navy Seal or a Ranger? Elite forces require a great deal more effort than boot camp for new recruits. Why would anyone want to agree to such pain and misery? I can see how an athlete might be willing to submit to a coach and endure pain for a better performance, but Rangers and Seals aren't training for fame or glory, they're getting ready for strenuous, hazardous, unpleasant, dangerous, difficult assignments that put them in harm's way on purpose for the sake of people they don't know. Makes me think of firefighters and those in law enforcement and the armed services. Why would anyone take on such work where your life is constantly on the line? I don't know. But I remember being at Jesus West Coast watching those young people streaming to the front, standing with their hands upraised, their faces turned heavenward, promising their most precious possession, their will, to the purposes of God. I remember those young people hastily rising from the dusty slopes, their feet hurrying to get to the place where they formally dedicated themselves with no reservation to the God Who, for their sakes, laid down His life for His friends.

The Waodani

I hated missionaries. I hated Christians. I had heard all about how missionaries forced different people groups to stop speaking their languages, forego their own culture, wear clothes, and behave like the Westerners who told them, "Convert or die." But then my husband went to Ecuador with Christian Chiropractors, and he brought back stories of the five men who were speared on a sandbar on the river, and how the men who killed them had become Christians because Nate Saint's sister, Rachel, and Jim Elliot's widow Elisabeth and her three-year old daughter Valerie, went back into the jungle to live with the tribe. That's a remarkable story in itself, but, considering my animosity towards missionaries I wanted to give you some information about the Waodani before and after. I'm not saying wrongs have not been done in Jesus' name, but an awful lot of good has also been done, and this is just a glance inside one of those stories.

A WORD ABOUT THE WAODANI.

The Waodani (wow-DON-ee) were the most violent tribe in Ecuador. They killed often and easily. And if you were a relative, a member of their tribe, or even their friend, if you angered them or did things they didn't like, you would be speared. The Waodani believed they gained strength by spearing, and they had to be very strong to leap the Giant Boa or they would be termites forever. Waodani children grew up understanding it's "spear and live or be speared and die." One anthropologist found that six out of ten Waodani deaths were from homicide. The jungles of Eastern Ecuador were known as the Heart of Darkness. It was there the Waodani lived, and if you went into their territory, you would never come out. They dominated the region with terror, their wildness and violence giving them power and control. They were volatile, unpredictable, and no one was safe from their spears—not women, not children, not friends or relatives, not babies or the infirm. Notice I didn't mention elderly. There were no elderly in Waodani villages. Few survived beyond the age of forty.

Anthropologist Clayton Robarchek said, "Originally I started out collecting genealogies. You'd ask someone what was your father's name or your mother's name and they'd say, 'Oh he was so-and-so and he was speared over here by the so-and-so and they stuck a spear in here and it came out here and when they pulled it out...' You get these incredibly bloody stories. It was an endless litany because virtually everybody's ancestors were speared to death. I asked, 'Why did they do that?' 'They were angry.' That was the answer." Why? He said their paramount value was autonomy. "If something comes along to infringe on your autonomy, this is a violation of the way things ought to be. The way one restores this sense of autonomy, this sense of control, is to kill. There is no precedent in Waodani culture for submerging your own self-interest in the service of a larger group. That idea just hasn't existed in the past. And so people are very unwilling to concede any of their freedom of action in service of the objectives of the group as a whole because the group as a whole never existed before."

Anthropologist Carol Robarchek stated, 'The Waodani have no institutionalized method for resolving conflict."

Clayton added, "Given that, there is no overarching mechanism for this behavior, people simply are able to do precisely what they please. Waodani are to an extent very much like us. They are independent, autonomous, self-reliant, brave—all those values that Americans hold dear the Waodani represent in their most extreme forms. Americans cannot help but admire them. On the other hand, there's kind of a cautionary tale there: If you carry this constellation of American values to its ultimate extreme what you get is Waodani."

When Dayumae (die-OO-ma) was a small girl, her father was speared. A Waodani warrior could demand that his children be buried with him, and Dayumae's mother was already ordering Dayumae's brother, "Put her in the ground!" As her father's life drained away, Dayumae wept and pleaded with him not to make her die, and after her mother left in disgust, Dayumae's father told her brother to help her get away where her mother would not find her. They ran through the jungle until they found some men who took the little girl out of the jungle to safety.

Wycliffe Bible translator Rachel Saint went to Ecuador to meet Dayumae, and through her learned the difficult Waodani language. She also heard the horrific ways this worship of power was destroying them all. Worshiping the wrong gods destroys us one way or another. And it always makes us less than we were created to be.

Dayumea became the first Christian of her tribe and was responsible for convincing the Waodani they should let the female missionaries live with them, and assured Elisabeth and Rachel that it was safe to do so. She also became the preacher, learning the Bible from Rachel during the week and teaching her people on Sundays what God said. She told them if they followed His trail, when they died they would find His house. They did not need to leap the Giant Boa. One by one, they came to know the love of God, and one by one they changed. The unbelieving of the tribe scoffed saying, "They've been tamed. I can see it in their faces." Men and women were being transformed by Jesus, and it even changed the way they looked. Theirs had been a culture of blood feuds and revenge. They had lived in constant, vigilant fear because nobody knew when they would be mercilessly attacked. Now they could sleep unafraid.

Nate Saint's daughter Kathy talked about two of the men who had speared the missionaries. She said, "Dyuwi, later on, realized what the pilots were trying to do—that they were trying to come and bring them the Word of God. He would say, 'to tell him about a different reality.'" Dabo was one of the older generation. He told Kathy, "We were almost down to two people. And if Nemo and Ggkadae (Rachel Saint and Elisabeth Eliott) had not come there would have been no one left." Kathy said, "That's impressive. He really thought if they had continued in their pattern of behavior of revenge and retaliation spearings, they would have killed each other off."

Anthropologist Robarchek stated, "The Waodani were able, in just a few years, to reduce the homicide rate by well over 90%. Nothing else changed. The ecological situation hadn't changed. They had no new techniques, no new tools available to them. There was certainly no biological change. What changed was the information the people had available

to them and on the basis of that they made a radical transformation in their social life. This pattern of vendettas that
we've been able to document that goes back at least five generations disappeared (snaps fingers) like that. Within a matter
of months, one group after another agreed, once they heard
that others were giving up the vendettas they agreed to do the
same thing. It was only when new information became available to them that they could see that there were in fact other
possibilities. Rachael and Elisabeth wanted people to believe
that there was a God and He wanted them to stop killing."

Kathy said, "The word in Waodani for believing or actually hearing, understanding, obeying, and several other concepts like that is *einglya*—To hear means, in that sense, to
truly take it in. Not just to hear but also to understand and
assimilate."

The anthropologist stated that the radical change in Waodani behavior was due to the information that had been made
available to them. I think he's accurate to a point. It was new
information that Rachel and Elisabeth brought, but it wasn't
new guidelines for social behaviors or better mechanisms to
resolve conflict. The information was in what Dyuwi said;
they brought them understanding of a different reality. A
supernatural one. A transcendent one. A transforming one.
Nothing else, no social reform, not legal edicts, no threats,
intimidations, or death, could change them so radically in an
instant. The Waodani heard, understood, believed God, and
truly took in His Truth, assimilated it, and obeyed. And God
gave them all new hearts, long and peaceful lives, and joy. You
can see it on their faces.

Kimo was one of the first converts. He said, "I don't spear
anymore. Enough spear killing. Just spear things to eat. Dayumae told us we lived without understanding. Then we understood."

When his aunt Rachel died, Steve Saint returned to Ecuador to attend her funeral. He was greeted as long-absent family by the men who had murdered the missionaries, who now expressed regrets. Mincaye took him down the river to the sandbar where the attack on the men happened, proving it to his friend by digging up the remains of the little yellow plane Nate Saint had flown. Mincaye told Steve as the missionaries were dying, he heard singing above the trees. When he looked up he saw bright beings in the sky. Others saw them too. "I speared your father," Mincaye said, "He was a great man. He leap the Giant Boa while he was still alive." Then Mincaye pressed a spear handle into Steve's hand and, putting the point at his own heart, opened his arms wide to receive his death. Struggling with years of pent-up emotions, Steve told the Waodani warrior, "You didn't take my father's life. He gave it." The spear dropped to the ground and the two men embraced each other.

Kathy and Steve were baptized in the river at the very spot Nate Saint had given his life. Kathy said all she could think of, as she stood in the water between two of the men who had killed her father, was how much she loved those guys. Steve Saint returned to live with the Waodani for a few years, and his own son, Jesse, became very close to Mincaye. In fact, he called him "Grandpa" in Waodani. And when it was time for Jesse to leave for college, the two men clung to each other and wept on each other's necks. Steve said he'd never seen a Waodani man cry. For Jesse's graduation, he requested that Mincaye be brought to the United States to watch him get his diploma. But that's another story.

I wanted to share these wonderful people with you, the changes in vicious killers that are almost beyond belief. After their conversion, the men who murdered the missionaries in 1956 lived in the astonishing peace of God for more than forty years—long enough to be grandfathers themselves. Three generations of missionaries invested in people who lived in the Heart of Darkness, who killed indiscriminately and en-joyed their reign of terror. They were everybody's enemies. Jesus told us to love our enemies.

When someone takes Him seriously in this matter, when we truly love our enemy, remarkable things can occur,. Mira-cles can happen. Glory can come down.

15

WALKING BY FAITH

When we first got our guide dogs, we were told to leave them on tie down when we went to meals. One evening after I returned from dinner, I noticed that Hedy was looking at me over the edge of the bed. I went over to greet her. She was sitting up, perfectly still. Then I saw that she was completely tangled in her tie down cable. It took me awhile to untangle her, but she sat quietly, not a bit of anxiety in her demeanor. I was impressed. I knew Guide Dogs for the Blind breeds their dogs to be calm and reliable, so I figured her steadiness was part of her heritage. Labs tend to quickly assess situations and surroundings, keeping their emotional equilibrium better than many other breeds. I concluded she had come that way. The trainers said they chose her specifically for me because she was assertive and confident. Todd, one of the head trainers at GDB, told me she was a "hard dog." He said she would always make a decision even if it was wrong. There were softer dogs in the group, but they could become bewildered and wait for their partner to tell them what to do. With my lifestyle of travel and different environments, I would need a dog that would not be incapacitated by circumstances.

So some of Hedy's behavior was because God made her that way and the trainers selected her to match my needs. However, after I started interviewing puppy raisers, I realized Hedy's steadiness was not just a personality trait; it was built into the foundation of her being by careful, methodical exposures to new environments, sounds, smells, visual stimulation. Hedy's raiser, Heather, was such a precise by-the-book person that she made sure she followed every protocol in the thick handbook of instructions provided by GDB. Sometimes she was frustrated because Hedy had obviously not read the book and had her own ideas of how she wanted to live her life. That's when Heather's sister Amber stepped in to help out. Their diligence in following the handbook from headquarters resulted in making Hedy practically unflappable. I believe she was so totally secure, so confident that help would come that she could wait in total peace without a wisp of worry.

For nearly two years, the girls carefully introduced Hedy to many sounds, movements and places so the puppy had a wide range of experiences. She tended to want to bite the vacuum cleaner when Heather's mom was cleaning, but she wasn't afraid of the household noises.

My prayer place is right across from the laundry room. Hedy liked to lie nearby in the narrow hall between the washer and the room where I sit talking to the Lord. Sometimes I would put in a load of wash and sometimes I didn't get it balanced. When the spin cycle came, the washer would begin to shake. The sound of thumping would get louder and louder, the cabinets would rattle, the floor would shake, and it felt as if the whole house would come apart, but Hedy, lying right in front of the thumping and shuddering, kept right on snoozing. The shaking never bothered her at all.

When COVID-19 spread across the world and confusion and fear broke out everywhere, I asked the Lord, "Did You do this?" He said "No, but I allowed it." It was part of the shaking He was doing so that only what could not be shaken would remain. He told me He allowed it "to dismantle self-sufficiency." He said it was the first birth pang, a phrase some translations render as "the beginning of sorrows."

As I write this, we are now in the second year of the pandemic and the stories and the experts keep changing their assessment of what is going on and how to best solve the problems. Chaos has not settled down. In fact, it seems to be getting more confusing, one thing compounding another. It makes me think of the disciples in the boat, the storm raging and Jesus asleep on the leather cushion (Mark 4:37-41). You know what happened. Jesus got up, rebuked the wind, it dropped down, the sea was still, and there was a great calm. Then Jesus said, "Why are you so fearful? How is it you have no faith?"

If I had been there, I'd know why I was so fearful. The storm was monumental. Bible teachers have said it was so furious that it was probably demonic. The disciples had done everything they knew to do and, seeing that the boat was filling with water, assessed their situation and probably concluded they were going to die. Were they?

We have the benefit of the whole story. And other stories like it. Every time, Jesus said things such as, "Don't be afraid." "Why did you doubt?" "Don't you remember?" Yeah, I've been through things and You've been awesome, but this is different, Jesus. I'm looking at a demonic storm that threatens to swamp us in this crazy chaotic sea. I'm looking at things that are totally out of my control and Jesus reminds me He's in the boat. He shows me Hedy wound up in her tie down cable, waiting patiently without thrashing, so confident that help will come that she can wait in peace, so aware of what the shaking washing machine means that the noise and quaking doesn't bother her at all.

Help will come. Jesus is there. He's coming to the wind-ravaged boat, walking on the water. That doesn't always bring confidence and peace, though. Scripture says, "they all saw Him and were agitated (troubled and filled with fear and dread). But immediately He talked with them and said, Take heart! I Am! Stop being alarmed and afraid." (Mark 6:50 AMPC) They didn't expect Him (and they didn't know He could do that) so they didn't recognize Him. They thought He was a ghost. Hence the terror. I think it's wonderful that He immediately talked to them. What did He say? "Take heart! I Am! Stop being alarmed and afraid (don't be afraid any longer). I AM. I AM Who I say I AM." If I expect Him, I will recognize Him and hear His voice even in the whipping winds. I will remember what He told me. Oh, it's just the shaking He said was going to happen as things begin to be cleaned up.

Over and over in the Bible God tells us not to be afraid. Before they begin the battles in the Promised Land, Yahweh tells Joshua, "Have I not commanded you be strong and of good courage. Be not afraid, neither be dismayed for the Lord your God is with you wherever you go." (Joshua 1:9) In the End Times briefings to His disciples, Jesus tells them over and over, "Don't be afraid. These things must happen." He told them birth pangs will come. You will hear of wars, rumors of wars, people groups will rise against people groups there will be pestilence, famines, earthquakes to shake up the world. There will be tribulation. Jesus told us. "In the world, you will have tribulation." And then He said, "But be of good cheer (don't be afraid). I have overcome the world."

"Don't be afraid. Don't you remember? When I fed the five thousand how many baskets of leftovers did you pick up? When I fed the four thousand how many baskets?" The disciples might have flipped through their memory cards and recalled the nine thousand fed with bread and fish, the lepers cleansed, the lame walking, the blind no longer having to beg, dead people restored to their loved ones. "Oh, yeah. Now we remember."

That's what the Lord showed me this morning. What was missing in the boat when the waves were raging? Faith. They forgot to remember what they'd witnessed first hand. God told me when I forget to remember what He has done for me, what I have seen over the years first hand, then I fear. Then I worry. Then I doubt. Then I forget to trust. But He wants to reveal Himself to me, He wants me to hear His voice.

He wants me to talk to Him. He is every bit the fullness of who He says He is. Without faith it's impossible to please God. Faith continues to come by hearing. Hearing what? His Word. His voice. His heart in the God-breathed text of His Divinely Authored Book. He who comes to Him must believe that He is. Period.

Hedy did not worry. She could wait patiently, knowing she was loved and help would come. She didn't fear when things began to shake and kept on shaking. She knew what it was. Nothing to fear.

Jesus told His disciples to cross over to the other side. Frankly, I don't know what they could have done that would have demonstrated faith. Maybe awakened Him sooner? Maybe not asked if He didn't care they were perishing? Maybe not tried to solve the problems themselves, trusting in their experience and expertise? I don't know. All I know is, when I talked about it with the Lord this morning, He reminded me of Hedy and a great calm came over me. She trusted she would have the help she needed. I need to trust the same.

My friend Bobbi had a vision that illustrates this principle. She found herself in the passenger seat of a careening car. Buildings were flashing by, cars swerving to get out of the way. When she looked to her left, she saw there was no one in the driver's seat. When she looked out the windshield, she saw terrifying chaos. Then she heard a tap on the glass and looked to the right out her window. There was Jesus, standing quietly. He pointed down. When she looked she saw His feet were on the ground. Nothing was moving. She looked out the front and there was the mad careen through the crowded city street, but when she looked back at Jesus, everything was perfectly still.

How do we keep from being afraid? How do we keep walking in faith? Keep our eyes on Jesus. Follow Him. Walk not after the flesh, trusting our human reason, our experience, our expertise, but after the Spirit. Where is He going? That's where we need to be. When He says, "Let's cross over the sea to the other side," He intends for us to get there. It may look impossible, but He says "Do not be afraid."

The Bible tells us to walk by faith, not by sight. It doesn't mean to walk blind; it means to walk with our eyes on Jesus. Faith is not in our ability to work up some confidence in what we can believe to happen. It's faith in God, trusting in, relying on, cleaving to, and obeying.

Here is a current real life example of walking by faith, not by sight. It's so fresh we haven't yet herd the end of it, but I felt the Lord wanted me to share it with you because it's such a stunning example of following the Lord into an unknown territory.

THE PUPPY PROJECT

Years ago when they were raising puppies for an organization that trains guide dogs, Matt and Amie Chapman founded a web series called "Growing Up Guide Pup." They then expanded to raising pups for other service dog organizations. Each season of their web series featured the socialization of a puppy who would be returned to the school to be trained for service.

I love puppy raisers. Early on I became involved in encouraging raisers in their work. They loved seeing how the strict protocols paid off in the working life of a real guide dog. But I also learned that only about half the puppies who are socialized by raisers ever become working dogs. Some simply don't want to do the work, but most are dropped for such things as fear, distractibility, or aggression. I began wondering if there could be a way to increase the percentage of successful dogs. That's how I began working with Amie and Matt.

For years now, I've prayed with Matt and Amie over puppies they were preparing for service work. Then we had a chance to pray for an entire litter of nine, and seven of them were matched with disabled people. So Matt and Amie started thinking and praying about a very big idea that had been pushing its way into their hearts. They reserved one of the puppies from that litter, a champagne-colored poodle named Pixie, to be a possible breeder for a big dream. They wanted to breed their own prepared puppies, prayed-over dogs who would be blessed and nurtured from their mother's womb. But when Pixie came into season, the Chapman's had a dilemma. Amie felt they should go for it, but Matt said there were too many ducks that were not yet in a row. They didn't have any of the finances in place. It would be expensive. There were other issues that I don't know—Matt just said it was like thinking of jumping off a cliff. So Matt went to talk to the Lord. When he emerged from his prayer place, he said he was going to go for it.

Excited and a little nervous, we prayed—over every aspect of the adventure. They called it the Puppy Project. Not one thing was done the usual way. For example, some pregnancies are brought about through artificial means. It's all about efficiency and expediency. The Chapmans prayed, found a fine gray fellow that we prayed over as well. Then the Chapmans had Pixie and him visit and become friends. Though Pixie stayed overnight, the sweet fellow did nothing till the next day, and only once. From that gentle interaction came seven beautiful puppies.

Many times puppy fundraising is done by letting each of the highest donors name a pup. But naming is a powerful thing. The Chapmans decided to name their puppies according to things in their yard that had special meaning to them, names with precious, significant, beloved and spiritual associations such as "Reed," "Fig," "Oak," "Maple," and "Ivy." They also didn't feed the mom the usual way. When Pixie refused to eat, Amie didn't assume she wasn't hungry. She thought about a morning sick mom and offered her other things till she found what Pixie would eat. One of the vets at the office where Amie works as a veterinarian technician warned her that Pixie could develop a food aversion. Obviously he'd never been a morning sick mom. Pixie did not develop any problems with food. Instead, she kept up her weight and was very healthy when she gave birth.

What impresses me most is how the Chapmans customized everything they did. They followed the leading of the Holy Spirit in partnership with the gifts of intuition He had given them, plus their experience and expertise and ability to solve problems outside the box.

Over the weeks after the birth of the babies, the Chapmans were so busy I didn't get many updates. When I did it was mostly to say the puppies were amazingly healthy and happy and how easy it was to care for this litter. Then, it seemed merely overnight, the puppies were being distributed to the raisers the Chapmans had found. They provided puppies to four different schools and we prayed about which puppies should be sent to which schools. Next thing I knew, they were dropping Reed off in Utah to be socialized for a guide dog school. I prayed for him, asking the Lord to bless him in this most demanding of all service work. The school's owner had been head trainer at two other guide dog schools and thousands of dogs had passed under his hands. Matt told me the trainer said Reed was the most remarkable dog he'd ever encountered and wanted to meet them to find out what they'd been doing.

Recently, Matt sent me this report:

"The pups are doing amazing. They turned five months old yesterday. We are getting awesome reports about all of them. I mean all of them! The Seedling Litter is amazing."

Here is a report from Lizzie. She graduated from Karen Pryor Dog Training Academy and is now raising and training Ivy for guide work, both as a service dog and our breeder prospect. Lizzie reported today, 'I can't say how much this puppy impressed me! I put her through tests that I wouldn't put a service dog in training through until at least a year old and at five months she's kicking all expectations out of the park!'"

Last week I got to talk to Linzey Zoccola, who founded Phoenix Assistance Dogs. She told me their mission is to train puppies to become assistance dogs for individuals living with a broad range of disabilities, people who are unable to train their own assistance dog. PAD also assists individuals in finding and training their own assistance dog if they desire to do so.

Matt and Amie are so impressed with Linzey and the customized work she does that they trusted three of their precious puppies to her. They even made the long drive from California to Pennsylvania to drop them off and meet Linzey in person. Linzey immediately knew the pups were special because of their confidence in a brand new environment. As the weeks passed, they have continued to be outstanding. Here is her report:

"Oak has shown so much maturity and growth in his 4 months with our program. He has embraced his partner and their disabilities like we never could have dreamed of. His environment is very unique and Oak not only learned quickly what was needed of him but continues to advance in training. Fig has a unique ability to connect and engage with individuals of all ages and abilities. He learns extremely fast and is such a clown when he plays! Maple has exceeded all of our expectations in both her temperament and ability to learn. She adapts to every new situation she's exposed to and has a strong desire to physically connect with her future partner who lives with limited range of motion and can't reach out to her."

At this point that's all I know. We prayed for God to design each puppy for a specific purpose for a specific person. We prayed for Him to pick each raiser and each school and trainer. And now we wait to see what will happen with this first litter in The Puppy Project that is totally dedicated to the purposes of God, a project that is uniquely blessed as the Chapmans continue in faith to follow Jesus wherever He may lead.

16

SONGS FOR THE SOLDIERS

I had just finished doing special music at a Full Gospel Businessmen's meeting and sat down to hear the speaker, Pauline Michael Mills, the grande dame of Christian music. She sang her world famous chorus, Thou Art Worthy, the first Scripture to have been put into a chorus. It had started a revolution in new music for the Body of Christ.

Pauline was like a small, energetic bird, her bright eyes dancing as her hands raced over the piano keys, her age-thinned soprano quavering with passion as she worshipped the Lord in His own words. It was mesmerizing. She was magnificent. You can see why I was rather shocked when she invited me to spend the next day with her.

It was Easter, 1980. As we sat in her small motel room, Pauline didn't waste any time. She fixed her bright eyes on me and said, "There's a very reputable prophet named John Mills who has said worship will become more popular than contemporary Christian music." That was a startling thing to hear. Keith Green, Randy Stonehill, and others had just begun rocking the foundations of acceptable church music with songs written and performed in the style of their generation. Contemporary Christian music was wildly popular. I couldn't imagine any music being more popular, especially not worship. "But," Pauline continued, "John said Christians will need songs in Scriptures that are not worship—songs for the soldiers to help them keep marching when things are tough." She let that sink in a moment, before adding with a meaningful and piercing look, "And I charge you to do it." I told her I'd never written a song in my life, but I'd do my best. I had already been collecting Scriptures for the couple of years I'd been a Christian. I was memorizing them, each with a significance that made me want to hide it in my heart. My favorite was Psalm 91.

For a year I tried. Every day I'd lay out my papers and sit looking at them, guitar in hand. I'd strum a little and try to make up a melody that would fit the words. It was awful. I'd been around music enough to know what was a song and what wasn't. These weren't.

My husband loved to dive, so we'd go to Anchor Bay every year, park our camper, and I'd paint or read or sing or walk on the beach while he looked for abalone. On this particular day, I remember looking out the window of our little camper. My husband was out diving, and I had tried yet again to write music for those Scriptures to no avail. The papers and my guitar were on the bed where I'd left them in despair. I stared out at the weathered driftwood log that marked the parking place next to ours and said, "Lord. I've tried. I've tried at least an hour every day for a year and I can't do it. I'm sorry. I just can't do it." There was a moment of silence and then I heard singing in my head, "Thou shalt not be afraid for the terror by night…" I grabbed the guitar and sang what I was hearing. He gave me an entire song.

I'm happy to say I was able to visit Pauline at her home and let her know the songs for the soldier were being written. She was then in her early 90s and frail, but as bright-eyed as ever, her enthusiasm for Jesus not the least bit diminished. I told Pauline God had given me the melody for Psalm 91. Then another, and another. She was delighted. I think that was a special gift God gave both of us. She had sown the seeds and there was going to bea bountiful harvest.

I never thought I'd be writing songs for Jesus. I'm kind of a mediocre musician. To me, this is purely divine enablement. I still don't feel like I write songs. Even the ones for Even In Shadow, the musical Dan and I wrote inspired by my mother's illness, those songs came out in one piece like birthing babies only faster and less painful. Creative work always has a sense of the miraculous in the process because it's that part of being made in God's image that feels the most like living in that divine atmosphere, but I also know when I have made something come about by the talent He gave me and my own understanding of the craft and something I cannot birth at all no matter how hard I try. To me, the Scripture songs that are not worship, but songs for the soldier, came about because I was willing and He did the rest.

By the way, worship music did indeed become more popular than contemporary Christian music. When Time-Life puts out collections of the top worship songs and advertised them on network TV, you know it's reached a significant level of popularity. Which also tells me that John Mills was right, and the songs I've been writing for the past forty years will do what He commissioned them to do for His people struggling in these troubled times.

I began spending two hours with Jesus every morning when my boys were in school. After two months, I suddenly jumped up and wrote longer songs that were not Scripture. They were usually to Him, but musings, not worship. And then, when I left the legalistic church and struggled with even wanting to be alive and every day I wished I weren't, He sent me funny songs that would break the hold of despair and give me enough courage to live one more day. Once He used a Christian copy machine repairman to say just the right things to lift my spirit as he worked on the recalcitrant machine. As soon as he left, God gave me a new song with that edifying truth imbedded in the words.

In 1990, I recorded the first album of Scripture songs "The Battle Belongs to the LORD, Songs for the Soldier #1." It was very basic, just me and my piano or guitar. It wasn't perfect, but ten years had passed since Pauline charged me with the task, and I thought I needed to put the songs out where they could be heard. Interestingly, the Lord did not release the songs until after I left the legalistic church and made it past the suicidal depression. As I said, it was basic and not perfect, but my friend Dale Enstrom had a Yamaha DX-7 synthesizer and laid down tracks of strings, French horns, electronic piano, organ, a snazzy new sound called "MetalX-press," and bass. They covered up my mistakes and added color that was always fitting for the meanings of the words.

One day Dale called and said he felt God was saying we should send 350 copies of the cassette to the soldiers fighting in the Gulf War. He was so sure of this that he said he'd help pay for it and do half the labor. I was reluctant. What if they were offended, thinking I was pushing my program? What if those used to rock and pop found it boring and rejected the meanings of the words because the folky style of my music was too soft? But there was something about the war that had to do with hidden terrors—maybe land mines—I don't remember now. This line kept coming to mind, "A thousand shall fall at thy side and ten thousand at thy right hand. It shall not come nigh thee." Psalm 91 is a song for war. "Thou shalt not be afraid for the terror by night, nor the arrow by day…" So we sent them, 350 little padded envelopes addressed "To Any Soldier." We prayed over them to find the ones God chose, and I secretly hoped I would not get hate mail back.

Letters started coming. They were grateful, generous. One said thank you, he had passed it to another soldier, but most kept them. One said he had seen three of his fellow soldiers taking it with them into the place they could relax at night, and he was able to lead them to the Lord. Still brings tears to my eyes to remember.

In around 2014, I was recording a new album of Scripture songs, this one with background singers from the youth groups from Dale's and Thomas' churches. Suddenly I heard a new song for Psalm 91. "He who dwells in the secret place of the Most High, he shall abide in the shadow of the Almighty…" It had parts. I'd never written a song with parts. I knew it was specifically for the kids in Thomas' youth group. Over and over, the girls sing, "You cover me," and the boys sing, "You deliver me." It's protection under His wings. It's protection from the snare of the fowler and the deadly pestilence. Do they still remember, those bright, talented young people? Sixteen years later, do they hear those words singing in their hearts? "I will say to the Lord You are my refuge and fortress. You are the God Whom I trust." More than ever, we need to remember He covers us with His pinions like an eagle spreading His wing over His chicks. He delivers us from the snare of the fowler. He will alert us so we don't get snared by the ones who would catch our foot so we can't fly. Psalm 91 was the first song God ever gave me, and it's on all three of my Scripture albums. God knew we would need that message.

Long ago I heard a report about some kids that were in grave danger. When enemy soldiers showed up, the children ran to shelter chanting Psalm 91. Though the soldiers fired at them with automatic weapons, all of the children survived. At that moment I decided to memorize that Scripture, and, as I said before, it is the first song God gave me back in 1981. Today, the message of assurance is even more powerful as we deal with a virus that has terrorized the world. Take a look at that psalm again. It says not to be afraid of the terror by night, the arrow that flies by day, the pestilence that continues to walk in darkness, and destruction that continues to lay waste at noon day. Though there are threats and dangers at every quarter of day or night, we are secure abiding in the only truly safe place: under the shadow of His wing.

When the pandemic began, I was suddenly shut off from my prayer partners and church. I felt bad because I had taught the congregation many of my Scripture songs and now I would not be leading them in worship or be able to encourage them with words specifically chosen to help them keep a faith-filled perspective. So I put my iPhone on the corner of my kitchen table and recorded a bunch of them, just me and my guitar. On one you can hear Hedy shaking her tags (if you listen very carefully) and on another the Lord provided the sound effects—real rain in just the right tone and quantity. There are more than forty Scriptures in the more than thirty songs, and each is chosen for its ability to uplift and encourage, strengthen and build faith in the listener.

The Message Is True is available on my website as a free download to help my brethren. That includes you. Please don't be shy. I want you to have these songs so you can more easily hide the Word in your heart. They're simple enough for your children, and there is room for parts. Feel free to harmonize, improvise, and soak in them. They were inspired by God Himself as He strengthened and encouraged His children in the difficulties of their lives long, long ago.

In the 1980s, God started giving me visions of the End Times. At the same time, we were getting prophecies about the coming perilous days. Prophecy, by visions or by words, is either foretelling (future) or forthtelling (bringing clarity so we know what's going on in the present). You can see both kinds in the prophecies in both Testaments. What I'm sharing here is the forthtelling kind, illuminating the present so we can understand what's happening and not be derailed by it.

This is the short version of one of the visions. I saw a shiny black snake with a wide opened sharp-fanged mouth. It was rigid as a stick and never moved, but somehow it was being propelled through the darkness. I couldn't see anything, but I knew horrors beyond horrors were going on in the blackness. It went on and on till I could hardly bear it, and then the snake rushed directly into a three bladed fan blade suspended in its way. Chop. Chop. Chop. The entire snake was chopped into pieces. Then the Lord said, "Evil will go on seemingly unchecked a very long time, and then The End." It's like when Jesus told His disciples, "When you see this, don't be afraid. These things must happen." He told them so they'd be aware and keep their spiritual footing because He let them know ahead of time it would happen. In this vision, He's telling us it will happen. Don't be surprised. It's part of what has to happen, just as sometimes He puts wicked rulers in power for His purposes.

In view of this, how shall we then live? The prophecy below calls us into a consistent abiding in Him in the secret place of the Most High, the only place of true safety. I want to add that, from there, we will be able to participate in the fulfillment of foretold events that are yet to come.

"As My Spirit calls, as My Spirit draws unto each one of you to come closer—closer, even closer, yet closer, in a newness where you've not walked. Yes, there are those who have come closer, but even closer, right under My very shadow, that is where you *need* to be. Oh know this—that you *need* the protection of the shadow. You *need* the protection of My hand covering you. You *need* the protection. Stand not away. Be not aloof from Me. Come closer. Come closer. Do not delay. You do not know what tomorrow brings.

17

MY STORY

Many of you have grown up in Christian homes and have always known Jesus. My friend Dan doesn't remember ever not believing in Him. John Lennox is the same. Lennox said he read C.S. Lewis to find out how it was to think like an atheist because he had no idea what it was like to live without connection to God. In this part, I want to share my experiences growing up without Christ. It's a look into living inside Eastern philosophies. It won't be like learning comparative religions by reading a book. It's what it feels like when it's part of you, when it informs your daily life. So if what I describe is not what you read in a textbook, that's good.

Many millions of Christians have been drawn to Eastern religions through music, drugs, gurus giving seminars and retreats, talk shows, and friends. So many of these seekers have left Christianity because it wasn't deep enough to satisfy their craving for more. Sadly, the More is there in abundance, but the faith of their fathers is familiar and lacking mystery, adventure, and power.

The average modern day Christianity omits the supernatural—the transcendent life that comes from closeness with the living God—even though the Bible abounds with it. Miracles are foundational to Christianity. Our very faith depends on our trust in the reality of it. Without miracles, we're missing most of what has happened, what can happen, and what's going to happen ahead. Without conscious awareness of the Divine Presence of God here and now, we won't expect God to intervene when we pray, or Jesus to come call us to meet Him in the air. We won't remain aware there's a reckoning, and an eternal Home without sorrow or death. Our lives won't have an accurate shape or meaning, and we probably won't recognize the voice of the Holy Spirit when He calls us to follow into a supernatural life on Earth beyond our wildest dreams.

Most Christians, knowing little or nothing about other religions, don't know the differences—and the advantages—of belonging to Jesus. I won't be giving you a primer on what each religion believes; I'm sharing my own experiences hoping it will give you insight into what these religions and their worldviews look like in real life.

CONFUCIANISM

I was born the second daughter of a Confucian scholar. When my dad was a lad, he was required to read Confucius' Four Analects every day. He incorporated that worldview into the fabric of his life. I grew up fed on Confucian ethics. Filial piety was especially emphasized—absolute obedience and devotion to my parents regardless of how it affected me personally.

Confucianism is not technically a religion, an attempt to please or appease God for favor, protection and provision. It's a philosophy, an ethical system in which each person has a pre-determined, assigned place in the hierarchy of family and society. Each person is like a column holding up the roof of the building. If you move away from your designated place, the structure could come crashing down. And it will be your fault. All decisions in life are made with everyone else, and society itself, in mind. My father used to say everything I did would reflect on me, my family, and all of China—so be a good girl.

I won't go into all the abuses that happen within that rigid and demanding system back in China and in my dad's life from childhood even into his years as a young adult with a family of his own, but the part you need to know is I was taught unquestioning obedience. My father used to tell me, "When I say 'Jump!' the only question you ask is 'How high?'" He also said, "You are too young to make good decisions. When you are mature enough I will let you know." To make matters worse, as the second daughter, I had no status at all in the family four. The hierarchy was Confucian-set: the father, the mother, the elder sister, and me, the caboose. If I ever tried to assert an opinion (even where to go for dinner) I was immediately overruled. There was only one Alpha, and I was not it. I learned early that alpha-hood was out of the question for me. Don't even think of it. Of course, never having had a chance to make decisions and learn from the consequences, I never learned how to make good ones, so by the time my father told me I was old enough to do so, I didn't know how, and of course I made very bad ones, which only proved I still wasn't mature enough to be trusted to decide anything.

TAOISM

The other philosophy I absorbed throughout my childhood was Taoism (the "T" is pronounced as a "D"). Taoism isn't about ethics or morality. It's more like a description of what can be observed on Earth. The Tao is an impartial and impersonal force. Humans are an insignificant small part of a huge whole. Things are neither good nor bad: they just are, and the job of humans is to find how to fit in and not get crosswise with the Tao, that powerful, inexorable Force.

This is the classic Taoist story my father told me.

A farmer had a horse, and one day it ran away. His neighbor said, "Oh that's terrible," and the farmer said, "You never know. It could be good, it could be bad."

The next day the horse came back, bringing with it another horse. His neighbor said, "Oh that's wonderful!" and the farmer said, "You never know. It could be good, it could be bad."

The next day the farmer's son decided to ride the new horse. It bucked him off and he broke his leg. The neighbor said, "Oh that's terrible!" and the farmer said, "You never know. It could be good, it could be bad."

The next day soldiers came through the village looking for young men to conscript into the army. Because the farmer's son had a broken leg, he was not taken to fight in the war.

Of course, you can go on forever—the son, overcome with guilt, becomes an alcoholic, etc., etc., But you get the idea. In Taoism, it could be good, it could be bad. You never know. It all depends.

The symbol of the Tao you see most often is a circle with a black curved raindrop shape wrapped in the curve of an equal white curved raindrop shape. In the center of the heart of each of the shapes is a dot of the other color. My father told me, in actuality, it's not a flat circle, it's more like a baseball in three dimensions, and the color, which are wrapped around the sphere, are black and red. Black represents the yin principle and red represents the yang.

As I said, Taoism is descriptive. *Yang* is the principle that includes hot, dry, sun, orange, aggressive, penetrating, outside, male (all males are *yang,* but not all *yang* is male), blustery, restless, anger, bright, hard, oppositional, decisive. *Yin* (not *ying*) is the principle that includes dark, moist, blue, cool, female, receptive, internal, intuitive, ice, calm, still, yielding, depression, deep, rest. There is also a sliding scale so there are varying degrees of whatever—temperatures or energy, foods, colors, personalities. Absolute *yin* is death. Everything is one or the other. Ginger is *yang.* Turkey is *yit hey,* rough *yang,* and should never be eaten when you're starting to come down with something. Raw pears are very *yin.* A weak female who eats too many may develop a shallow, stickery kind of cough, because she has become too *yin.* A little ginger boiled ten minutes in chicken broth will balance her back up. I learned this balancing of *yin* and *yang* in my mother's kitchen. And I learned the balancing of energy from my father and my husband, Dennis, who were both acupuncturists.

Traditional Chinese Medicine is based on restoring order, function, and flow in the body's systems, all of which God brilliantly designed. It is no more occult because of its origins than pharmaceuticals are based on witchcraft, though the word in the Bible for witchcraft—*pharmakeia*—means the use or administering of drugs (Gal 5:19). I have to add that many Christians are afraid of acupuncture and think terms such as *yin* and *yang* are demonic. My first pastor used to say acupuncture is evil because demons could get into the body through the needles. That's pure rubbish.

In the second half of the twentieth century, scientists did experiments with acupuncture meridians and photography, discovering, to their amazement, that the ancient system of Chinese medicine had mapped the body's energy lines accurately, even the loop the kidney meridian makes around the ankle. I'm bringing this up because Christians miss out on some medically verified treatments that could be helpful for them, and also pass on this fear of foreign invasion to others which reveals ignorance that, as a Christian, I find kind of embarrassing. Now, there are some acupuncturists who may do Buddhist things in their practices, but you don't have to go to them. Dennis used acupuncture in his practice and also prayed for his patients and led a lot of them to Jesus. Energy medicine is not automatically "of the devil."

Since Taoism is mostly descriptive with no standards of ethics or behavior, and its founder Lao Tsu's book, the *Tao Te Ching* (pronounced dow-day-ching) is written in lovely, poetic language, it's very difficult to resist. In fact, it was required reading at a local high school. I know because a Christian father called me up to ask about it, saying his daughter and her friends were very excited to read it. I gave him a quick course in what's wrong with it and the dangers that make it deeply treacherous.

Taoism is so lovely that God, Himself, had to reveal its lies to me. After I became a Christian, I had a hard time giving it up. I could find nothing wrong with it. So I asked Father God, and He showed me the lie. In the symbol of the Tao, there is a drop of yang in the center of the yin and a drop of yin the center of the yang. There is nothing pure. But God told me He is the Father of Light in Whom is no variableness or shadow of turning. In Him there is no darkness at all. Furthermore, in Taoism, it could be good, it could be bad, depending on your point of view and happenstance. In Jesus, no matter what happens, God will work all of it together for good for those who love Him and are living for Him. We have security. "Surely goodness and mercy will follow me all the days of my life, and I will dwell in the house of the Lord forever. (Ps 23:6)"

There is no Supreme Being in either Confucianism or Taoism, no concept of sin, accountability of choices after death, and nobody to pray to. My father's mother used to throw the *yarrow* sticks each morning to see her fortune before she would dare to step out the door. When there's no God, and you're on your own to figure out how to navigate your life, you can become very superstitious, afraid to trigger a cascade of ill fortune with no One to appeal to for help.

In Taoism, there is no concept of sin. I realized this as I sat rehearsing the *Kyrie* from Bach's B Minor Mass with the Occidental College Glee Club and chapel choir. I remember it clearly. We had just sung *Kyrie eleison* ("Lord have mercy"). Dr. Swann looked at us and said, "I don't care what you believe. You need God's mercy." I was mystified. What does that mean? Why do I need mercy? I'd heard the word "sin" before, but it always made me think of a drunk in the gutter. I didn't know it's an archery term that means "missing the mark." Not hitting the bullseye. It would be many years before I understood the significance of sin, what it does, and why I wouldn't want to. I already wasn't a drunk in the gutter. How can anyone know what is sin and what is not?

Well, the Bible goes into that in detail, but there's a really easy way to find out what is sin and what is not. Did Jesus do it? We know He didn't commit murder, lie, steal, sleep around, or profane the Name of the LORD. But I now realize there are other "missings of the mark" I wouldn't automatically consider. So I ask myself, was Jesus ever retaliatory? vengeful? self-centered? dominating? power-hungry? short-tempered? malicious? rebellious? Did He belittle others? Did He mock, ridicule, scorn, or demean? Was He selfish? obsessed with His comfort, convenience, or insistent upon getting what He deserved including dignity, respect, and honor? Was His life all about gain, privilege, validation, control? Seems to me He left vindication and validation in the hands of His Father. After four decades of living with the Lord, I no longer need the world to validate me, but I still struggle with flesh. So, in this way of looking at sin, I have to say I need mercy. I sure do! Lots of it! And the good news, the Good News, is I have it. New every morning. In abundance. I have it because Jesus already paid for every one of those sins. *Kyrie eleison.* Thank You, Jesus! In that mercy, in the abundance of forgiveness, there is freedom from the penalty of sin, freedom to make mistakes and learn, freedom to go to God and reconnect, realign, and reconcile (the way everything is right when you get all the numbers to agree on the ledger sheet).

But back to my story. My parents decided early on not to try to indoctrinate me in any religions, though I was thoroughly steeped in Confucianism and Taoism. You can't help conveying your beliefs to your children. It's expressed in everything you say and do. When my friend Janet left for school, her parents would say, "Have fun." When I left for school, my parents would say, "Be good." I have to say my parents did take us to a Protestant church in town, hoping to help us be better Americans and fit in. All I remember was the building was pink. We went once or twice and suddenly stopped. Many years later I found out why. My mother had heard one of the Elders saying in a stage whisper that black birds are not welcome in the white bird's nest. It was the times. In the 1950s, Chinese were not welcome in White neighborhoods. The Anti Chinese Exclusion Act of 1882 had been repealed only about a decade before, and hatred for the yellow peril was still alive and well, even among Christians. I still remember answering a knock on our door. I opened it and saw a middle-aged white woman standing there with a sour look on her face. "You're going to hell and all your ancestors too because you don't believe in Jesus," she snapped. Then she spun around and left me standing there in shock staring after her. I was a little kid. I knew nothing of Jesus. And after that, I didn't want to. After that, I started hating Christians and Jesus too. If that's what His followers were like, I didn't want anything to do with any of them.

As a freshman in college I thought someday I would have to figure out what I believed about God. I remember looking out of my dorm window thinking, How about now? I decided that God, if there was one, got everything going and then stepped back and let it work itself out. God, if there was one, was much too big and important to bother with Earth and us insignificant beings upon it. After that, I studied world religions. In class, I learned that human beings, trying to understand their circumstances, developed religious systems that would explain the life they saw around them. I was particularly attracted to Hinduism because it was the oldest. I always liked originals. To me, they had more credibility because they were the first. I was also attracted to Buddhism, which came out of Hinduism and shared some basic tenets such as reincarnation, but I wasn't drawn to the easy kind that the masses followed. I liked Zen Buddhism. It required more discipline and was very artistic. The best calligraphers were Zen Buddhists.

As I said, it's one thing to read about a world religion in a book, and quite another to see it in practice. In 1967, my parents sent me on a university ship for a semester at sea. I took world religions so I could go on field trips to the most sacred places in India and Japan.

HINDUISM AND BUDDHISM

It was dusk when I began walking the streets of Bombay with my shipmate Margaret and the Indian man who was one of the directors of tourism in charge of greeting our students. He had taken an interest in me and offered to give us a tour of the city. So he chose for us wonderful foods from the vending carts and told us about the architecture and history of the ancient city. I noticed emaciated people in rags lying on the streets and in doorways, barely visible in the dimming light. They seemed to be the color of dust, almost indistinguishable from the hard surfaces on which they lay. Our guide said, "Pay no attention to those people. They all have jobs. They just prefer to sleep on the streets and in doorways." Confucian-trained to unquestioningly respect and accept whatever Teacher said, I believed him. But then I found out that every morning some people would come by and pick up any body that didn't move and throw it in the back of the cart. So much for my romance with Hinduism. On the dirty streets of Bombay, I had a first-hand look at what reincarnation translates to in real life.

Here is how reincarnation works. You have this thing called karma. It gets sticky when you do something bad and loses its stickiness when you do something good. When it's sticky, it picks up stuff that weighs it down. When it's less sticky, some of the heavy stuff falls off. When you die, whatever you weigh at the time determines how you will be born the next time around. The more you weigh, the lower your life form. If you're a bad man, you might come back as a woman or a dog. If you're good, you can be born a human in one of the castes, the highest being Brahmin (they're the ones with the dot on their foreheads) followed by the Kashatrian class, which is the warriors. I don't remember the others. The lowest of the low are the untouchables, because they've been so awful they don't even deserve to be in a caste. And if you're very, very good, you will come back as a Brahma bull.

The thing about karma is it's utterly inexorable. You get what you deserve. There's no forgiveness, grace, mercy, or extenuating circumstances. What you weigh is what you get. Therefore, if you have a low birth, you must work off your bad karma by suffering to make up for all the wrongs you've done. Blindness, physical deformities, low economic status all indicate less than stellar performance in your former life.

In a documentary I saw two blind kids making their way through a crowded Tibetan street when an old woman yells at them, "You deserve to eat your father's corpse!" One of the boys says to the other, "I wonder what I did. I don't think it was too bad, though. I don't think I killed anyone." The parents are affected too. It is thought they did terrible wrong in their previous life since they are cursed with a useless blind child. It's really an ugly system when you see it in operation. And I want to point out that this exchange happened among Tibetan Buddhists. For some reason, Westerners seem to be especially impressed with Tibetan Buddhism and I think it's important to see religious systems as they really are, as they are believed and practiced.

But wait! It gets worse. Since reincarnation is a belief that says you are what you deserve to be, and you must work off your past bad behavior by suffering, no one is inclined to help you. It's not a character flaw in other people; it's an expression of their worldview. In their religious system, to help you would be to interfere with your process and actually hinder your coming back next time in a higher life form. So, by necessity, there is a lack of compassion. In Pearl S. Buck's memoir of her childhood in China, she wrote if you saved a drowning man, not only would you be responsible for the man, you would also be responsible for his entire family because you interfered with the ending of his present life and the completion of the suffering that was, perhaps, sufficient to give him a better life next time.

You can guess that the caste system is rigid and unforgiving. If you're privileged, it's because you deserve it and you can justifiably look down on everyone else. Lower castes deserve their lack of status, and your destain actually helps them suffer, thus causing more paying off of the consequences of their wicked former life.

Our guide was of the Kashatrian caste. He regaled Margaret and me with lovely stories of tumbling with his siblings in their beautiful home, their travels to fascinating places, his excellent education. He was very, very nice to us, but when his "man" came to the taxi window to ask for instructions for his next task, our guide was so curt and rude to him that we were shocked. The man was trying to do his job, but he was interfering with our departure to the next interesting place, and our guide verbally cuffed and kicked him as you would a bothersome dog who got in your way as you strolled in the park.

You can learn a lot about a religion by how the people act, and especially how they treat other human beings. Of course, the Christians of my early life were more like stink weeds than flowers releasing the fragrance of Christ, but I found out later that was not Jesus' fault. Nor is it characteristic of Christianity. In fact, when I began interviewing my parents for books I was writing on their lives, they told me about a number of Christian people who had put themselves at risk to help them. Many of them were white, and several became their lifelong friends. I mention this because it's too easy to lump people together in categories and make a case for offenses and wrongs that are unforgiven and require restitution. I don't feel that way. In my talks on the Chinese-American experience, I often tell the audience not to feel guilty about how their people might have treated my people. I say, "As a representative of my people, I forgive you." Enough of this blaming and complaining and demanding. Back in China, the Chinese were mean to each other, even in the same village. There is no one righteous, no not one. We all need to be forgiven. However, in the lands where reincarnation isn't a romanticized, watered-down concept of past lives and multiple opportunities to learn and do better, there is no hope of forgiveness. And the manifestations are surprisingly heartless. I heard there's a sect of monks that beats dogs so they can be born higher next time.

In reincarnation you experience the consequences of your choices, for good or for ill, and you pay for them the next time around. But no worries. If you're a dung beetle because you've been very bad, or blind, or mentally inert, you have a lifetime to learn, suffer, make better choices, and be born better next time. In this way, you can continue learning, improving, and finally get to the point where your karma doesn't weigh you down at all. At that point, you don't have to come back anymore. You float on up to Nirvana, a state of total bliss, a raindrop returning to the ocean, your individual life disappearing into the great oneness.

There's always a drop of truth in the lie. The truth is, our human hearts long for total oneness with God. And God longs for total oneness with us. Jesus says it in John 17. It's the kind of connection that knows no separation, that soulmate closeness that humans long for in a mate, the kind of unity a jockey feels with a 1500 pound race horse when they are roaring down the track, moving together as one. You're not absorbed in the other, and you do not become one another, yet you are so joined together you are no longer two entities but one.

In Buddhism, you don't get Nirvana. When you're good enough, you become a bodhisattva, a god in human form. Let me explain something here. In Buddhism, everyone can become a buddha. It represents a state of being where you have reached the Middle Way in a perfection of non-involvement with the vicissitudes of life. You don't get worried, you don't get afraid, you don't get angry or frustrated, or excited about anything. You live in a peaceful tranquility as exemplified by the slightly upturned corners of the mouth of the statues of Gautama Buddha that represent him in his enlightened state.

"Gentle Guan Yin" was my favorite story in Frances Carpenter's book, *Tales of a Chinese Grandmother.* I still remember one of the lines. "She thought only good thoughts for nine years, and at last she was perfect." But as she was about to enter into Heaven in her new god-state, Guan Yin heard the cries of humans in distress and turned back to help them. She is considered the goddess of compassionate hearing, and a favorite bodhisattva to this day.

According to this system, anyone can become a buddha or a bodhisattva, you just have to be good enough to be perfect. Of course, Gentle Guan Yin thought only good thoughts for nine years. I can't even do nine minutes. Not much chance of goddess-hood for me!

So what's the lie here? By extreme discipline you can become perfect. You can become a god. Not "you can become like God," but you can become a god and be worshiped. What's wrong with this picture? Do you hear hissing from the Garden? Trumpets blaring to call you to bow down to Nebuchadnezzar's golden statue? Anti-christ's declarations on the threshold of the end of all Time? Scripture does say we are joint-heirs with Christ, which is rather elevated and spectacular when you think of it, but human beings as gods? Nah.

THE ZEN MASTER

As I said, I was drawn to Zen Buddhism, and there was a living Zen Buddhist master and calligrapher that I greatly admired. It so happened that one day when I was in San Francisco, I noticed a poster that said he was going to be speaking at the campus of a nearby college. Delirious with my good fortune, I eagerly arrived early—early enough to be in the front of the cluster of adoring disciples who crowded around this popular man.

The poster had said we would be meeting in a particular room, but when we arrived, it was obviously too small, so the master called the school to change the room. When the young woman arrived to escort us and unlock the new room, she was in an agitated state. I don't know why. What did the illustrious Zen master do? He laughed at her. Then he ridiculed and berated her. The more flustered she became, the more he derided her for being upset, for not being tranquil the way he was. It was ugly. As we walked to the new room, the Zen master continued to make fun of the woman's distresses. She had obviously no idea of how to maintain tranquility in any situation, the Middle Way where nothing bothers you. I felt sorry for her. And Zen Buddhism, in person, lost its shine. Even I, a floundering, confused young woman, knew that wasn't the way to treat other people, especially when they're having a bad day.

God does want us to be able to have His peace no matter what the circumstances, but that comes from knowing He will take care of us no matter what. But that's a different kind of peace from detachment. That peace comes from secure attachment to the One Who holds our times in His hands and will work it all together for our good.

Incidentally, this flat-line, seemingly serene existence is not life and more abundantly. Jesus wasn't a flat-line person. He threw the money changers and merchants out of the temple—more than once. And He told the Pharisees they were a brood of vipers and whited sepulchers full of dead men's bones. Not very polite, tolerant, or nice. But the Greek word for meekness is *prautes*, strength under control—like a great war horse completely under the control of its rider. As Greek scholar William Barclay put it, it's never being angry at the wrong time and always being angry at the right time.

Once I asked Jesus why He said such awful things to the religious leaders of His people. It was because that's what it took to shock them out of their complacency. "Neither do I condemn thee. Go and sin no more" would not have done the job. They had to be shocked, the way an exposed wire from a worn electrical cord can give you a small, but very unpleasant jolt. It makes you aware something is wrong, and might motivate you to investigate what it is and figure out how to fix it. Nicodemus and Joseph of Arimathea were high-ranking members of the Sanhedrin. Not all the religious leaders in Israel were so invested in their power and status and righteousness that they did not become open to radical Truth, especially when He was there in person telling them where the dangers lay.

By the way, I used to think of Hindus as extraordinarily detached from this world, sitting in lotus position for hours, serenely working out their karma with private meditation. Recently I learned that Hindus have murdered thousands of Christians in India. And Buddhists can be violent against Christians as well.

There's another thing about Hindus. It seems the outcasts, the untouchables whose lot in life is to starve, be shamed, and rot, are coming in droves into he arms of Jesus Christ. What a shocking freedom they must have, what delirious joy must be theirs when their worldview opens, transformed with spiritual eyes to see a different reality—the generous grace of God's forgiveness for every wrong, and their adoption with honor into His Family!

I thought it would help you to know about this, because every so often we hear how awful Christianity has been to other cultures, peoples, and religions, especially in the Crusades. I'm not defending what wrongs have been done in Jesus' name. I hated Him for it, remember. But it's worth noting that the murders that have been done because of atheism worldwide far outnumber what the Church has done in all its years of history. And you may include in that count millions of babies, their mothers having been assured they are nothing more than blobs of cells, "the product of conception."

THE OCCULT

So I abandoned Hinduism, Zen Buddhism, and moved to the occult, the hidden knowledge that is mysterious and supernatural. That was the rage in the 1970s. Some of it wasn't new to me.

In the 1950s, playing with Ouija boards was common. We had them in our house. My sister was really good at it. My friend (let's call him Sam) also grew up playing with that, he and his sisters. They were fascinated. They had a friend who did tarot card readings, and when they were adults, they went to seances and anything that was otherworldly. There is a lot of danger in consciously opening yourself up to the dark realm. When you deliberately yield your will to something you know is not God, you are giving legal permission to demonic involvement in your life and your family line.

Sam's sisters continued to be fascinated with anything supernatural, as long as it's not God, and they were beset by bizarre manifestations in their lives, the lives of their children and grandchildren, and on their property and in their houses. On one occasion, it got so bad in the house they had it "smudged." This gets rid of the demonic manifestations for a little while. Why? Because the dark side would rather give you a little relief from harassment in exchange for your trust in rituals and people of spiritual power instead of in the true and living God, especially when His name is Jesus.

There are other very serious open doors that come in the guise of harmless rituals or procedures purported to bring about more peace in the heart and mind. One is in meditation. The Bible tells us to meditate, ruminate, chew over the things of God, think on things that are good, pure, lovely, true, etc. That's a good kind of meditation, one with only blessings and no risk. But blanking out your mind can be dangerous if you're being led in a group and you are just going along with the instructions of the leader without being aware of what's going on.

I remember going with friends to a relaxation class. While we imagined a tranquil scene and were in our most receptive state, the instructor told us to let someone come into the scene. In fact, we were told to invite someone who would help us in times of turmoil and troubles—a spiritual guide. It was a very dangerous practice, but I didn't know it and, in my case, I was never good at visualization and couldn't settle down long enough to get tranquil, so I never saw anybody. Years later, Jesus told me He had protected me because, the way I was, I could have ended up going places from which there was no way back.

I had grown up with astrology. My mother used to read our newspaper horoscopes to us every morning, though we didn't take it seriously. We could tell they were so general they would fit almost anyone. Nevertheless, Mom bought each of us, including her grandchildren, mugs with our signs on them and a brief description of who we were star-destined to be. Those descriptions became part of our identities.

Aren't newspaper horoscopes just a harmless amusement? No. At the very least, reading daily horoscopes is input that is not coming from the God Whose entire desire for us is His best for every day. He knows the end from the beginning. Why would we look elsewhere? It's a diversion—not as something that's entertaining, but as a stream is diverted from its proper course, resources are diverted from their intended recipient, attention is diverted from the One Who knows how to guide us through whatever comes into our day. Why would we look elsewhere?

At the very worst, astrology can lead to deeper study and become an open door into other occult knowledge. That's what happened to me. I was trying to align with the stars to insure my future and establish the best configurations of compatible signs in my surrounding relationships. It was deadly. Astrology pigeon-holes people, turning them into categories of expected behavior, instead of seeing them as unique individuals. I ended up divorcing my husband because I was sure we could never reconcile our differences since our signs were so incompatible.

Isaiah 8:19 says: "And when they say to you, 'Seek those who are mediums and wizards, who whisper and mutter,' should not a people seek their God?" Well, yeah. That's a very good thought, except I had no idea there even was a god, much less *The* God, so I never thought to seek Him. Plus I already knew I didn't want to have anything to do with Jesus— white man's God. However there seems to be a drawing to the supernatural, a sense there's More, so I started looking. It didn't take long. In the 1970s, Eastern Mysticism was becoming more and more popular, with saffron-robed gurus showing up on network TV, their India-accented voices sounding wise and tranquil. My life was anything but tranquil.

It was an era of experimentation with the paranormal. One fad was astral projection (the spirit leaving the body and tootling around in other dimensions). LSD and peyote were big too. I didn't use hallucinogenic drugs—or any drugs. I didn't even drink. Nevertheless, curiosity about personal power seems to be like blood in the water to the sharks of that dark realm, and soon I was being mentored by a psychic with startling violet eyes whose office was just down the hall from mine. I was seeking more power in my life because I had lost all control over it, including my mind. Having given up on my marriage, I ran away, leaving my two little boys with my parents, telling them I would return for them when I had my life together. Why would I do such a thing? As I studied astrology and developed my healer skills, I became less and less in control of my life. I kept dreaming about killing my sons and I was afraid I would do it someday. This may seem creepy to some of you, and I don't lightly share it, but God told me you need to know, so here goes. Actually, I'll give you the short version.

Dr. Dennis Greenlee and I were having dinner in a nice restaurant. He had hired me to work in his office and was interested in getting to know me before I left my present job and went to work for him. During the conversation, Dennis mentioned that his life's dream was to be a missionary. A missionary for Jesus! Those people who force their Christianity on other cultures, insisting that they conform to their standards of morality, forbidding their own heritage, telling them they were all going to Hell and their ancestors too, because they didn't believe in Jesus! I threw my hands over my ears and said rather too loudly, "Don't ever say that name to me again!" I said a few other things, but you get the point.

Dennis quietly got me to calm down. He promised. No more Jesus. I sat back down, and he encouraged me to talk about what I was interested in. I told him I was being mentored by a powerful psychic and was about to go astral projecting. I told him I was learning how to make energy balls and tune in to supernatural realms. Dennis listened without comment, but unbeknownst to me, shortly thereafter he asked his Gideon brothers to pray for me. "Pray that the little Chinese girl will see what she's dealing with and that Jesus will reveal Himself to her."

Not long after that, Dennis and I were visiting in my apartment. All of a sudden, I felt as if we were being encircled by something so terrifying I could hardly speak. It was like being in a circle of campfire light with wolves from the dark pressing in from every side, only much scarier. I told Dennis I was going to pull up my auric shield, but I couldn't get it above my knees. Calmly, he said, "I can get rid of them."

"Do it!" I ordered, shaking harder than I knew was possible.

"You won't like it," he said with maddening calm.

I barked, "Do it anyway!"

"Okay," he said. "In the name of Jesus, I command you to leave." Like a wave withdrawing from the shore, the "things" withdrew and disappeared.

The next day, I went to see the head psychic. I could tell there was something—a seven-foot tall something—following me. "Something is here," she said. "It doesn't mean me harm, but it means you harm."

"I know," I said. She had to answer the phone so I sat on a stool and said in my mind, "Jesus, I don't know you and I don't like you, but I saw something last night, and if you're who he says you are, get rid of this thing."

The psychic got off the phone and said, somewhat surprised, "It's gone."

I said, "I know."

That was the beginning.

So now I knew there was a realm, an invisible one, inhabited by beings that were real and powerful and terrifying. I had also seen a power much greater than theirs, that they had to obey, but that did not force itself upon me. I knew it was Jesus because that's the name we called on for help. I didn't see or hear Him, no light in the corner, no voice in the room, but He came and the other things left. I didn't fall at His feet and worship. Instead, I felt a kind of reserved amazement. Oh! You do exist. I wonder what that means. When you've spent your life hating someone, you don't automatically fall in love with Him. I take that back. Some do. Recently I watched a documentary about five Muslims, each from a different country, who were in deep anguish for one reason or another. Each got to the point they begged God to reveal Himself, and Jesus showed up. Each of them was radically changed, but they already believed in God and had been devout and serious followers of their faith.

My coldness of soul was from no consciousness of God at all. It's like the kittens in the experiment I heard about. Researchers put young kittens in an empty room with horizontal lines painted on the walls. After a few weeks they put the kittens in a normal house, and the kittens bumped into the legs of the tables and chairs. I was like that with God. I couldn't see anything vertical. No neural pathways from exposure, so I simply couldn't comprehend it.

Not long after that, I started working as a microcurrent therapist at Dr. Greenlee's office. Dennis went from room to room, adjusting patients who were already gowned and face down on the table. It took about two and a half minutes. He was fast and he was good, and there was a waiting list of people trying to get in to see him. My schedule was also packed, but my treatments took longer to give. I'd see a patient every fifteen minutes, twenty-five patients a day. Even though it was forty-five years ago, there are two patients I remember quite well. They were middle-aged white women, Marge and Myrtle. When I think of it, they were about the same age and look as the one who showed up at my door when I was a little girl—the one who told me I was going to Hell and my ancestors too. But Marge and Myrtle weren't like that.

Marge had those lumpy knuckles of osteoarthritis—very painful. I could see the pain in her eyes, but she never complained. Myrtle was a caretaker for some grown men with mental disabilities. She called them her boys and always spoke of them with immense fondness, though I know they were sometimes difficult, and she was not young or strong. She, too, never complained. These two women would come in and tell me about Jesus. I don't remember what they said exactly, I just felt the acceptance and care, and also noted that they said the same things—about how God loved me and had a purpose for my life. Really? Could it be true I wasn't the randomly birthed second daughter of the Confucian scholar? The invisible, the inept, the untalented, the plain, the unremarkable? I knew they didn't know each other. I thought they must be reading the same book or something because they consistently said the same words. And they never told me what a wretched sinner I was—though I really was. I had abandoned my children. I was still in the occult. I was rebellious, defensive, profane, lawless—a person still believing I would have to construct my own value within the overwhelming meaninglessness of life.

Marge and Myrtle were regulars. Each of them had an appointment every week. And whenever one of them had an appointment, whatever day or time, the patients on either side of their time slot would cancel. I'd have forty-five minutes with one of those sweet women, hearing and feeling the love of Jesus week after week.

They loved me into the Kingdom.

Looking back, I know God intervened. Even then I knew something was fishy about those cancellations. It was the first I noticed the fingerprints of God on my life, evidence of His Presence and love as He waited to be wanted. I'm telling you this for several reasons.

I didn't believe in demons. I thought there was just the Tao, and power could be good and it could be bad. Since my intention was to heal people, I was sure the forces I was cultivating and controlling were good. It never occurred to me there might be malevolent entities on Earth that would actually be controlling *me*, and make me, the original peacemaker, want to kill my children. It was the twentieth century, for

Heaven's sake. Well, I found out demons are real whether you believe in them or not. And they aren't your friend.

Even though I was rude to Him, the Lord of the Universe was patient and loving with me. Gently and graciously He began to open my eyes, particularly through the love of Marge and Myrtle, and, about a year later, I finally gave Him my heart.

Jesus defeated death, hell, and the grave. He made a public spectacle of all of the demonic realm when He conquered them on the Cross and was resurrected as proof that every single sin was paid for in full. So we certainly don't need to be afraid. There is also a lot in the Bible about the supernatural power of God. The invisible realm operates by authority. All power in Heaven and Earth has been given to Jesus. And He has given it to us. Demons always have to obey, which is why Dennis didn't even have to raise his voice. It was the authority of Jesus' Name he was using, not rituals, incantations, or personal power.

When you see people deeply invested in terrible things—the occult, witchcraft, demon worship, or even if they're just different races and religions, remember I was one of them. Many of them have been brought up with an atheistic worldview, reduced to situational ethics, animal instincts, survival of the fittest, and horizontal thinking. They can't comprehend the vertical. They've been taught there is no God. How could they then see His fingerprints or hear His gentle call? I couldn't. Like me, they struggle through the confusions of these chaotic and maddening times, unaware there is a personal God Who loves them and understands their emptiness. As I thought about this, the Lord said, "They're crying. But their tears are softening the hard-packed ground." Right now they lack the vision and neurological connections that would enable them to comprehend and perceive Him, but we can pray for those tears to prepare the foundations of their lives for the flowers to come.

And remember you can pray what the Gideons prayed for me and know it's God's heart you're sharing when you do, for the lost are His creations and as precious to Him as you are. I often thank the Gideons in my heart and ask the Lord to bless them, because they prayed for me when I was hostile and unreceptive, and God answered by showing me the truth of the spiritual reality that exists beyond what we can see, and rescued me.

During my unguided search for truth, I had no idea what "personal God" meant. I thought, if there was a god, he made everything and, being much too big and busy to bother with us puny, insignificant humans, left it all to work out itself. After I became a Christian, Jesus surprised me by saying, "Honey, it takes a much bigger God to know every hair on your head and the thoughts and intents of your heart." I didn't know, when I was a freshman in college, deciding what I thought about God as I looked out my dorm room window, that He was listening—waiting for me to discover the depths of His love.

I wish my parents had taught me about Jesus because, though I eventually came to know Him, I made a big mess out of my life first, and wasted time I could have spent growing in the love of God. But we were Chinese and nobody told us. On the other hand, when I was thirty, Jesus sent Marge and Myrtle to love me into the Kingdom and, years later, I was able to bring both of my parents to Christ.

Looking back into those early years, I have an impression of a young woman desperately pretending to be alive. More accurately, I feel the truth of the Scripture that says we were once dead in our trespasses and sins. For thirty years I sat in darkness under the shadow of death, but the Dayspring from on High came and shined His Light on me and guided my feet in the ways of peace. I have now spent more than half my life in the company of the God of the Universe. I have never felt such love. I have never enjoyed my life more. I am gloriously, overwhelmingly, eternally grateful. Someday I will see His dear, beloved face and be with Him forever, and, as C.S. Lewis wrote, that will be the beginning of my real story, the Great Story in which every chapter is better than the one before.

18

NEW LIFE

So now I'm a Christian, whatever that means.

The first thing I did was apologize to my boys. When I think back on it, they didn't have to believe me. I had hurt them probably worse than anything they'd faced before in all of the years of their young lives, and I certainly wasn't a very reliable source of stability and sanity for them. I kept moving from apartment to apartment depending on employment, and I'd pop in and out of their lives sporadically and infrequently. They didn't know I was wrestling with my own demons (literally) and afraid to bring them into my chaos, but I couldn't explain that to them. John was eight. Thomas was seven. Only after I started getting to know Jesus did my life begin to be less frightening. Only then did I feel I could risk contacting them more consistently.

So there we were, sitting together with Dennis in my apartment while I told them about my encounter with the wolves and with Jesus, and Dennis explained the Gospel to them because I was too new to even know how to say anything beyond that Jesus had shown up and rescued me. The real miracle in all of this is they believed it—that Jesus is God and they could be His—and both of them have grown up to be outstanding men of God. Recently when I asked Thomas why, he told me it was something that happened to him that day in my apartment. This is what he said:

"During that time things were very unsettled. I didn't know when I was going to see my mom. I didn't know where I was going to be when I did see my mom. I felt like every time I saw her she was somewhere else.

247

"The mental picture I had of life at that time was just swirling darkness, and maybe if you picture fog and funky lighting so you could see it swirling and unsettled—kind of like being in the middle of the ocean but there was no water that you could identify. It was just swirling darkness. And somehow, in the middle of this darkness, I came upon a rock. It was very clearly a rock. And I remember the mental image of me just hanging onto this thing. It wasn't huge. It wasn't like the Rock of Gibraltar popping out of nowhere. It was big enough for me to hang onto and not a lot bigger than that. But it didn't move. I could see the swirling around me. I could feel the swirling around me and I could feel that the rock didn't move, so I clung to it. It was very clear in my head. Jesus was the rock that I could cling to, and that was enough for me at that point in time. I expect to have that picture etched in my memory for the rest of my life."

THE LEGALISTIC CHURCH

God often puts people who have been in the occult in legalistic churches to help them get their bearings, like braces on legs to help you walk straight. After my conversion, my family and I spent ten years in a legalistic church where the emphasis was on performance and absolute, unquestioning obedience. Does that sound familiar? Having been reared to be a dutiful Confucian daughter, it was easy for me to submit to the pastor. I became a devoted disciple, giving all my time and talent to the church. The pastor made me Minister of Music and I began leading the congregation in song on Wednesday evenings and all day Sunday. I took all of this very seriously. In that church, serving in ministry was proof that you were truly committed to God. Being given a position of ministry was an honor, a validation of your worthiness (and righteousness) before the Lord—and everyone else. What could be more legitimatizing than endorsement by the Most High through His representative on Earth?

We were told God required sacrifice, and nothing—not work, vacations, children, marriage, exhaustion, illness, emergencies, or anything was to keep us from fulfilling our sacred duties. We were also told that faith in God was proven by trusting Him, not doctors, for healing, so I did not go to the doctor when I had pleurisy and pneumonia. It nearly killed me, but in the six weeks I was in so much pain I could barely breathe, I never missed a service. I sang anyway.

It's not new, this idea of sacrificing everything for God. Missionaries were expected to. They often parked their kids at boarding schools with other missionary kids, seeing them infrequently. It was the accepted, expected, respected thing to do. Not all children of missionaries ended up crashing on the rocks—either from abuses in the boarding schools, or from growing up in an institution instead of with their parents, but many stories are told of the damage done by this kind of extreme putting God before all others. My sons suffered from it.

My dear friend (let's call her Mary) was married to a pastor who was often gone on God's business. He diligently served the Lord and was worn and preoccupied by the many demands of his ministry. It was the way it was. Ministry required that much. The wives stayed home with the children and tried to keep things together. The children saw their father infrequently, and, when they did, there was often nothing to talk about because they were strangers to one another. Mary's eldest son (let's call him Charles) was badly damaged by this. He longed for his father's attention, but their personalities and interests were too different. For years Charles tried to make contact with his father. At last he found something he and his dad could do together, and they had a brief time of sharing that passion before the cancer came. They prayed, the congregation and Charles and his mom—to no avail. The man who had given his life for God had now done so literally. Mary told me soon after that Charles went off to college where the full force of scientific materialism hit him. She said he called and told her he no longer needed God. He had science, and science had answers. It has been decades, and Charles has still not recovered. I wonder if he felt he could not take his troubles to God because it was God's work that was taking his dad away. How could he tell God he felt sad and lonely? It would be complaining because his dad was obeying God. But was he?

Mary was the daughter of missionaries. She expected this kind of life herself. She had grown up seeing her mom hold things together the best she could while her husband was out serving others. The children didn't have much time to get to know their father. That's why she was shocked when, many years after her own children were grown, she heard a speaker say God's first priority for a man is his family. Really? That's not what churches have traditionally taught. But that's what the Bible says. A lot. God has entrusted these precious lives to us parents and, as any of you who are older know, those little ones grow up very fast and are soon gone.

I felt the need to bring this up because—first, I did it myself, and second, my parents did it to me. They weren't pastors, but they were very busy all the time. They were health professionals, and when they weren't taking care of their enormous patient load, they were hosting research scientists, experts in electronics, Cal Tech engineers, PhDs investigating the properties of Ultra High Frequencies (UHF). Every night after work, Mom would feed us, put us to bed, and then prepare for guests who started arriving soon after. They stayed till the wee hours in the morning, and this happened seven nights a week and all day Sunday for at least four years.

My mother entertained the wives, who would never have put up with any of this night after night except my mom made sure they had a wonderful time. She even made a fresh cake from scratch every day—with butter cream frosting. I think she would have preferred resting quietly in the evenings, but she believed in what my dad was trying to do, and she felt her duty as a wife was to support her husband, so she helped in the best way she knew how. The result was the research went on at a blistering pace with my father facilitating major discoveries in UHF. It was a significant, world-changing contribution to technology, and I'm very proud of both of them. But it cost something. My mom told me she saw me go out into the crowded room, find my dad, and climb up on his lap. Without even a break in his sentence, my dad removed me from his lap and set me on the floor.

See? This kind of sacrifice of everything for the project or the ministry or the job or the career or the art—it's acceptable, admirable, even approved and applauded in our society. But it causes deep and long-range damage. It kept me in a cult-type church for a decade because I craved the approval of a father figure, and Mary's son is still angry with God and wants nothing to do with Him, even though Father God knows how to heal his heart—and would—if he'd give Him a chance.

In order to save my sons from the evils of the world, I helped found a Christian school that we held in the church. Since it was a Christian curriculum, the science was creationist, with all the latest scientific discoveries. We loved it. I led worship at the school every morning and taught art, music, writing, and drama. I loved that too. I had always wanted to be a teacher, but had failed abysmally in my first teaching job, which was in South Central L.A. in "the ghetto," as it was called in those days. With seven periods of as many as 45 thirteen-year-olds in one room, and me looking about twelve, I could never keep order. It was horrible. But at the Christian school, there was order and respect and a chance to ignite the fires of the love of learning, and I got to teach the really fun subjects.

One of Thomas' classmates was Stephanie, a sweet little girl who loved to draw, but didn't think she had any talent for it—until she went through my course on right-brain drawing. Suddenly she could draw astonishingly well. Shockingly well. And she loved it. She also loved horses. We hit it off immediately. Stephanie's mother, Carol, was one of Dennis' patients. She came to school functions and especially enjoyed the musicals I wrote and directed with both Stephanie and her sister Christina in starring roles. Rhonda, a tall, slender blonde, came often to our Sunday afternoon services. We thought she was kind of a church-hopper because she went to other churches as well. We didn't know she was so hungry for God that she went wherever a service was being held, soaking up all she could of this amazing Living God to Whom she had recently given her life. An auburn-haired young woman named Debra also came sometimes to our church. She was a new believer trying out various services to see what felt like home. Eventually she started working in Dennis' office. We all became good friends. Back then we were new in our faith—floundering and finding our way. We never would have guessed that, forty years later, we would be closer to each other, deeper in Jesus, and a sisterhood of faith and love that has sustained us through many hard times.

Our whole life was the church. All of our friends were in the church. All of our celebrations and social activities were with the church. When Dennis took his vacation scuba diving on the North Coast at Anchor Bay, the church came and camped alongside us, singing praise songs to Jesus around the campfire after feasting on fresh abalone, ling cod, and red snapper. It was glorious and delightful and insular and restrictive and we had nothing to do with people on the outside. They just weren't committed enough to Jesus to be good company.

You may wonder how fairly intelligent people could put up with such demands on their lives, but churches like that are very close-knit families. It's the "us against the world" kind of mindset that creates powerful bonds. If we stick together, we'll be safe. My son John said, "I remember church feeling homey. It was loving and welcoming and family." I, myself, felt so loved, accepted, appreciated, and, best of all, the pastor approved of me and elevated me to second in command. I was a shining disciple of Christ, so serious about my faith that I assiduously kept all the requirements. And when I heard Jesus was interceding for me, I told Him He really didn't need to. He could use His time to help others that needed it more. My goodness! (literally) I was practically a bodhisattva! Move over, Guan Yin!

Changes

At first it was glorious, but as the years passed, things at the legalistic church were getting more and more strange, and one day God told me to cut back my hours of teaching at the school. I knew immediately I would lose the favor of the pastor, who took any reduction of service as a withdrawal of devotion to God, and to him as God's representative. But even then I knew Who was God and who was not. My obedience to God brought about the swift wrath of the pastor, a stripping of all my ministries, and public humiliation. Unbeknownst to us, Pastors Jim and Sheri Lujan had been praying for years that Dennis and I would be delivered out of the false teaching, and God answered their prayers before I became any more insufferable. John and Thomas were in college, so, once again, I had to make my apologies to them. Thomas was at Le Tourneau in Texas, so he got a phone call, but Dennis and I drove to Bethany Bible College, several hours away, to tell John in person.

John said he immediately knew something was up because it was a Sunday and we never went anywhere on Sundays. He remembers that we stayed for the service and I cried through the whole thing. Afterwards I told him that everything I had taught him about God was wrong. Recently John said, "I've spent the past thirty years trying to find out who He really is."

In a way, I'm also still on that quest. Who is He really? We pick up so many bogus ideas from a multitude of sources. But trials have their way of revealing what is true and what is not. For the past year, John and his wife Shelly have been going through the worst trials of their lives, but, through each new terrible thing, John and Shelly keep finding Him to be bigger and better than they thought.

After a time of shock and demoralization, Dennis and I began attending the Calvary Chapel the Lujans pastored, and it was at their church that I met Bob Cull, who came out from Maine twice a year to do worship concerts in Lake County and visit his grandma Bea. God chose Bob to be my mentor—the best person to show me the true heart of God—a musician, Bible teacher, and artist who spoke Jesus in my language. I tried to make him my guru, still trained to follow and obey whatever Teacher said, but he quickly squelched that, saying, "We're all just bozos on the bus." Absolute obedience and devotion are reserved for God alone.

I had been taught that we must not "heap to ourselves." Everything we had—all our time and resources—were to be sacrificed to God through the church. Spending money on ourselves, buying anything nice or the slightest bit better than the barest necessities, was selfish and soulish. Everything was about Spirit. This view is rather insulting to God when you think about it. He invented matter. He invented beauty, pleasure, fragrance, touch, aesthetic appreciation, music, color, sex, humor, emotions, curiosity, and the human body. He intended human enjoyment of life. You can see that in the Garden. Things were lovely and smelled good and were designed to be pleasant and delicious. By the way, Christianity is the only religion that doesn't say matter is evil.

God created the universe so well-suited to the comfort and flourishing of human life that it has been called the Anthropic Principle—so dubbed because natural scientists haven't been able to escape the obvious Fine Tuning of everything to make it perfect for human life. Some have called it the Goldilocks Principle. Plus, when God created it, He pronounced it good. And when He created humans, He said that was very good. Obviously God didn't think it was evil to be human in a physical body. We are made in His image. It's very special to be a human being, much more than we realize. Why else would He have deigned to be one? And, even more astonishing, He has chosen to remain one. Think of that! When we get to Heaven, we will find a Man on the Throne. Did you realize that? I didn't—till I started listening to Bible scholar Chuck Missler. Before that, I kind of thought Jesus took off His divinity, did His work on Earth as a human being, redeemed us, then returned Home where He took off His human suit and put back on all of His Deity, whatever spirit form that might be. But it doesn't say that. Revelation specifies what John sees is Jesus in His transcendent form—as a Man. Hard to fathom. But that's what it says. And, of course, He comes back riding on a white horse and then rules and reigns a thousand years on Earth—as a human being. Does that strike you as hard to understand? I love my guide dog Hedy, but I would never become a dog to save her and her kind, much less stay a dog once the deed had been accomplished. I admit, I really don't understand, but then, He's God and I'm not.

STAYING ALIVE

I forgot to mention that, after leaving the legalistic church and before being mentored by Bob Cull, I spent a year and a half wanting to die. We had been told we were going to Hell (though they didn't say "and your ancestors too") because we were totally deluded by the devil and sliding rapidly to the Pit. I didn't really believe that (though I wondered). It was more the horror of realizing what I had actively taught my students and friends about God was completely wrong. I, who prided myself (operative words) for being accurate and thorough in every aspect of my Christian life, now realized with shock after shock how unrighteous I had been. I was devastated. I felt like a bear coming out of its cave after being asleep all winter—now blinking in the strong sunlight. I knew something was wrong, but I didn't know what. And I didn't know how to find out. So I just kept trying to make it through, deciding each morning to be alive one more day.

Another person who was also struggling was Dale Enstrom. I met him in 1982 when I was Minister of Music at The King's Place, a Christian coffee house in Clearlake. He and his friend Bob Fischetti came up to play their original music for us, and share about Jesus. Keith Green, Randy Stonehill, Phil Keaggy—they were breaking new ground in Christian music, but Dale's melodies and messages were different, and I wanted to know what he had. So I asked him. I knew it was something I didn't have, and I wanted it. Turns out it was a love relationship with Jesus. It flowed through his lyrics and lyrical melodies like living water—because that's what it was. It was First Love—Bride of Christ. What does that mean? "Well," he said, "it's like when you marry someone. You get his name, his home, his checkbook…" That concept was totally new to me, but it watered my soul in that time when the legalism was sucking the vitality out of my relationship with God. The letter (the Old Covenant of the Law) kills, but sometimes it's a slow dehydration. Now I had a little stream of my own, one I could cultivate in my private times with the Lord.

I was good friends with Bob and Dale through the years at the legalistic church, and they often made the two and a half hour drive to come minister at the coffee house. Eventually Dale started making that long drive every week to record tracks for my music projects in the little studio Dennis had built for me, staying the weekend at our house to attend church with us and play his B3 organ to enrich the music for the service. He came to worship with us because he figured out his own church was a cult, and wanted strong, straight teaching. He believed he was getting that now, and was willing to give his whole weekend to get it.

Dale was still around years later when I was trying to decide whether it was worth going on. Both of us had figured out the legalistic church wasn't teaching the truth either, but I don't think we would have seen it had the pastor not started swinging the hatchet at me from the pulpit at every service. He even delivered a sermon on the fall of Lucifer, the Minister of Music whose pride in his talent and beauty led to the stripping of ministry and loss of his privileged place in Heaven. No longer an archangel, Lucifer sank to the depths of degradation. He became Satan. Dale and I had been new Christians when we started attending our churches, and we both had believed everything we'd been taught. Now we were confused and bewildered. The only thing sure was we wanted to keep hanging onto Jesus, whatever that meant. By then, neither of us knew.

BLESSING AND CURSING

One day I was driving down the little, rarely-traveled side street that intersects with the street that runs right in front of our former home church. It was their time of prayer and I knew they would be "praying" for us, the deluded, rebellious, backsliding unfaithful. I knew what they would be saying. I had been at many such prayer sessions. "Oh Lord, please send a messenger from Satan against them to expose the errors of their ways so they will return to us. And if they won't repent and apologize, then take their lives before they lose their salvation."

They were basically cursing us. I wasn't angry. I knew the drill. I had done the same thing many times, and I understood they really believed they were praying scripturally for our good.

As I paused at the stop sign, the Holy Spirit said, "Bless those who curse you." So I did. Right there at the stop sign.

To my surprise, I saw my words, looking like sabers, going out from me and their sword-words coming from the upper room of the church. They met in the middle of the street, flashed in a short flurry of swordplay, then turned around and returned to the ones who spoke them. It was a rather graphic vision of what happens in the invisible realm.

I was stunned. I think when Jesus tells us to do something, there's more to it than symbolism or ways to keep our hearts clean from bitterness. There's something literal going on in the invisible realm, and I saw it in vivid detail. I could almost hear the clanging of steel against steel.

Scripture says death and life are in the power of the tongue (Proverbs 18:21), and spoken words are much more powerful than we imagine. It was a startling revelation of the wisdom of what Jesus said—"love your enemies, bless those who curse you, pray for those who despitefully use you." And it showed me one more way God has given us to overcome evil with good.

RESTORATION

In the meantime, Bob Cull and God were feeding me spiritually nutritious things—books by George MacDonald (C.S. Lewis' literary hero), teachings of Gayle Erwin (a good friend of Bob's, and eventually one who had a profound influence on my future as a writer and publisher), and tapes of his own sermons sent to me on a regular basis. He also gave me a verse—Isaiah 61:1-4—which he said was what Jesus did, then what He's doing for me now, and what I am then to do for other people. It became my life verse. Here it is:

The Spirit of the LORD God is upon me because the LORD has anointed me to preach the Gospel to the poor and afflicted; He has sent me to bind up the brokenhearted, to proclaim liberty to the captives and the opening of prison doors to those who are bound, to proclaim the acceptable year of the LORD, and the day of the vengeance of our God, to comfort all who mourn, to grant consolation to those who mourn in Zion, to give them beauty for ashes, the oil of joy for mourning, a garment of praise for a heavy, burdened, and failing spirit that they may be called trees of righteousness, the planting of the LORD, that He might be glorified. And they shall rebuild the ancient ruins; they shall raise up the former desolations and renew the ruined cities, the devastations of many generations.

That last part—about the rebuilding places that have been in ruins for years, the raising up of that which was previously desolate, and renewing of ruined cities so people will have places to live that are safe, secure, peaceful, and cooperative— it just tugs continually at my heart. I want so much to help stop the devastations of many generations. This book is part of that calling.

In the legalistic church, we were taught that ministry is a sign of God's favor. If you aren't in ministry, it's because you don't qualify anymore. You're not good enough to serve the Holy and Righteous God. For three years I was out of ministry before God put me back on the platform leading worship. Just before Bob's time of mentoring me was finished, he said God had not taken me out of ministry to correct my doctrine about Him. He said God had me spend three years learning to sit on His lap. Now that I think about it, that's the one thing I wanted most when I was a small child in my parents' house. I wanted to be on my daddy's lap.

Bob's grandma Bea Cull lived only a few miles from my house. She was delighted to continue the mentoring for me. Sharing Jesus was one of her very favorite things, and she was full of bright life and joy, even in her eighties, which is when I met her. My dear friend Stephanie had been my student at the Christian school and needed spiritual resetting as much as I, and we went often to visit Bea, who was still teaching Sunday school and giving music lessons, loving to be in the middle of the activities whatever they might be. Stephanie and I spent hours discovering through Bea what the abundant spiritual life in Jesus really looks like. Her answers to our questions were never what we expected. One time Bea told me Jesus wants to put on my life and go about loving people through my personality. It was a surprising image, but it really helped me understand what it is to embody Christ to a dark and dying world.

CONNECTIONS

The Lujans took me to Calvary Chapel retreats where Bob Cull was teaching and leading worship. There Bob introduced me to his friend, Gayle Erwin, a bunch of Calvary Chapel musicians, and Chuck Smith. Each man had a quality God had told me would be evidenced in the life of any man who truly surrendered his will to Him. At those retreats I got to see what Jesus looks like expressed through a number of strong men of God with their unique, individual personalities. Definitely not cookie-cuttered.

Jim Salinas was worship leader at the Clearlake Calvary Chapel. After a while, I joined the team and became friends with his wife Sophie and their three boys, Jeremy, Dustin, and Corey.

One day Jim gave a concert of his original music. He had a raspy, but kind of golden voice, and I really liked his songs, particularly, "I Get Lifted Up by the Love of My Lord." Because of that song, I felt moved to invite him to record an album at my studio. He was happy to accept, but there was a problem. I didn't have a recording engineer. My engineer had decided he wanted to move on and left me stranded, saying God would send me someone even better. I didn't see how that was possible, but there was nothing I could do. I decided to try to run the 12-track myself. Jim said he thought we could figure it out together. We did manage to record all his songs—all the synthesized instruments, all the vocals, and then we realized we had another problem: we didn't know how to mix. But Jim was dauntless. We dove in and did our best, finishing in time to enable him to deliver cassette tapes to friends and family for Christmas. It wasn't great, but we figured we could try again in January and send out new tapes when we got it right.

One day in summer, I was shocked when I walked into my studio. Jim was not alone. I had given him a key, but not permission to invite others there. I was getting increasingly annoyed with him for this intrusion when he flashed his Salinas smile and said, "This is my best friend, Danny. If anything happens to me, I want him to mix my music."

I paused briefly, thinking Jim and I had been trying for six months to remix his album, and it was still awful. I said, "Why not now?" I gestured to the 12-track. "Let's see what he can do." In five minutes, Dan produced a mix that was better than what we'd managed in six months.

I'll give you the highlights of the short version. Dan drove two and a half hours every day to come mix Jim's album. After six months, he said God had told him to "help Carolyn" and moved to Lake County. He became the recording engineer at my little studio, Earthen Vessel Productions, and God truly did send me someone better than I thought was possible.

For thirty years, Dan has expanded Earthen Vessel beyond what either of us could have imagined. He taught himself how to use PageMaker and we published my mom's memoir of growing up in her parents' Chinese laundry. After that I decided to continue publishing my own books rather than trying to go through the big houses in New York. One of the deciding factors was what Gayle Erwin did. He had started self-publishing his books because it gave him total control over his work, and if he wanted to give books away, he could. So I wrote books and we published them. And when God sent us authors with stories He wanted known, we published them too.

During my mother's illness, I went often to Southern California to help my dad take care of her in their home. My watercolor teacher, Milford Zornes, and his wife Pat lived only five minutes away, so Milford's friend and colleague, Bill Anderson, would pick me up and I'd go spend the day picking their brains on the creative process. God gave me that very special gift of time with these gentle, inspiring men, and it refreshed and restored me during the stress and sorrows of caring for a mom who was so heartbreakingly ill. These interviews turned into our first hard cover, full color book, *Nine Decades with a Master Painter*. Instead of all the other timelines and lists of award-type biographies that were out on Milford's life, this one was a conversation between two great artists and friends. I was delighted when Milford told me it was his favorite book on himself. Earthen Vessel published four books of Milford's work, plus two that were written and organized by his son-in-law, Hal Baker with the patient input of his wife Maria. The best part has been the friendships that developed with these artists and writers that have been so cherishing and enriching to me for more than twenty years.

To our surprise Earthen Vessel has become a small publisher with more than fifty books in print. We've done several albums of our original songs and projects for a few others (at God's direction).

At the start of the Millennium, Dan and I found ourselves co-producing Summer Theatre Workshop, a teen theater group that would put on a full main stage musical in just eight grueling, but wonderful weeks. I wanted to do it because Lake County has one of the highest teen suicide rates in the country, and kids out here in the boonies get pretty bored in the summer. It was quite the adventure, but it also brought about a deep friendship with a quiet nineteen-year-old named Nathan, who was in charge of set design and construction, and became my spiritual son. In his penetrating search for verification of his Christian faith, Nathan found the Veritas Forum, lectures and interviews of the most brilliant thinkers of the faith. One of them is Dr. Eleonore Stump, who changed my thinking about the Book of Job when she pointed out the multitudes of references to birthing and nurturing God revealed to Job from the whirlwind. I'm still listening to those insightful and astonishing talks. I love hearing what really smart people say about Jesus Christ.

Summer Theatre Workshop also engendered *Even In Shadow*, an original musical that Dan and I wrote together against impossible odds. We wrote it, as it were, running from the wolves, always behind in creating the script because my mother was so ill and I was spending time in Southern California helping my father take care of her. Miraculously, we managed to make it on time to opening night. I knew it was one of the best things I'd ever done, and I wanted to make it available to other theater groups, but my mom was ill, I lost my sight, I went to guide dog school, and started working on other things. But I always wished Dan and I could rewrite it and get it ready for other theater groups to put on stage.

Stephanie graduated from college in fine arts and came to work at Earthen Vessel, illustrating and laying out books, designing covers, and co-authored with me a course on right-brain drawing using exercises I invented way back when she was a student in my art class. Her own horse drawings as an eleven-year-old are in it as examples of before and after learning to see this new way. We called the course *The Art of the Seeing Eye*, in honor of the Scripture that says the hearing ear and the seeing eye, God has made both of them.

One of my most memorable times with Stephanie was when Elisabeth Elliot came to Sacramento to talk about parenting. As you can imagine, the place was packed. Many of us knew she had taken her three-year-old daughter Valerie into the jungle to live with the people who had speared her husband. I had read quite a few of her books, her clear-eyed Christianity startling me out of many of the wrong teachings I had learned in the legalistic church. In one account Elisabeth told of losing a year of translation work in a suitcase that was lost on the river. We had been told if we were obedient and righteous, God would protect us and everything connected to our work for Him. He would also make our path straight and smooth, and we would prosper in everything we did for Him. *A Path Through Suffering* decimated that false teaching. Suffering is part, an important part, of the Christian life. Everyone I could think of—from people in the Bible and Jesus Himself, to martyrs and Believers such as Eric Liddell, suffered, but God brought about new life, spiritual life, through the loss of what the world calls good.

Stephanie and I sat in the big auditorium, excited to learn what Elisabeth would say. What would this courageous woman tell us about parenting? She told us she was extremely strict with Valerie in her first years, and then she never had to correct her again. Her spiritual compass had been so well-established that she governed herself easily and unerringly aligned with God's moral and spiritual laws.

Afterwards, as Elisabeth signed my copy of *A Path Through Suffering*, I thanked her for her books that had helped me understand God's ways after being taught very wrong in a cult church. Elisabeth's head snapped up and she fixed her penetrating eyes on mine. "You're not still in it are you?" she said in alarm. I assured her I wasn't.

We corresponded for years, her husband reading my letters to her at the breakfast table. She always sent the words to a hymn she found particularly meaningful to her. She had a generous spirit, still pouring out her life for the good of the

Kingdom, and Stephanie and I were so blessed that we had a chance to meet her.

Early in the Twenty-first Century, Nathan came to work at Earthen Vessel doing a variety of jobs. As he developed as a photographer, we hired him to design covers for books and albums, and to do portraits for websites and book illustrations. He also had a skill with video and made several of those for us too, as well as documenting Milford's workshops and interviews with the Bakers for projects I was working on. Nathan, Stephanie, Dale, and Dan became drivers for me, and each of them made possible multiple trips the long hours to my parents' house during my mother's and father's illnesses. All of these dear friends were accepted as family, and I believe their loving presence helped both my parents feel what Jesus is like when human beings invite Him to be their God. My parents had always warned me sternly not to be friends with my employees. "Even your best friends will stab you in the back," they said. And theirs had. Various trusted ones had stolen money, given away business secrets, lied, and started competing companies with my father's schematics. I had written the accounts in my *Eternal River* books, so I knew they knew what they were talking about. But here were three of my employees, and they were helpful and honest, giving and gracious. My mother even commented about it. These faithful friends converted her heart and eased her mind. She knew I would be safe trusting them with my business and its future. I believe all four of them had a part in drawing my mother and father to Jesus.

After leaving the legalistic church, Dale found a great Calvary Chapel near him and started sending me tapes of his pastor's teachings. The verse by verse study of the Bible is still going on, and now I can tune in online and get course corrections and inspirations from that Holy Spirit-inspired teaching. Dale also played keyboards on all of my album projects, including collections of my Scripture songs. The youth group at his church became background vocals for one of them, and Thomas' youth group and his wife and daughters, were another set of background vocals. To my utter delight, John made a surprise trip down from Oregon, just in time to lay down a track for the album. Thus, God gave me my heart's desire—an album with both of my sons on it and wonderful young people, including my granddaughters Anna and Gracie, singing my songs.

Fast forward to the present. After 38 years of writing, and 20 books of my own in print, I have received new orders from Headquarters. This will be my last book. It's time to move on. I will be returning to music, recording more of those Scripture songs He commissioned me to write so many years ago, along with the funny ones He gave me when I wanted to kill myself. I want to return to painting while I can still somewhat see what I'm doing, and one more thing. You'll never guess. Remember Jim and Sophie's son Dustin? He's now an actor, singer, dancer, choreographer, director, and filmmaker. When I asked his mom to find out if he would be willing to help Dan and me work on *Even In Shadow*, he replied, "Dan and Carolyn? Sure. They're family." I'm telling you this because it just delights the cockles of my heart. I have so longed to bring this musical back to the stage. For nineteen years I wished it could be done, but something always got in the way. Nineteen years ago, Dustin was a little kid. Now he is a professional with two degrees in the performing arts. And all his expertise is in areas where Dan and I are lousy. Sometimes God is so cute. He never ceases to amaze me.

So many remarkable turns, new directions, enriching adventures, and wonderful people have blessed my life in these years, and I wish I could share them all with you, but the book would be 1,500 pages long and even then there would be more.

Comparing my life of God-ordained divine guidance and perfectly timed connections with my previous existence in a random, undirected, unguided, meaningless floundering in a universe of pitiless indifference, or inexorable reincarnations or detachments, or alliance with demonic power, I have no doubt I've made the best possible choice for myself in saying Yes! to Jesus.

WHAT WE HAVE

As a former Taoist/Confucian/Buddhist/psychic healer, and super Pharisee, I feel compelled to enumerate here what to me are some of the most important riches of Christianity—things that deeply affect my worldview.

1. He's really there.

It started before the beginning of time. Scripture says from eternity past we were in His heart and mind. He—God of the Universe, Maker of Heaven and Earth and all that is therein—personally designed each human being and wants to communicate with every one of us. I think of a father cradling his newborn in his arms. For nine months he has been waiting to see the face of this new little one, and he is already thinking of the time those eyes will open and see him, recognize him, respond to his voice, and love him beyond all others as beloved one and only daddy. A.W. Tozer said, "God waits to be wanted." God waits for us, newly born again, for our eyes to open, see His face, recognize Him as Father, and rest in the security of His embrace, trusting Him and responding to His voice in that very special relationship Almighty God chose to have with us, whom He created to be His children.

2. We are loved.

One time I was apologizing to God for having sinned a particular way yet again. He stopped me mid-shame and said, "Honey, the reason you continue to sin this way is you simply don't know how much I love you." He didn't say, "You don't love Me enough." He said I didn't understand how much *He* loved *me*. I realize every sin I commit has at its root the truth that I simply don't know how much He loves *me*. Many times we don't feel lovable and most of us have been imperfectly loved, people around us (such as parents) being flawed human beings with baggage of their own. But He cares about each of us and knows our deepest needs. Many times, having grown up the second daughter, the invisible, the unfavorite, the overlooked, I don't feel very special. Knowing that, once He said to me, "You're My favorite." Dryly I replied, "You don't have favorites," whereupon He said, "You're my favorite Carolyn Wing Greenlee." Well, that shut me up! It's best not to argue with God.

He loves. He watches over us. He teaches us and strengthens us. He wants our best and shows us how to get there. He rescues us, lifts us up when we fall, deepens our understanding, shares His wisdom, opens surprising doors and windows, takes us beyond what we as humans can comprehend, turns our worst to the best, and lavishes us with His love. In other religions, devotees spread a table for their gods. In Christianity, God spreads a table for us, His beloved children.

3. We are secure.

In the legalistic church, we were taught to scoff at the idea of Eternal Security. Having established our own righteousness by our right behaviors, we thought those who clung to the idea that once they are saved they cannot lose their salvation were lazy and looking for excuses to live in the license of "greasy grace." After leaving that church, I started watching Charles Stanley, who taught the scandalous doctrine of salvation by grace, which was almost impossible for me to comprehend. One day, Dr. Stanley was teaching on Eternal Security. He said it was so important that our whole lives were affected by whether we believed it or not. I told God I did not want to be in a relationship that I had to stay in no matter what. I had to be able to leave if I wanted to. Jesus answered gently, "Honey, you may choose to leave if you want to, but I'll love you so well you won't want to." At that moment, I knew I was eternally secure. And that gracious worldview has made a huge difference in my life.

One last memory as I review my life over the span of nearly 75 years. Long ago, when I could see pretty well, I was looking through a book of photographs of the West, moved by the beauty of the landscape. I don't like deserts, but one picture was taken at sunset when sky and land were shades of purple and blue. Stunning! And there were other pictures of canyons carved and sculpted in layers of autumn colors. I told the Lord they were so lovely, and He said, "Yes, and I knew what they would look like before the Flood." As I thought about that, He added, "Living without meaning made your life a desolate wilderness. You were deeply gouged by grief and shame. It was never meant to be that way. You were meant to be a garden. But through your choices and the choices of others, you struggled through barren wastelands and canyons of regret that still trouble you, but I will transform them into places of breath-taking beauty."

He has. And He continues to do so.

19

THOUGHTS ABOUT THE CHRISTIAN LIFE

You've heard my story. Now I want to share some of the things I had to wrestle with as a Christian trying to understand the heart of God. A lot of this came from being in the legalistic church, which taught us that God was demanding and exacting. After we came out of that false teaching, the words that were used to beat us triggered reactions in me, so I made a point of rethinking what the Bible means when those words are used.

THE FEAR OF GOD

Of course, you can imagine what fear of God meant in the legalistic church. However, in our age of tolerance, I think we've gone too far in the opposite direction. Even Christians shy away from the words "fear of God," preferring a more amicable version of supreme being. "Fear of God" is reduced to "reverential respect." I did that myself. Really? What about "our God is a consuming fire?" Ever been around a fire? Here in Lake County, we've had five seasons of devastating wildfires. When the summer winds begin to blow hot and dry, do you think we're afraid? It's not a reverential respect for fire. It's fear. And it makes us careful when we have to do anything that could cause a spark, and we keep alert and quickly report if we smell or see smoke. We know our safety depends on this healthy vigilance and fear of the power of fire. Proverbs states the fear of the Lord is the beginning of wisdom. God is not a bully or a tyrant. He is good in all His ways and He loves us deeply and completely. But He is not our buddy, the Man Upstairs. God spoke and two hundred billion galaxies shot across the emptiness of space, each containing hundreds of billions of stars settling into spirals and beautifully colored clouds, each held in place by the word of His power. And He calls each star by name. It's a smart human being who recognizes what C.S. Lewis understood: "He's not tame, but He's good." The quickest route to true humility is an encounter with the Living God. Ask Job. God is not lenient, lax, or indulgent. He is just and merciful. And He is always Good. In addition, having a powerful dad is a source of security and peace for the child who adores him. The bigger, the better. It doesn't frighten the child; a big, powerful, wise, good and godly father is a source of admiration, emulation, and respect, with maybe just a touch of healthy fear. Child-like trust. That's the beginning of wisdom.

Here are some Scriptures that exemplify this kind of good fear.

"Oh, how great is Your goodness, which You have laid up for those who fear, revere, and worship You, goodness which You have wrought for those who trust and take refuge in You before the sons of men! In the secret place of Your presence You hide them from the plots of men; You keep them secretly in Your pavilion from the strife of tongues." (Ps 31:19, 20 AMPC)

And here's another: "Who is the man who fears the Lord? Him shall He teach in the way he should choose." (Ps 25:12) Guarantee of turn-by-turn guidance. Very handy in the fog in the night, or when there's so much smoke you can't see the lake and aren't sure what's real and what's hidden behind all the confusion.

"The secret [of the sweet, satisfying companionship] of the Lord have they who fear (revere and worship) Him, and He will show them His covenant and reveal to them its [deep, inner] meaning." (Ps 25:14 AMPC)

Want to know what's really going on? Ask the One Who knows. He tells His secrets to His friends. Here's biblical proof:

Abraham and God talking about the impending destruction of Sodom and Gomorrah (Genesis 8:16-33). God says, "Shall I hide this from Abraham?" But He doesn't. He tells him and they talk. And here's a New Testament confirmation from Jesus Himself. "You are My friends if you do whatever I command you. No longer do I call you servants, for a servant does not know what his master is doing; but I have called you friends, for all things that I heard from My Father I have made known to you." (John 15:14-15 NKJV) And then He does tell them, including the betrayal, the ugly things to come, and the good things too, but they don't understand it till afterwards. That's instructive to us. Sometimes we want to know the future so we can prepare, but some things are so far out of the range of our experience, expectations, conjectures, reasonings, or imaginations, that there's no way we can understand. Till afterwards. I think that applies to the days we're living in now, but He will give us the guidance we need to get through each new thing. I even think we can be a little more accurate in understanding what He's telling us if our ears are open, if we're not full of our own thoughts, demands and complaints.

THE BAD GUYS

We have an advantage over those first disciples: we have the whole story. In the Bible, God has revealed His complete plan, Beginning to *Telos*—intended End. The disciples kept getting caught up in their frustrations with Rome, so they completely missed what Jesus was telling them in detail about the events that were about to happen. If we're willing to let the Holy Spirit open our understanding, we'll navigate the coming days with grace and power—if we're willing to trust Him and not focus on what looks to us like the bad guys. Believe me. Those aren't the real bad guys. The real bad guys are bigger and badder than the humans doing their bidding. And they're not their friends. And their destiny will not be pretty. It doesn't matter how much money they grab. They're going to leave it all behind. And then there's a reckoning with the One Who gave them that life. So remember that when you're tempted to frustration and fury over what it seems certain people are getting away with, nobody gets away with anything, not even us. As Christians, we have legal forgiveness. But we didn't get away with anything. The Judge offered us grace and we said, "Yes, please."

As for the urge to do something Waodani-like to try to restore order in your part of the jungle, here's something that helps me keep my heart aligned with God's. Picture the worst person, the one who makes you most crazy, frustrated, furious, disgusted. Now picture that person in Hell. If you're happy about that, you're not sharing the heart of God. He went to extremes to make a way so people would not be eternally lost. I think even Judas would have been forgiven if he had asked. "But," you say, "Satan entered him." Yeah, but lots of people have had demons in them and gotten saved. Remember the demoniac in Mark 5? He was inhabited by a Legion. That's a lot. And even though demons are not as tough and powerful as their boss, satan is no match for Jesus. They're not equal. They're not brothers. Jesus is creator. He made Lucifer. Then after Lucifer fell and tricked Eve into doubting God's goodness, Jesus defeated him thoroughly—both in His human temptations in the wilderness, and on the cross. Satan is no match for Jesus.

A word about the lake of fire. It's real. Jesus talked about it a number of times, and it's mentioned all through the Bible. It was not intended for humans. God made it as a place of punishment for the devil and his angels. They will not be there with pitchforks torturing the damned. They won't be in charge; they'll be in torment. By the way, God does not send anybody there. They choose. Free will, remember? God does not force people to love Him. To insist that they live with Him throughout Eternity would not be loving to those who hate Him. Or those who don't want to surrender their lives to Someone else, no matter how good he may be. They'd rather stay on their throne, thank you very much.

So what good is it to think of your worst enemy in Hell? It helps you see them from a Kingdom perspective. It elevates you from horizontal thinking down in the weeds where you can't perceive anything except what's in front of your face. If you look at people from God's point of view, what do you see?

Here's an example. Consider a powerful organization whose policies and wickedness make you feel crazy. More is going on behind those fortressed walls than we know. Within the edifice of impenetrable unity, there are those who see things—memos, emails, documents, procedures. Eyes begin to open. Minds begin to see the truth, begin to wonder, falter, feel the ache in their moral compass and realize this isn't what they want for their lives. I assure you, some of those who look like active parts of the ravening horde are having those pangs in their heart of hearts. Some have gotten to the point that they not only left those organizations, they've told us about them. Meanwhile, you can be sure the Holy Spirit is calling to them. Why? Because people are praying for them, just as the Gideons prayed for me. We can pray their spirit will hear as we cry out to them, "Wake up before it's too late!" This life is not merely power and wealth and the exhilaration of feeling you can buy and sell entire countries or people groups because you're so amazing. There really is a King Whose Kingdom goes on forever. These kingdoms of Earth? They're a drop in a bucket, a few grains of dust on a scale. They have no weight, no substance, and they're not going to last very long. But you have an invitation from the KING OF KINGS to be a joint heir with Christ, a beloved child of the King Himself. You still have a chance to live an extraordinary life bringing Kingdom power and purposes to Earth here and now. He made you for so much More than this.

See, the great thing about letting go of retaliation mentality is it frees you to walk in the much bigger Reality where the stakes are eternal and the One Who made it all is completely aware of what's going on at all times. You can have confidence that He is doing things the best way possible. You can trust that. Proverbs 3:5 says, "Trust in the Lord with all your heart and don't lean on your own understanding." His ways are higher than ours, but we can participate in His purposes. More than one Roman soldier gave his heart to Jesus. Even Centurions and members of the elite Praetorian guard. Members of the very household of Caesar himself changed their allegiance. We know Jesus paid a huge price so nobody has to go to Hell. When we value what He values, He will share His secrets with us, His thoughts, His plans. Why? Because we care about what He cares about. We are His friends and we can be trusted to pray and act in harmony with His heart and not take matters into our own hands. Scripture says the wrath of Man does not work the righteousness of God.

Psalm 37 is worth reading—all of it, but I'm including only a few verses here, the ones that apply directly to this subject because it seems to be an area in which Christians get snared, and it yanks them out of alignment with God's heart. Psalm 37 was written by David, who dealt with a lot of opposition, wicked people, sculduggery, treachery, and betrayal, even in his own household, even from his own son. David had problems with his temper (which you'll see in the next section) but God also called him a man after His own heart, so I figure he got this part right when he wrote this psalm.

1 *Fret not yourself because of evildoers, neither be envious against those who work unrighteousness (that which is not upright or in right standing with God).*

2 *For they shall soon be cut down like the grass, and wither as the green herb.*

⁷ Be still and rest in the Lord; wait for Him and patiently lean yourself upon Him; fret not yourself because of him who prospers in his way, because of the man who brings wicked devices to pass.

⁸ Cease from anger and forsake wrath; fret not yourself—it tends only to evildoing.

⁹ For evildoers shall be cut off, but those who wait and hope and look for the Lord [in the end] shall inherit the earth.

⁴⁰ And the Lord helps them and delivers them; He delivers them from the wicked and saves them, because they trust and take refuge in Him. (Psalm 37 AMPC)

A friend of mine was being harassed by a very public figure who humiliated him whenever he could. We prayed. The next time I heard from my friend, he said the man had completely changed. Now he was cooperative and tried to help him in every way he could. I was stunned. Who knows what burr was under that man's saddle? Maybe no one had ever prayed for him in his life. We asked the Lord to bring him His peace. We prayed with God's heart for that man, and it change him. Wow! If you're furious and fretting about a person, place, or thing, pray—for the unrighteous judge, the self-serving county supervisor, the abusive professor, the berating boss... It could change their lives.

Here's what Paul says about getting into harmony with God: "Do not be conformed to this world (this age), [fashioned after and adapted to its external, superficial customs], but be transformed (changed) by the [entire] renewal of your mind [by its new ideals and its new attitude], so that you may prove [for yourselves] what is the good and acceptable and perfect will of God, even the thing which is good and acceptable and perfect [in His sight for you]." (Romans 12:2 AMPC)

PSALMS

Another thing that bothers us. There are glorious, inspired, and even prophetic words that lift us when we're devastated, strengthen us when we're weak, and inspire us with the majesty of God. But there are things such as calls for God's vengeance on enemies that include violence to babies. Those who read Psalms thinking this is how to worship can be shocked, close the book, and walk away. What kind of God approves of such violence?

David was a man of war, fierce and passionate. He worshiped extravagantly, and he could go from one end of the emotional scale to the other in six seconds. Most of the psalms are his songs to God, and they reflect his honest expressions to the One he trusted most.

God is not given to flashes of temper, but David was. In Psalm 15, David described the upright as those in whose eyes a vile person is despised. Jesus said, "Love your enemies. Bless those who curse you. Do good to those who hate you. Pray for those who despitefully use you." On the cross, many vile persons were mocking him. What did He do? He said, "Father, forgive them, for they know not what they do."

Because David was a man of war, God chose to have His temple, proposed by David in His honor, built by Solomon instead. That should tell us something about the heart of God. Jesus is the exact expression of God's nature, wisdom, and intent. He's not into dashing babies against the rocks. So why are those words in these songs that were part of the worship services in the Temple? If anything, those mystifying psalms assure us that we can be brutally honest with God, pour out our hearts fully, and trust Him to understand. It can open a dialogue that will bring us back into alignment with Himself and His best for us.

It also helps to remember that the Bible is an accurate record of human beings in all manner of circumstances; it isn't a template, a collection of accounts that show us how we're supposed to live. Having been brought up on books that always had admirable people in them, I thought I was supposed to learn how to act by doing what people in the Bible did. What a shock when I read The Book of Judges! Even the early church, apostles, elders, and faithful followers are not our model. The Bible gives us a window on the interactions of people who watched the Messiah walk among them before and after the resurrection. That didn't suddenly make them super saints zipping around Earth in rip-roaring power. They still had to deal with their humanity, old patterns, and former beliefs.

In the legalistic church, we were taught to keep nothing to ourselves, as per the early believers in Jerusalem who had everything in common. But the Bible doesn't tell us we must do what they did. In fact, a few chapters later, you see that the Jerusalem church is broke. The Bible faithfully records what the church members chose to do. It is not telling us we are to do the same. They are not our model.

OBEDIENCE

Obedience to God's laws—it sounds so Old Testament, so harsh and hard and grim. In our world of emphasis on independence, license, and lawlessness, obedience can be seen as restrictive and diminishing. In the legalistic church, it was. In Confucianism, it is all of that and worse. But God does require obedience, just as good parents teach their children to stay out of the street and not touch hot stoves. Rather than fences that restrict freedom, God's laws are like guard rails on a narrow, winding mountain road. The first level of obedience training is for our safety. But wait! There's more to it than safety. I'm thinking of gymnasts in training for the Olympics. They willingly submit themselves to pain and suffering, long hours of practice, and obedience to their coach. How far do you think they'd get if they were satisfied with whatever they thought they'd done magnificently because it felt good? Or if the coach, wanting them to feel good about themselves, said, "Close enough." When Olympic scoring is done in tenths of a point, "close enough" will never get you anywhere.

In guide dog school, we learned to do an obedience routine that was called, surprisingly enough, "Obedience." Here's what it looks like. Hedy and I will demonstrate. It starts with Hedy a few feet away facing me on a Sit Stay. I give the command for a recall saying, "Hedy, come," Hedy walks till her left shoulder is next to my left knee. Then she swivels her rear end around till she's aligned with my left side with her right shoulder at my left knee. Then she sits down. It's awfully cute. Then we do "doggy push-ups"—a Down, then a Sit three times. This routine is done every morning, and establishes both who's the Alpha and keeps the guide sharp because it has to do each movement perfectly. We were not allowed to reward our dog for approximations. Hedy tends to hover instead of going completely flat on a Down because she knows she's going to be told to sit shortly thereafter. Or she'll pop up right after the Down, since Sit comes next. I have to wait till she gets it right before I give any reward or praise. On the Recall, I must make sure her rear end is not off at a 45 degree angle, but aligned with me. Why? Because I have to be able to reach down and find her harness handle. Imagine locating your dog with your eyes shut. A blind person must be sure the dog is precise in these movements otherwise we won't be able to find our guide when it's time to go.

During their training, guide dogs are taken to all sorts of places with sounds and smells and movements. They take all sorts of transportation and learn to stop at any change in elevation—stairs, curbs, thresholds, holes in the street. Hardest of all, they have to forego normal doggy behaviors such as sniffing, grazing, or greeting other dogs. With guide dogs, everything they do is for our safety. Other service dogs do great work such as pulling wheelchairs, opening doors, picking dropped things off the ground, but guide dogs are responsible for making decisions, and they have to be vigilant all the time. When I was at GDB, I saw a guide pull his person back to the curb when a distracted driver turned right just as the blind person stepped into the crosswalk. Guide dogs have to be precise. "Close enough" won't cut it. That's why we were taught not to reward unless it's perfect. Otherwise, we confuse the dog. Reward is the consequence of doing it right. Consistency is crucial in dealing with dogs, and humans too. There's security when you know what to expect, and what's expected of you.

Labs are very food oriented, so they're especially motivated when there's a treat dispensed for a task well done, but I realized that it wasn't just the kibble that Hedy enjoyed. She loved the work. She loved doing something for me. Service dogs are like that.

You can't force a dog to work; they have to want to. In fact, they love it. It fulfills them. Hedy's puppy raiser said she knew right away that Hedy needed a job. She was happiest when she was working. It was who she was. She was bred for it. It was part of her God-given divine design. Our morning Obedience time was like an anchor for her, a reminder and assurance that she had purpose and had done her job. This was especially evident when we got locked down and could no longer go places. It wasn't a matter of simple boredom; it was a feeling of not quite being herself. But after the morning Obedience was done, she settled contentedly into the day.

What's the reward for all this training, obedience and precision? The privilege of freedom! They get to go places no other dogs go. They get to spend their entire day with their favorite person, and the bond is something none of us guide dog partners can describe. In the Kingdom of God, obedience brings freedom to enter new realms of experience and partnership with God as Friend to friend.

I want to add that GDB taught us what to expect after we graduated and went out into the world. There was a whole session on "The Public." We were told we are ambassadors for all guide dog teams and to always remember that how we deport ourselves will affect the people around us—for good or for ill—just as my experiences with Christians first drove me away and then drew me into the Kingdom.

As Christians, we are ambassadors for Christ. As ambassadors for the Most High God, we're always on a mission, our ears open to that Holy Spirit nudging us to pray for the overworked checker or the cranky customer. It's fun to look for God opportunities wherever we go. It makes each outing an adventure. Every day at work or in the neighborhood God can show us people who could use caring words or silent prayers. There's something truly wonderful about living for the King instead of for ourselves. It's like what happened when the Woodlawn football team dedicated their season to Jesus. Offensive tackle Reginald Greene said. "It was about something bigger than all of us. We felt a part of it." Those young men no longer thought only about their high school and the championship they might win. Their efforts resounded in the realms of invisible kingdoms, and it gave them fulfillment on the scale of eternities.

My son John is going one day at a time through his own catastrophic loss. What do we do when we feel our guts have been torn out? He and his wife Shelly are struggling, each of them seeking the Lord in ways they've never needed to before—when things were normal, not wrong-side-out and upside-down. You find out a lot about a person when the rug's been ripped out from under them and they're on their face on the floor. To my utter astonishment, I received this email from my dear son who is thinking, not just of how much pain he's suffering, but in how he can bring honor to God, letting the people around him know there is a good God Who cares and can be trusted even in this.

John said, "One of my prayers lately was discussing with God the many opportunities that we have now to show God's mighty hand in the worst of times. I've already casually mentioned to some people that the only things keeping me at peace right now are worship music and prayer. It's amazing how readily people accept this type of thing from someone who is going through a very trying time. I keep praying that God's purposes be accomplished both with Shelly and with me. As painful as it is, it's also rather exciting. I again recall the words of Bethany Bible College's president when he prayed that he was on his tiptoes waiting to see what God will do. I also am on my tiptoes.

Much love, John"

FAILURE

My friend Carol used to attend a church where the main theme of all sermons was "You could be doing better." I can almost hear the crack of the whip from my past years at the legalistic church. The altar was always full of weeping people after the sermon because we had heard we had, yet again, sinned and come short of the glory of God. Like sheep we had all gone astray, each of us seeking our own willful way. Our hearts were deceitful and desperately wicked, and we were failing God—again. Every service this happened, and you were considered in danger of backsliding if you didn't acknowledge your guilt and go to the altar and repent.

Recently it occurred to me I could ask God if that's how He sees us. I got a very fast and emphatic No. Several things came to mind immediately:
  - Little green apples
  - Time in the chrysalis
  - You are the Potter, I am the clay

- He Who began a good work in you is faithful to complete it
- Be not conformed to this world, but be transformed by the renewing of your minds
- From glory to glory
- You weren't the first to fall

Let's take the last one first. What does that mean, "You weren't the first to fall"?

In the Garden, Eve was tempted by the serpent. That means there was evil already, and Satan was right there to try to destroy humankind at the start of our history. As you know, God did not create our arch Accuser. He created Lucifer, the covering cherub, dazzlingly beautiful and talented especially in music. He was one of the top cherubim and lived in the very presence of God. God had loaded him with gifts, and the most precious gift of all was free will.

A short digression here to explain something. There's a lot of wondering about free will and God's omniscience. Does God know everything ahead of time? If so why doesn't He prevent things that could go wrong? Or does God choose to not know certain things so free will is more meaningful? This explanation by Dr. Eleonore Stump, biblical scholar and doctor of philosophy, makes the most sense to me.

Regarding time, Stump draws a black line from left to right and puts a red dot in the middle. The red dot represents our present. Everything to the left is the past. Everything to the right is the future. We go along, the red dot moving on the black line in the direction of the future. Then she takes a red pen and draws another line. This red line is above and parallel to our time line. This is God's line. She calls it "the eternal now." That's where God is. For Him, all time is Now. Every moment of eternity is Now. So the reason He knows what I'm going to do is He can watch me do it. He can see Judas betraying Jesus for thirty pieces of silver, and tell His prophet Zechariah to write that down. Was Judas a hapless victim, born to destruction, fated to betray his Master and kill himself? I don't think so. It doesn't ring true to me that God would do that to someone He created in His own image and loved. It's free will. Judas had it, and he chose his own course.

Personally I believe Father God knew, but Jesus as human being did not. I don't think Jesus chose Judas because He needed one of the twelve to betray Him. I think Father told Him who His disciples should be, and any one of them could have done it. Why do I think that? Because of the way they all reacted at the Last Supper when Jesus said someone would betray Him. And they all ran away in Gethsemane, even John. And, as we know, Peter denied him three times. I think The Holy Spirit told Jesus what Peter would do and then He told Him to tell Peter ahead of time. So Jesus spoke the prophetic words (including the cock crowing) so Peter would know it wasn't a surprise to his Master, and also that Jesus wanted him to know he could turn around afterwards and strengthen his brethren.

So when God created all the heavenly beings, He knew some would rebel. My friend Dan asks, "Why would God create something that powerful when He knew it would cause so much suffering?" I have a perfect answer: I don't know. When I ask God, I get echoes of, "Where were you, little one, when I laid the foundations of the earth." My point in this part is simply to say, God created free will and we weren't the first to fall. Pride entered Lucifer's heart big time and he not only challenged God for the Throne, he talked a third of the angels into rebelling with him. Didn't he know he couldn't win? Apparently not. And I think he still thinks he can defeat God's Plan for the redemption of all He created. I guess pride can blind a being that much. It also shows me there's a lot of motivation in that dark heart to destroy us and prove God a fool for ever giving such weak and puny creatures free will, favor, and something ineffable inside made in the very image of

God. He also gave us something He never offered the angels that fell: forgiveness.

Of course, God already had a Plan in place before the foundations of time, which means to me that He knew it was all going to happen—all the rebellions, all the disobedience, all the evil and suffering, and thought it was worth it. He made a way to transform the destruction into something better than it could have been, because the Lamb was slain before everything even began. How can that be? We're back to the "Where were you…?" question. I don't know. He's God. I'm not. But I do get whispers of the real nature of the battle, and that we're a far more significant part of it than we think. God created a universe in which free will is one of its tenets. And when He laid out all the ordinances for how everything would function within His creation, He factored in our failings and struggles and the transformations that happen by His Spirit as we slosh our way through the muddy waters of these confusing times.

Here's the deal on the way it works in our lives. On a healthy apple tree, when the fragrant blossoms fall, tiny bumps begin to come out of branches where the flowers used to be. They slowly increase in size till the tree is covered with little green apples. They're small and hard and sour, and no one would pick them or expect anything different. They are exactly what they're supposed to be at this stage in their development.

After a few months, the apples grow large and red and sweet, and in the fullness of time, they are ready for harvest. But until then, they're not done. If you were the farmer, would you berate the little green apples for being small and hard and sour? Of course not. You know that's appropriate. In fact, it's expected and important for their process on the way to maturity.

Many of us Christians berate ourselves because we're not "better," especially when troubles come. It helps to remember that we're all little green apples, and it's in our spiritual DNA to keep developing as long as we're still connected to the Branch. Scripture says He Who began a good work in us is faithful to complete it. That means He will get us there. After all, He is the potter, not us. We're just a lump of clay. We can't foresee what we're going to be. That's in the potter's mind. All the lump needs to do is stay on the wheel. It may be a mystery to us because we don't see what He intends us to be, but we can feel His strong, sure touch even while our world seems a spinning whirl of confusion. On the other hand, there are times that are much more scary than when we are developing and growing, or when we are being shaped by the Master's hands. I think the hardest time for us as Believers is when we are most helpless. Within the chrysalis, the caterpillar has to go to complete soup before it can be transformed into a butterfly. And sometimes we feel like we're nothing but soup with no strength at all—formless and void and dark in the flimsy shell of our personhood. But God understands process. He invented it. He's changing us from glory to glory, not yucky to glory. What He created in each one of us is good. We are made in His image, and He's committed to getting us where we are meant to be. There will be refinement, chastisement, course correction. You'd expect that from a good Father. We just need to keep saying Yes to Him, and letting Him be the Master even though we often don't understand.

I'm not saying we will "arrive," a kind of Christian bodhisattva-hood where we are magnificent in our maturity. We will always need our Daddy. I remember Be Cull, who was in her early 90s at the time, telling me she thought she had this faith-thing pretty down pat. But she had just received notice that her Social Security was going to be cut, and she immediately worried about how she would survive. Chagrinned, she said she guessed we never have it all together. Then she added, "That's a good thing because we will always need to depend on Jesus."

Right now, God is exposing our weaknesses. In our weakness, His strength is all the more obvious to us, and it causes us to be willing to listen and let Him show us what we need to see. Sometimes it's an unhealed wound or an ungrieved grief that He wants to heal. Sometimes it's a false value that we need to see doesn't yield the good fruit. Sometimes we're going our own way and we need to see it's a dead end or a dangerous road. In that case, we repent—turn around, change our minds, agree with God, and walk with Him in His way. At the same time, He's developing our confidence that He is there, a very present Help in trouble. He will unwind us from things that ensnare or tie us up. He will explain what's happening so we don't worry when everything around us rattles and shakes. He wants to let us know because we are His children and we are His friends. Jesus, Daniel, Isaiah, Zechariah, and others told us what is happening. I think the most important thing to remember is Jesus said these things must happen. Don't be afraid. Don't be deceived. He also said He's shaking so that only what cannot be shaken will remain. He's showing us in our lives which beliefs, behaviors, attitudes, habits, and priorities have no value. We are laying aside weights and sins so we can run unhindered and participate in the greatest adventure of all time.

I've talked to you about obedience, the fear of God, the privilege we have of participating in His purposes in prayer. I'm closing this chapter with a prophecy that encourages us to keep walking closely, habitually with God, Who wants to bring about through us the kinds of things He enables His disciples to do.

Resting heavy on My heart in the coming days, resting heavy on My heart when I continue to say to you do not deviate from the things I have told you. Do not deviate from your obedience, My children. Do *not* deviate from your obedience, My children. It rests heavy on My heart.

The world will pull. There will be tugs. There will be those things that make you want to look aside. There is no right. There is no left. There is nothing but Me. I am all that will stand. I will stand now and tomorrow. I will be there into infinity. Children, do you know what infinity means? Do you know these little trials that you go through now are but opportunities? They're opportunities to equip you. Oh, children, heavy on My heart rests that matter of faith, the faith I need to see in My children as they walk. And in the walk of obedience, the power with the signs following, children, the power with the signs following are at hand for an obedient people.

20

Walking Circumspectly

Walk circumspectly, not as fools but as wise, redeeming the time for the days are evil. (Eph. 5:15)

Quite a few of my friends are having a hard time with the present situations. They're frustrated with what's happening in the world, and for good reason, but it makes them not want to get out of bed, wonder why they can't bear to be alone, or struggle with depression and anger. One man has been so angry he has been unable to think or sleep. He was having problems with his stomach. No surprise. Who needs to digest or sleep when they're running from the bear? All he talked about was the horrors and the new horrors and more horrors—and what he would do if somebody did that to one of us. He lived in a state of rage, and his words were full of it. As a man thinks in his heart, so is he, and whatever fills a man's heart comes out his mouth. The only things he was talking about were bad. And it made him feel bad as well. But it didn't stop there. It also made others feel bad too. Whenever I saw him, he had a new terrible thing to tell me, piling higher the mountain of conclusive evidence of the wickedness and idiocy of this industry, this company, that political something. It's easy to criticize, accuse, condemn, find fault, mock, ridicule, blame... And I can agree on how awful it is, where it will lead and what is sure to destroy us because of greed and selfish agendas. So now there are two upset people and, since we're in agreement about how terrible they and everything they do is, we feel better. Sort of. But it's just talk. Just complaint. As C.S. Lewis said, two plus two doesn't put any money in your pocket.

The wrath of man does not work the righteousness of God. Psalm 37:8 says, "Do not fret, it only causes harm"—to both you and others. I'm not saying we should ignore injustices, violations, insanity, acting as if everything's fine, but there are things that we can do that are powerful and much more effective than flesh. Romans 12:2 says, "Do not be overcome by evil, but overcome evil with good." God will show you how.

I was praying for my friend this morning. A picture came to mind. A car had run off the road and was trying to get out of the mud. The more the driver hit the accelerator, the faster the wheels spun, flinging red mud into the air, splattering everything nearby with sticky, staining dirt.

In view of all this present insanity, how shall we then live? Two memories came to mind. "Fritz" was a young German shepherd descended from a line of champion police dogs, but he was donated to a guide dog school because he refused to bite. When I met him, he was being prepared for training at the school. Fritz was smart and willing, but whenever he saw another dog, he would bark furiously, growl, lunge, and bare his teeth. A guide dog can't do that. First, aggression is not acceptable in any service work, and second, he would totally forget to take care of his partner, who was relying on him to keep her safe—not from dogs passing by, but from obstacles, holes, irregularities in the street, traffic, and changes in elevation.

So here's the deal. Fritz had a job to do, but he was so distracted whenever he saw another dog that he totally forgot what he was supposed to be doing. My friend loves Jesus and has astonishing insights and awareness of God and His ways, but he's so distracted by all the dangers around that he focuses on those things instead of on what God has designed him to do. It's a two-fold loss. Not only do those around him get splattered with mud, we don't get the benefits of the giftings

God has given him to help us decode and navigate safely this time of landmines and bear traps. So I pray. I prayed for Fritz and he was able to joyfully serve in the work he was born to do, and I am praying for my friend, that he would not be deceived, the Word of God choked out by the cares of this life and the ugliness around us, but that he will keep his eyes on Jesus, see what He's doing, and follow the Spirit. See, if you're doing what you're not called to do, you're not doing what you are called to do. Concerning the End Times, Jesus kept telling His disciples, "Don't be deceived." It's like the magician doing slight of hand. Your eyes watch the hand that's doing the movement while his other hand is doing the mischief. Lord, help us not be deceived in these times! Don't let us be fooled, distracted by wickedness we can't do anything about while the evil we could be confronting in the real battleground goes on without hinderance from the people of God. We have weapons of warfare that are mighty, but only if we use them. Greater is he that is in us than he that is in the world. We're not helpless. Remind us what You've said. Help us stay on the road! Keep us out of the mud!

All throughout the year 2019, the Lord kept telling me, "Enjoy normal because, starting next year, there will never be normal again." Boy! He wasn't kidding! This morning I was sitting in my prayer place, spattered with red mud, feeling totally unable to deal with the evil that is rushing towards us like a huge, dark wave. I'm like one of Tolkien's hobbits, peace-loving, longing for a quiet life of family, friends, and good food. I told God I really wish I were not living during this time. And God reminded me of what I've been writing in this book: He designed me for this time. He planted me in this time. I have something to do and I will be good at it. Then He reminded me of this story.

Dan was walking near the studio one morning when he heard a woman yelling, "Help! He could tell it was coming from a couple of streets below us, so he jumped in his car and drove down to find out what was going on. He saw a number of people standing around. A car had slid off the road and down an embankment into ground cover next to a neighbor's garage. It was balanced precariously, half-way off the retaining wall. Someone had called 9-1-1, but rescuers had not yet arrived.

The driver had been thrown from the car and the lower parts of his legs were pinned under it. The corner of the open door was digging into his upper thigh. Dan went over and lifted the door as mush as he could to relieve the pressure. The man mumbled, "Oh, thank you. That's better," but he was pretty out of it so he didn't say anything else. Dan thought he'd hold up the door till the rescuers got there, but it felt like it took forever. He was in an isometric position and getting exhausted. The others were trying to figure out what to do, walking around, examining the circumstances, but nobody offered to take Dan's place or help him hold up the door. Meanwhile, Dan was struggling with his own muscle fatigue and the strain on his back, but whenever he relaxed his hold on the door even a little, the man yelled in pain.

After about ten minutes a fire truck arrived, then a police car and an ambulance. Firemen were examining the car, assessing the situation, deciding what they'd have to do. Dan couldn't tell what they were doing because he was still holding the door off the man's leg, but he thinks they secured the car with a winch and used an air jack to lift it. Dan said, "Finally a fireman comes over and says, 'Let me help you with that,' and lifts up the door and closes it." Dan wondered if he could have done that himself, but he figured it took equipment he didn't have, power from another source that could lift the car so the door could be closed. Dan had done the only thing possible under the circumstances, and he held up his end till it was safe to let go.

A lot of people were there that day, all of them trying to figure it out. They called for help, but it hadn't arrived. So this guy is pinned under the wreck and Dan goes over and holds the door off him till the rescuers come. Before they arrived, Dan was doing all he could to help. The others had good intentions, but mostly they talked about it, evaluated, reasoned, conjectured, and guessed. Not one of them helped Dan.

I bet you can see the spiritual lesson here. It's easy and safe to stand around talking about a problem, but each of us is designed to actually do something. When you see a wreck, God has equipped you to help. Dan was strong enough. He was determined enough. He had the character that caused him to hurry to see what he could do, and then the *hupomeno*, the ability to persevere, endure, to literally bear up under pressure, until the crisis had passed.

That's what God showed me this morning. Each of us is here to make a difference, and it will take everything we've got, but divine help will come and bring a different energy into the situation. We might even hear Him say, "Here, let me help you with that."

Don't worry. It's not all up to us. God doesn't expect us to defeat the enemy. He already did that. We're just helping work out the details. God keeps reminding me it's an honor to be on Earth at this time, being part of a select band of Christians designed for this extraordinary period in human history. Yes, but I'd really rather it weren't so scary. I'm just a little person and I'm not very brave. I thought I was pretty steady, but this is like my worst nightmare. I feel like a chicken in a flock of peregrine falcons.

Now, here's the good part. Most of the time we can cope with our lives with all the mechanisms we've developed over the years. We feel normal and reasonably in control. But something that shakes our foundations, makes us feel trapped, and shows us how not in control we really are…well, it brings out all sorts of things we didn't even know were there. When the pandemic began, I asked the Lord, "Did you do this?" He said He allowed it. Why? "To dismantle self-sufficiency."

The thing about the Holy Spirit is He never shows us things about ourselves to make us feel bad. He shows us because He wants to heal it, and we have to see it first. So if something is bugging us day after day and we're horrified and embarrassed that we're like this, it's because we needed to be able to see it clearly enough to be willing to let Him make it right.

Okay, but I've been admitting it to God and I'm not any better. "Acceptance," God said. "You don't accept My acceptance—of you with all your failures and struggles. You don't accept how fully you are accepted in the Beloved." Part of it is input—you are what you eat, and that includes words and images and things you take in regularly, particularly in the messages of the media. But it's mostly deep inside—inability to feel the security of Father's love. Once God told me the reason I kept sinning this particular way is I simply didn't know how much He loves me. I had to work on that. I had to counter my own negativity by grasping the truth and hanging onto it. I had to build new ways of thinking about Him, His love for me, and my acceptance from Him. I had to come to the point that I knew I had nothing to prove—that He accepted me and loved me and enjoyed me as His child even if I struggle and repeatedly fall on my face.

I'm not saying He's telling me "good enough"—an indulgent Father approving of whatever the kid feels like doing. It's a security of knowing I'm so accepted in the completed work of the Beloved on the cross that nothing can discourage me—not even the committee in my head. Then I'm free to follow Abba, my dear Papa God, my hand in His, my eyes on Him instead of on the things that I'm afraid might be on the road ahead.

James says to count it all joy when you face trials of all sorts because the trying of your faith produces something valuable. It's a steadiness that you get when you find God really is as faithful and trustworthy as He says. My son John has found this out as he continues through his trials. Not only has he found God a very present help in trouble, he's been living this saga in front of his co-workers. And you know what? As they go through their own severe fears about pestilence and chaos, they have been asking him how he has been able to be so calm through his. He tells me he has never had so many open doors to share the goodness of God with people who have never felt the need to know Jesus before.

Do you know what keeps a diving bell from being crushed on the ocean floor? The pressure inside is slightly higher than the pressure outside. Do you know why a dandelion can poke through a crack in a sidewalk? Turgor pressure. That's when every cell in the plant is completely full of fluid. It's what makes a carrot crisp instead of limp as an earthworm after the rain. Human cells also have turgor pressure. Psalm 1 says, "Blessed is the one who walks not after the ungodly, stands in the way of sinners, sits in the seat of the scornful, but his delight is in the Law of the Lord, and in that Law he meditates day and night. He shall be like a tree planted by the rivers of water, bringing forth fruit in its season. Its leaf will not wither." (A better translation is "wilt.") Steer clear of the world's ways—mocking, scornful, self-absorbed, ignoring God, missing the true aim of life, which is God. Keep taking in that Living Water, soaking in the Word, letting it fill every cell of your being, and you'll have turgor pressure in all your leaves, and your fruit will be sound, full, and sweet. Even in the drought. Why? Because He planted you by the river.

Actually, along those lines, it helps to put this in clear biblical perspective. Colossians 2:9 says, "In Him dwells all the fullness of the Godhead bodily, for it pleased the Father that in Him should all fullness dwell, and we are complete in Him." Did you get that? He's full of the Godhead—completely full—and *we are complete in Him.* In Greek, "to complete" includes the word *telos*—end, goal. Not merely to end it, but to bring it to perfection or its destined goal, to carry it through. There's something supernatural going on here, something we can't comprehend with our puny, worried human hearts. We've got supernatural spiritual turgor pressure, and it keeps us from being crushed no matter what pressures are exerted from the outside.

Bible scholar Spiros Zodhiates gives us insight into what God has provided for us—spiritual fortification that is supernatural and so needed for us humans as our world presses in upon us. Both of these words are found in Luke 1. Mary has just arrived at the home of her cousin Elizabeth, who is six months pregnant with the miracle baby who will grow up to be John the Baptist. Mary greets Elizabeth, and Elizabeth says, "Blessed art thou among women, and blessed is the fruit of thy womb." (Luke 1:42) The word in Greek translated "blessed" is eulogemene—to speak well of or eulogize—well spoken of. Zodhiates says, "When we ask God to bless us or speak well of us, we are asking Him not merely to approve our plans, but to interfere in our lives. God's Words are God's actions." Something to keep in mind when we ask Him to bless our day...

The other word occurs when Elizabeth says in verse 45, "And blessed is she who has believed there would be a fulfillment of the things that were spoken to her from the Lord," the Greek word translated "blessed" is makariotes, to be indwelt by God and thereby to be fully satisfied. Elizabeth is recognizing Mary as indwelt by God (rather literally).

This verse, and this particular Greek word, are something we can cling to. Many of us have received promises from the Lord that seem impossible. God reminds me "with God nothing is ever impossible and no word from God shall be without power or impossible of fulfillment." (Luke 1:37 AMPC) It was what Gabriel told Mary when she asked how she was going to be a mother, all things considered. It's supernatural. What God says will come about is sure to come about. Some promises take a long time—20 years for the birth of Isaac, over 2000 years for the return of Jesus for His Bride. In the meantime, He has given us makariotes indwelling Spirit blessedness that helps us have the peace and satisfaction we need no matter how impossible it may seem, no matter how long it may take.

Here's more clarification of what God wants for us in makariotes blessedness. According to Zodhiates, James 5:11 is seriously mistranslated. "We count them happy which endure…" Zodhiates says, "Happiness has absolutely nothing to do with makariotes—blessedness, an inner quality granted by God. The word 'happiness' in its equivalent in Greek and used in the Classics is 'lucky' and it never occurs in the New Testament. The Lord never promised happiness, good luck, or favorable circumstances to the believers, but makariotes blessedness. This means His indwelling and the consequent peace and satisfaction to the believer no matter what the circumstances could be." The proper translation would be, "Behold we recognize those who endure as blessed." Zodhiates writes, "That is to say, having been indwelt by God and in Him finding their full satisfaction in spite of their suffering."

That's what John is doing at work. That's what we see in my steady Hedy. Inner strength. Internal security. Diving bell ability to bear up under extreme pressure. Spiritual turgor pressure.

SHARPSHOOTER PRAYERS

Another thing that makes us mad is the feeling of being trapped, having no choice, being helpless. But what if there's something you can do that you would never get to do under any other circumstances? We've been praying for a friend who is incarcerated. She deals daily with a spectrum of personalities and disorders of other inmates. There's always turmoil and drama and our friend tries to stay out of it, though it's not always possible. Meanwhile, we're praying for her and we've given names to the ones she describes. We name them according to women in the Bible whose character is the opposite of what the inmate is exhibiting. There are no walls or bars that can keep the Spirit of the Living God from bringing His love to these women.

Another friend is losing sleep because her neighbors get visitors in the middle of the night. Up drives a car and the driver honks its horn. My friend has lost many nights of sleep, both because of the noise and also because of the anger of being rudely jolted out of sleep. But what if it's a golden opportunity to pray for them? There's a spiritual principle that gives you legal access to anyone who has violated you. So now, when a driver pulls up and the horn wakes her up, my friend can ask God to love bomb that person. Maybe pray what the Gideons prayed for me. The Holy Spirit might even inspire her with words of knowledge, information she would have no way of knowing, so she can pray wise, sharpshooter prayers on their behalf. It's not flimsy words in the air. There's Omnipotent, Omniscient, Omnipresent Deity hearing the requests of His precious little daughter, and He loves those night visitors who are leaking their lives out on the ground like blood from an untended wound.

You see, thrashing does not help. There are things you are positioned to do, and you have access nobody else has. My friend knows about the drug dealing in the house next door because it's her neighbor. She knows precisely when each drug addicted human being drives up to add more destruction to their precious, God-given life. She is now aiming her anger at the enemy and the love of God at the person the devil is doing his best to destroy. When we have God's perspective, we can use our anger to fuel prayers with fervency that have effects in the supernatural realms. Scripture says the fervent prayers of a righteous person avail much. Actually, King James says "availeth" much. They keep on being effective.

We have no idea how profoundly effective our prayers are, or how important to God. When the Apostle John is transported to the throne room in heaven, he sees elders holding golden bowls full of the prayers of the saints. They're right there in the presence of God. It's not empty words. Especially when we pray Scripture, there's supernatural power traveling with our breath. The Bible says the Word of God always accomplishes that for which it has been sent out. When God created everything, He used words. Jesus, Himself, is the Word of God. Let's not underestimate the weapons of our warfare, which are mighty through God for the pulling down of strongholds, casting down imaginations, and every high and lofty thing that exalts itself against the knowledge of God.

So much of what we encounter these days is lies, fabrications, manipulations, deceptions. Imaginations and proud things flaunting their power, mocking the ways of God. How do I know? The Bible tells me so.

For a time is coming when people will no longer listen to sound and wholesome teaching. They will follow their own desires and will look for teachers who will tell them whatever their itching ears want to hear. They will reject the truth and chase after myths. 2 Timothy 4:3-4

The context of the verse is the intrusion of apostasies, but it also applies to patterns of deceptions. The Hebrew mind thought in patterns that had multiple layers and times of fulfillment. It's one of the things that makes the Bible so relevant to the time in which it is being read. Scripture tells us people will be making things up and others will be believing them.

Those who don't want to know the truth will believe the lie. They seek it. They want it. How is this information helpful? Because we get warnings all through the Bible of what will be coming. We're told so we won't be surprised, but also so we'll have confidence that everything else that is prophesied is also going to come true. In view of this information, how shall we then live?

Scripture says to keep our eyes on Jesus. Keep The Main Thing the main thing. Remember Who He is, what He's done, what He said, and what He's doing now, not to mention what He's going to do in the future. He really is coming back. It's not allegory, myths, fables, fairytales where the prince comes riding on a white horse to rescue the fair maiden in distress. There is a Divine Return, a final reckoning, a judgment, a wrap up of all evil, and accountability to the One Who knows every thought and intent of the heart.

This is not all there is, now or to come. Remember Jesus is in control of everything. He has already saved us.

"She will bear a Son, and you shall call His name Jesus [the Greek form of the Hebrew Joshua, which means Savior], for He will save His people from their sins [that is, prevent them from failing and missing the true end and scope of life, which is God]." (Matt 1:21 AMPC)

Did you see that? Jesus came so we wouldn't miss out on the purpose and scope of life. He came so we would have access to God, in prayer and partnership now, and in presence for the rest of Eternity.

WHO'S IN CONTROL?

Jesus was born into a world hostile to God. It was crowded with idols, and even the truth He had spoken into the holy Scriptures had been corrupted and reinterpreted into a litany of demands that no one could meet. There had already been a succession of horrible Herods, one of whom had murdered his own family to secure his throne, and the present one would soon murder all the babies in Bethlehem that were two years old and under. It was a time of political intrigue, creepy alliances, and massive injustice. The people had no rights, no power, no security, no status, no freedom to live without Roman rule looming over them at all times.

The government was cruel and crooked. Rebellions were quickly and succinctly squashed.

Into these trying circumstances came the Creator of the Universe, trusting enough in Father that He would submit to birth as a human baby, totally dependent on His parents and God for protection, unable to control anything at all.

Fast forward thirty-three years. Now He's standing before the ones who can (and will) condemn Him to an agonizing death. But now He's in complete control. For fear of a riot, none of the rulers wants to deal with Him during Passover, but Jesus forces the issue when He presses Judas at the Last Supper, so the arrest happens earlier than planned, and the Passover Lamb is pronounced not guilty by Pilate on the very day and at the very time priests are examining spotless lambs for Passover. Herod, Pilate, Caiaphas—all are worried about holding on to their power and prestige. They all want to know "Are you king of the Jews?" What does Jesus say? "My Kingdom is not of this world."

A fascinating side note just to show Who's still in control. When Pilate writes "King of the Jews" in Hebrew, Latin, and Greek on the sign that is nailed over Jesus' head on the cross, the first letter of each word in Hebrew, which is read right to left, created an acronym. The Jews didn't miss the significance of this and were highly upset, but Pilate refused to change it. Saying what he had written will be forever written. Do you know what it said? YHWH.

Fast forward more than two thousand years. What do you think? Is there lack of control, corruption everywhere, people in power manipulating and maneuvering to protect their positions? Jesus reminds us He came, went through all the sculduggery and evils against Him, died and rose so we could have citizenship in a different and transcendent Kingdom. Because our King has defeated death, hell, and the grave, we have access to heaven through prayer, a chance to affect the course of events, and freedom inside the circumstances of the current days, no matter how limiting they might seem to be. God tells me, "It's not a box. It only looks like a box." He also reminds me the battle belongs to Him. It's not by might or by power, but by His Spirit that the mountain of opposition is removed. (Zechariah 4:7) Not only are we not victims, huddled trembling behind heavily bolted doors, we are His divine army, we have work to do, and He has given us everything we need to do it.

We have armor—the armor God provides. One crucial piece is the Shield of Faith. It quenches the fiery darts of the wicked one. The enemy is busy firing flaming missiles at us, but when we block them with trust in God's power, wisdom, and goodness, that spiritual perspective shields and protects our hearts and innermost beings.

Why am I telling you this? Because this is our opportunity for clarifying the times, viewing them in the context of the Mind of God. He wants us to know what's coming, and He wants to make sure we're ready. If there are holes in the armor, they need to be fixed. If the sword needs to be sharpened, this is a good time.

As this pandemic continues, as more strange information floods our brains with contradictions and scary stories, more fears and furies are showing up. Strong emotions are being triggered. They are like signal flares revealing the weaknesses in our faith. Here are some in people I know: fear of the future, hating to be told what to do, feeling helpless, feeling trapped, victimized, confused, depressed, hopeless, anxious, insecure, unprotected.

In my case, I found myself wanting desperately to run away and hide.

As you know, my dad was a brilliant inventor. He had a restless mind that he'd change because something came up that caused him to decide another course was better. The problem was, he didn't think to tell me. I was too young to understand that he hadn't actually promised anything, and he would have been shocked to think I had counted on things he had said. But he left behind a litter of what felt to me like broken promises. As an adult Christian, I have been able to understand and forgive him, but the wounds of my childhood left me struggling to trust Father God in significant areas that I wasn't aware of until my insecurities were triggered by this prolonged time of increasing weirdness.

Ensconced in my prayer place, I asked Papa God why I was feeling like a small child wanting to run away. Alone with God in the quietness, I came to recognize the reason I didn't trust Him had to do with not being able to rely on the promises of my dad. I asked for healing from the fear of sudden changes of the rules, of promises nullified because I didn't qualify to receive them (though I never knew what I had done wrong), of insecurity because the rules changed without warning and I'd find out only after I'd broken one. "I'm not your earthly father," He said. "I can be trusted. I do not change."

I can honestly say I am grateful that the deep weakness in my ability to trust God was exposed. God is doing this for every Christian I know—letting us feel the full force of our worst weaknesses so we will get alone with Him and find the source. He wants to heal it. He wants us whole. We need indwelling *makarios* Spirit-full turgor pressure in our innermost beings. No imploding. No wilting. He has something for us to do, and we will be good at it. We were born for such a time as this.

BECOMING BATTLE READY

Horses are flight animals. Their first reaction to commotion is to run away. That's me, my *modus operandi*. Just call me "Chicken Wing." But horses can be trained to be battle ready, steady when there are things flashing around them, loud and scary and very close by. God is making us battle ready so we can stand our ground in the chaos and not bolt and flee the battlefield in fear. We were born for this. We are being trained for this. It will be the most amazing adventure of all time.

Here's the passage from the Bible that I think gives the clearest picture of what we're really dealing with—the real enemy—and what supernatural armor God has provided for us.

"...be strong in the Lord [be empowered through your union with Him]; draw your strength from Him [that strength which His boundless might provides]. Put on God's whole armor [the armor of a heavy-armed soldier which God supplies], that you may be able successfully to stand up against [all] the strategies and the deceits of the devil. For we are not wrestling with flesh and blood [contending only with physical opponents], but against the despotisms, against the powers, against [the master spirits who are] the world rulers of this present darkness, against the spirit forces of wickedness in the heavenly (supernatural) sphere. Therefore put on God's complete armor, that you may be able to resist and stand your ground on the evil day [of danger], and, having done all [the crisis demands], to stand [firmly in your place]. Stand therefore [hold your ground], having tightened the belt of

truth around your loins and having put on the breastplate of integrity and of moral rectitude and right standing with God, and having shod your feet in preparation [to face the enemy with the firm-footed stability, the promptness, and the readiness produced by the good news] of the Gospel of peace. Lift up over all the [covering] shield of saving faith, upon which you can quench all the flaming missiles of the wicked [one]. And take the helmet of salvation and the sword that the Spirit wields, which is the Word of God. Pray at all times (on every occasion, in every season) in the Spirit, with all [manner of] prayer and entreaty. To that end keep alert and watch with strong purpose and perseverance, interceding in behalf of all the saints (God's consecrated people)."
(Eph 6:10-18 AMPC)

That's God's armor, private issue to each of us. Right now He's revealing to us where there are weaknesses in it. It's a kindness, because we still have time to get alone with Him and talk it out. In our understanding of truth, in our faith, in our salvation, in our Gospel of peace, in our confidence in the Word of God, in the righteousness of Christ, in our prayers for one another—where in this armor of God are we vulnerable?

What will repair it? Worship and Surrender. Worship includes the idea of magnifying the Lord. When you magnify something, you see it bigger, more clearly, and in greater detail. When we worship the Lord He is magnified in our minds and we remember He is big and no problems we face are bigger or more powerful.

The other is surrender. When we do, paths open up before our feet that would not be available under any other circumstances.

The Chinese word for "crisis" is made of "danger" and "opportunity." Once we see God in His bigness, clearly and in detail, we can surrender to the circumstances and let Him show us the possibilities, opportunities, and ways we can bring His love into whatever He opens before us. Here are some examples:.

Lilias Trotter went to a country she knew nothing about, not even the language. There she looked for opportunities to bring people the love of God. She told one woman, "You love that child."

The woman said, "She is my eyes."

Lilias responded, "That's how God loves you." The Holy spirit gave Lilias a way to reach across cultures into the heart of a woman who could understand the love of God in the context of her love for her child.

Eric Liddell was thrust into a camp with 1799 other prisoners of war. There he looked for whatever need God showed him. He had been taken from his chosen mission field and imprisoned in another where the needs were even greater. In that harsh confinement, he was able to deeply affect teenagers, international businessmen, opium addicts, entertainers, tourists, and others who might have never otherwise encountered a man of God like him.

When my mother was diagnosed with an incurable, terminal, degenerative neurological disease, I never could have guessed it would lead to the healing of our difficult relationship and her salvation. In my life there have been times of struggles and sorrows, but God has revealed, as He did in the Batu Caves, stunning beauties I would never have seen except for following the light of my guide through that long darkness. "I will give you the treasures of darkness and hidden riches of secret places," says the Lord, "that you may know it is I, I AM, the God of Israel, Who calls you by your name." (Isa. 45:3)

Lord, Who do you want to be to me now that You could not be under any other circumstances? Help me follow You trustingly. Let me hear You say, "This is the way. Walk ye in it."

Scripture says, "Be strong in the Lord and in the power of His might." It's not our might. If we're doing this in our own power, we'll find ourselves frustrated, furious, fretting, and fearful. Nope. It's not up to us. It's a supernatural battle and for that we need supernatural armor. And we have it. It keeps us sure-footed no matter how much the ground shakes. No matter what earthquakes rattle the world, we know where our stability lies. We are safe under the shadow of His wing, and He says, "Do not be afraid. The battle belongs to the Lord. Keep watch. Stand your ground. I am with you always, even to the end of the age."

DON'T BE DECEIVED

Years ago, I watched the film Batman Begins. Scarecrow has plans to take over Gotham City by lobbing bombs into its streets. The bombs release a Phobia Fog that causes people to see whatever they fear most. Some see other people as malevolent clowns. Others see gigantic, hairy tarantulas. People are going nuts, attacking one another because all they see is what they fear. Only two people have the antidote—Batman's girlfriend and the one good cop.

As chaos increases, there's a moment when a terrified little boy is running through the mayhem on the streets, and as he's about to rush past, Batman's girlfriend catches his hand and pulls him gently into her arms. "It's not real," she says in a soothing voice. "It's not real." As I watched the little boy calm down, the Holy Spirit said, "It will be like that. You'll be doing that." There will come a time when everyone will see their worst fears coming to life, but it's not real. It's a spiritual phobia fog lobbed in by the enemy, and you have the antidote. You know the Truth, and He will make people free.

You can't give what you don't have. Your faith in God shows up in your words and actions and even your thoughts.

Those around you will pick them up like satellite dishes. Through you, they'll know whether God can be trusted, whether the words in the Bible are true, whether there is truly a realm beyond this one, a supernatural realm more real than this, a place from which Help comes in supernatural ways. I think it's totally supernatural when we can have peace, joy, inspiration, and offer compassionate help to others even when everything around us looks like giant, hairy tarantulas or malevolent clowns.

My father used to quote to me this line from a poem: "Four walls and iron bars do not a prison make." He would say, "The real prison is in your mind." When I think of Paul writing about rejoicing and all those uplifting words that flowed from him in the letter to the Philippians, it helps me to remember he was in a prison cell, a very nasty place to be in those days. But he was free. Feeling joy and freedom while in a stinky, dank, comfortless place—that's something worth having. Can we get it in these days of deception and confusion? Maybe. Apparently it's something God wants for all His children, this blessedness that comes from the indwelling of God. But a lot of us have been taught all our Christian lives that God wants us to be happy, prosperous, comfortable, etc. External circumstances can change in a moment. We found that out with a surprising virus. That kind of security is easily shaken. But this kind of indwelling by God that leads to inner peace, that's true freedom.

Another thing that gets us wound up in a knot is all the voices contradicting one another with force and piles of "evidence" to show they're right. I'm suggesting to you that there's no way to know what's really true. I think God wants us to ask Him what we should do, walking not after the flesh of human reason, but after the Spirit. Along those lines, I want to tell you something I learned in guide dog school. This one changed my life. Maybe it will help you align with God in these days.

Because I had some residual sight, I was blindfolded, and before I could begin the assigned route, Hedy did a fishtail and spin and I had no idea where I was. "Your near parallel is on your right," the instructor said. I knew that should instantly orient me accurately, but I was busy trying to retrace Hedy's physical squiggles on the sidewalk and I couldn't comprehend what my instructor said. Finally, after several minutes of this, with her hints getting more and more revealing, yet my understanding continuing to be non-existent, I finally took off the blindfold and found I was exactly where I'd been before Hedy did her squiggle. My instructor said, "The problem with you analytical types is you waste a lot of time trying to figure things out—what you did wrong, what you have to do to get right again. You have to forget all of that. All that matters now is asking yourself, 'Where am I now, and where do I want to go from here?'"

It really doesn't matter why we're in the mess or what it really is. What we need is something only God can give: Clarity. We need to know what God would have us do. And we won't ever know what that is as long as we're being barraged by the voices of the world and our minds are crowded by all the scenarios of how things could be done better or what we think should be done to stop the mayhem. Only One Person knows the truth about what's going on. And He knows what we are meant to do in the midst of it. We must know His voice and follow it alone.

Why does this matter? Let me tell you another story. This one is from Michael Hingson, whom I met at Guide Dogs for the Blind. We were both graduating soon with our new dogs. Mine was Hedy. His was Africa, a replacement for his beloved Rosell. I sat on the couch talking with him and asked him to tell his story.

One autumn morning, as Michael and his colleague David were preparing for a presentation to customers interested in their data storage systems, a loud, violent crash rocked their building. When David looked out the window, he saw smoke and fire coming from the stories above and millions of pieces of flaming paper falling past the window. The building swayed twenty feet. Furniture slid, ceiling tiles fell, and the men wondered if they were going to die. Then slowly the building righted itself. What was happening? It made no sense. Immediately Michael began to pray, listening for anything God had to say. He said, "Listening is the most important part of prayer. It's how I try to live my life, constantly asking, 'Am I doing the right thing? Is this what I'm supposed to do? Is this the right path?' It's the maintaining of a profound awareness of the presence of God moment by moment no matter the situation."

Michael and David began to secure the office, but then stopped. There was a sudden sense of urgency. They felt they had to get out of the building.

The sighted man was in a panic, but the blind guy was calm. He knew something David didn't. Rosell had come out from her snooze under his desk and was sitting quietly beside him with her right shoulder at his left knee. She was calm, which meant she was sensing no danger. Michael reached down, grabbed her harness handle and began evacuation procedures. Then came the long descent down the central stairwell of World Trade Center Tower #1—1,463 steps from the seventy-eighth floor to the street, the smell of jet fuel giving Michael a vague idea of what had happened. Nobody had a clue, and there was no cell service inside the stairwell.

I won't go through the whole story here. It's very well presented in Michael's book, Thunder Dog. What I will say is Michael needed turn-by-turn guidance.

Finally Michael, Rosell, David, and all the others made it out of the stairwell and onto the street. There they paused to catch their breaths, grateful to be alive. But almost immediately they heard a roar like a waterfall of breaking glass. A policeman shouted, "Run! The tower's coming down!" A cloud was rising up three hundred feet high, quickly enveloping them in dense smoke, toxic gasses, vapors, and pulverized concrete dust. They were blasted by sand and gravel, and metal and glass fell around them. People scattered, running in all directions.

Once again Michael wondered if he was going to die. He cried out to God and immediately God answered 'Don't worry about what you cannot control. Focus on running with Rosell. The rest will take care of itself.'" Michael recalled, "I'd never before heard God's voice so close and so clearly. Immediately I feel peace and a sense of protection. My mind and my heart begin to settle down and I start to focus on Rosell."

The cloud was so thick that no one could see. The street was full of people running blind hoping to find safety. Running with Rosell, Michael commanded, "Rosell, right! Rosell, right!"—the command for a moving turn. The guide looks for the first opening—a street, a stairway, a tunnel, a doorway—any open place in the direction requested. I wonder how many followed the blind guy and the dog as Rosell found the first opening on the right and swung into it. A short way in, Rosell abruptly stopped. Michael felt with his foot. They were at a stairwell. David read the sign. It was a subway tunnel. Grateful to be out of the cloud, they clattered down to the subway platform. A lone worker led all of them to the employees' lounge where there was a water fountain and good air to breathe. From there they made it home.

Michael had desperately needed turn-by-turn guidance. Timing was crucial. Direction of flight was crucial. From their decision not to continue securing the office to the direction they fled once they got out of the tower, each decision helped save their lives.

Michael didn't spend any time in survivor's guilt. He figured if God saved him, He had a reason, and Michael, who had made a practice of consulting with the Lord in all areas of his life, asked Him once more for guidance. So it was that he left the high paying job with the huge corporation in New York and moved all the way across to the other coast to serve as a representative for Guide Dogs for the Blind, the school from which he'd received each of his wonderful guides. The high-powered, high-paying job had lost its appeal. Now Michael wanted to put his energy into an organization that helped others in their time of need.

A word about Rosell. One of the instructors had told me GDB dogs are carefully bred for good temperament, stability, intelligence, willingness, conformation, teachability, stamina, health, sound structure, and beauty. Standards are high. Client safety is of paramount importance. But nothing in Rosell's breeding or training prepared her for 9-11. She had to keep calm in a closed stairwell with a bunch of terrified humans and the toxic fumes of jet fuel, then guide Michael through a street littered with shards of twisted steel, broken glass, pieces of buildings, a hazardous, dangerous, incomprehensible mayhem with fragments of broken city invisible in the overwhelming thick, gray cloud. They were running, Michael following Rosell, the dog skirting fallen objects, listening to Michael's voice, "Rosell, right!." She kept her focus on him instead of the shrieks, screams, and crashing cacophony. She did her job. She didn't panic. She didn't quit. She found the first opening on the right and stopped before they tumbled down the stairs. Head trainer Todd confirmed that Rosell's behavior that day was exceptional, far past what any guide dog has ever been asked to do.

What makes this all the more remarkable is Rosell is afraid of thunder. Early that morning, the low rumbling in the dark caused her to shake. She shook so hard that Michael rose before dawn to comfort her in this anxiety she always showed when there was thunder. I know the towers roared as they collapsed that day. The sounds of humans and destruction could have turned Rosell into frozen confusion, but she did her job and never faltered or stopped till they were safely home.

Personally, I suspect Rosell's puppy raisers had prayed over her. Some of them do that. Hedy's did. And I prayed a year for God's best choice of a dog for me. I suspect Michael, who tends to do all things in communion with God, also asked Him for His best choice of a dog when it came time for a new one. I believe God, in the Eternal Now, made sure Michael's dog would be a steady guide that he could follow through the chaos to safety, and I think God saved others that day as they followed the blind man running with Rosell.

There's no way anyone could have guessed what would happen that morning in 2001. And no one could have guessed what the years 2020 and 2021 would mean to billions of people around the world. Many of us Christians are wondering where we are now and where does God want us to go from here. I can tell you His leading is not hard to find. He is not hiding. He wants us to know. We can find it as we walk not after the dictates of the flesh, but following the Spirit, the Called Alongside One Who is our Strengthener and Guide, listening to His voice, not the cacophony and confusion around us. Meanwhile, all around us are others who are wandering blind in the thick, confusing smoke. As we run the race with endurance in God's way, perhaps they will want to follow, turn to the Right, and discover, to their delight, there is help waiting, a place to rest with clean air and a fountain of cool, life-giving water.

21

Walking in His Way

Cause me to hear Your loving-kindness in the morning, for on You do I lean and in You do I trust. Cause me to know the way wherein I should walk, for I lift up my inner self to You. (Psalm 143:8 AMPC)

Three Things To Help You Understand Walking In His Way

First, Warrior was a war horse that fought in World War I. His owner was General Jack Seely, who rode him into every battle during every charge. Seely said he knew this horse was special because, even when he was very young, he was able to stay calm as Seely rode him deeper and deeper into the moving water of the sea. Water to the fetlocks. Water to the knees. Water to the chest. Seeley said, as the water rose higher on Warrior's body, he would tremble a little, but not bolt or even shy away. He was totally under the control of the General, who loved him. Later, in battle, with shells and guns and bayonets, screaming horses, screaming men, Warrior stayed in place until Seeley told him to move.

There was only one cavalry unit in world War I, a collection of every horse that could be gathered up, their riders not polished troops of highly trained soldiers, but cowboys, Mounties, clerks, and General Seely was its leader. Whenever they went into battle, Warrior and Seely were in front leading the charge. To the soldiers in the cavalry that team was their encouragement and inspiration.

One day word came that the Germans were in Moreuil Wood. They had been sweeping across the land, and now were establishing themselves in a key position. Three times—yes,

314

three different times—the cavalry was told to get ready for a desperate attack on the Germans. It was dangerous and they knew most of them were not likely to survive. Three times they had to get themselves mentally ready to charge and die. Can you imagine? And three times the word came that the orders had been changed.

Then came a fourth call. They would be charging into the woods directly into the enemy's line of fire. Seely gave the command, and everyone rushed forward—1,000 horses ridden by a mixed brigade of willing and determined riders. Warrior and Seely led the cavalry charge, galloping at speed for half a mile on muddy terrain. The morning of March 30, 1918, supported by 190 bombs dropped by the Royal Flying Corps, the cavalry battled the Germans. By evening, it was over. Surprisingly, Warrior and most of Seely's command survived, and the Allies were able to take Moreuil Wood, stopping German advancement and turning the tide of the war.

Warrior trusted his master totally, even in the thick of the battle. In the chaos all around him, he did not bolt, shy, panic, or whirl in a frenzy of fear. Warrior not only enabled General Seely to fight without distraction, he kept the cavalry, both men and horses, secure because they saw he was there, solid, stalwart, and strong.

It's a cosmic war. The Bible tells us so. It's bigger than we can imagine, and God has each one of us placed strategically for His purposes. We don't know the entire Plan, but we don't need to. All we need is absolute trust in our Master, obedience to stay in our place without bolting, wandering, or being wildly reactive—caught up in the confusion of the turmoil around us. God knows everything that's happening. We don't. We just need to trust and obey.

Obey what? I'll get to that.

This second thing is something Dennis told me many years ago. My guess is you won't like it, but I felt strongly God wanted me to tell you because the message is so important. Dennis had a patient who trained German shepherd attack dogs. The patient told Dennis he paid careful attention to each dog's demeanor, including the look in his eyes. If the dog was too eager to attack, the trainer had him put down. Too dangerous for everyone. And he could never be a pet.

God has to be able to trust us to follow His orders in the right spirit with ourselves under His control. If we're too eager to attack, we're too unreliable to be trusted with dangerous assignments. You don't give a bazooka to the volatile, violent, angry, aggressive, rebellious, hair-trigger, reactive, easily offended, explosive person who is without self-control. I've heard some Christians say they just want to "kick the crap out of those people." Really? That's horizontal thinking exactly like the world. It adds to the conflict and turmoil. It doesn't change it with weapons that are mighty through God for the pulling down of strongholds. And it certainly doesn't make anything better.

The opposite of a German shepherd who can't wait to get his teeth into somebody is *prautes,* Greek for "meekness," or "gentleness," but it's not weakness in any way. A being who has this character is *praus.* Warrior was *praus,* strength under control. Moses is called *praus,* the meekest of all men, and I'm sure none of us would have wanted to be around when he came roaring down Mount Sinai as the Israelites danced around the golden calf. In his *New Testament Words,* William Barclay says, "A man who is *praus* is one who is under perfect control. It is not a spineless gentleness, a sentimental fondness, a passive quietism. *Prautes* is never being angry at the wrong time and always being angry at the right time. It is a strength under control." He says it's wrong to think this is attainable on our own. A person who is *praus* is not perfectly self-controlled, but God-controlled.

A person who is *praus* is gentle, gracious. Righteousness does not tolerate injustice, but neither does it stoop to the methods of the world. Jesus was *praus*.

As I write this chapter, I am only four days up from six weeks of being in bed. It wasn't COVID; it was the seasonal flattening I always get at this time of year. So I took my father's Chinese herbs, kept warm, drank lots of water, and lay around till I was strong enough to get back to work.

When I felt better, I was thrilled to be writing again, my mind finally cleared to the point I could think coherently, so I resumed my usual way of writing, which is a combination of typing, listening to what I wrote and fixing what I hear needs rewriting. That was fine until I realized my three days of being up were not as normal as I expected. I finally had to face the fact I was feeling dizzy again and my thoughts were starting to be scrambled. This morning I admitted I had relapsed, took a cup of my father's herbs, and promised the Lord I would stop writing whenever He told me that was enough.

As you read this, I am waiting for my lunch to finish cooking, the Lord having stopped me mid-paragraph. It was an exciting place in the narrative and I really didn't want to stop, but I felt a definite nudging from the Holy Spirit, so I stopped. God has power but it cannot flow through us unless we're aligned with Him.

"It's turn-by-turn guidance," He told me as I put my lunch into a pan. "Tell them this is what it looks like so they'll recognize it when it happens to them."

Okay. I'm back at my computer, lunch having been consumed, time having been provided off the work to give me a spacer to hear the Lord, not just my own thoughts. I didn't lose a thing by stopping when I got the nudge. But in the past, I wouldn't have listened. I didn't need to. Things were normal. I could do what I always did. I could ignore my body's warnings and override nudges and whispers from the Holy Spirit. But now that a seasonal cold can turn into something much,

much worse, I'm paying attention. I don't want to relapse. I don't want to spend another six weeks in bed, not having the brains to think and finish this book before Jesus comes. (That's a little joke.)

I was thinking you probably don't need guidance to tell you when to stop writing in order to keep from relapsing, but the guidance I'm talking about is all about practicing the presence of God. It's contact with Him throughout the day. It's willingness to stop and change directions rather than keep on pressing through, which is what I usually do when it comes to writing a book, especially when I'm on a roll. I love writing, but I see I'm like one of those German shepherds with too much fire in his eyes as he sits, quivering, more eager to attack than listen to the master.

Third, a look at God's order of things. Moses has died. Joshua is in charge. He orders the tribes to leave the encampment at Mount Sinai and follow the ark, keeping it in sight "because you have not passed this way before." Now they have just crossed over the Jordan on dry land. Scripture says the inhabitants were terrified of them and their hearts were melted within them. So what did God tell Joshua to do? The world would say, "Go get 'em! Strike while the iron is hot. Mow them down while their hearts are melted and there's no strength in them to fight." But that's not what happened. During the wilderness wanderings, none of the males had been circumcised, so, before they went in to fight in the land, all of them had to be reconsecrated with this sign of the covenant Abraham had with God. Now every one of your fighting men is curled up in pain. Does that seem like a good battle plan to you?

I asked the Lord what He wanted us to know about this strange choice of signs. He said it is visible proof you don't look like the rest of the world. It requires a painful cutting in the most protected area of your life, and it's a constant reminder, in private times, that you belong to Him. And it's painful. You have about three days of not being able to think of much else. But you also know you are about to go into the most serious battles you've ever faced, and you need the assurance of that covenant bond with Almighty God. Three days you have to contemplate these things. And then you have a Passover, full circle from where your people began, blood on the doorposts, Death passing over because of the blood of the Lamb.

I think one of the hardest things for all of us right now is feeling totally incapacitated. We need clarity and the peace of heart that comes from hearing God instead of the world. It's the preparation from circumcision of heart that enables us to keep our eyes on Him. This clarity means focusing on re-consecration with God, realigning till we care about what He cares about, and being willing to follow His directions even if they make no sense to our normal human minds. In World War I, those cavalry soldiers had to be willing to not charge three times, but they had to be thoroughly committed each time. When the fourth call came, they were ready to charge with all their hearts. They knew they had a place in the war, and they did what only they were qualified to do. And their valiant efforts turned the tide of the war.

We have a place in this war, and we are not alone. Our Commander has gone before us, and He is with us every minute, always close by. Moses spoke these words to the people as they approached the land they would have to fight to secure. "Be strong, courageous, and firm; fear not nor be in terror before them, for it is the Lord your God Who goes with you; He will not fail you or forsake you." (Deuteronomy 31:6 AMPC)

We must always remember the battle belongs to the Lord. Ultimately, crass commercialism, greed, human trafficking, slavery, wicked governments, crooked legislators, abusive authorities, persecutors, the perverse, the unjust, and all the systems of the world that act in opposition to God will be destroyed. The last chapters of Revelation describe it in detail. It only looks as if they're getting away with things. Therefore, we can concentrate on our little corner of the world, bringing as much light and salt as we can manage as we do whatever He calls us to do.

I want to encourage you to reset your focus. And also to know it's not just you who can make a difference. Your kids can too. They may not be able to change legislation or stop a violent mob from destroying all the businesses on a quiet, peaceable street, but they have friends, and friends influence friends. Remember who we followed in the Batu Caves. Not the guy with the man-made light. When all the other kids are freaking out because of the instability of their parents and the craziness on the news, your kids can walk in the peace of God that passes all understanding. Do you think anyone will notice? When Warrior held his ground in the midst of the battle do you think the cavalry soldiers saw him? It gave them courage. Your kids can change the way their friends read their lives, and it starts with their own powerful example, walking in the Light as He is in the Light.

But wait, there's even More. Here is one of those delicious surprises in Scripture that you may not know. This is a *rhema* word spoken directly to us—personal communication from the Commander of the LORD's hosts for such a time as this.

In Zechariah 10:3, the LORD says, "I will change this flock of sheep into charging war horses." Really? God is going to change His sheep, who aren't very bright and too timid to drink if the water's moving—He's going to transform us into war horses? We'll be like Warrior, battle ready, not stampeded by the confusion around us. We'll be like the cavalry that stayed in place, waiting for orders that will tell us when to charge. We'll be like trustworthy German shepherds whose desire is not to attack, but to please our Alpha (and Omega). And we are using this time to get straight with God, reconsecrating ourselves, renewing the covenant, remembering His

promises and His faithfulness through all our wilderness wanderings. What that prepares us for is His Plans, which will
not be anything we (or the enemy) could have figured out no
matter how smart we are. At this level of warfare, we must
have what only God can provide, and He is glad to supply
everything we need, including peace of heart and mind and
confidence to follow our Leader in whatever He directs. We
may feel puny, but the weapons of our warfare are supernatural, and they're mighty through God. In our weakness, we are
much more willing to let Him lead, relying on Him instead of
our smart strategies or personal power. His strength is able to
complete, accomplish, perfect what concerns us and bring it
all to His intended end.

The Apostle Paul knows all about it, and this is what he
says, "I have learned to be content [and self-sufficient through
Christ, satisfied to the point where I am not disturbed or un-
easy] regardless of my circumstances. I know how to get along
and live humbly [in difficult times], and I also know how to
enjoy abundance and live in prosperity. In any and every circumstance I have learned the secret [of facing life], whether
well-fed or going hungry, whether having an abundance or
being in need. I can do all things [which He has called me
to do] through Him who strengthens and empowers me [to
fulfill His purpose—I am self-sufficient in Christ's sufficiency;
I am ready for anything and equal to anything through Him
who infuses me with inner strength and confident peace.]"
(Phil 4:11-13 AMP)

I love Paul's emphasis on God's strength and sufficiency.
One thing we're finding out is how not self-sufficient we are,
how not strong, how not brave. It helps me to know Paul
struggled with that too. "He said to me, My grace My favor
and loving-kindness and mercy) is enough for you [sufficient
against any danger and enables you to bear the trouble man-
fully]; for My strength and power are made perfect (fulfilled

and completed) and show themselves most effective in your weakness" (2 Cor 12:9 AMPC)

Yeah, but I still want stability, security, predictability. I want the earth to stop shaking so I can just get on with my life. Scripture assures us we aren't the only ones. Jesus, Himself, had to make a choice. He really didn't want to drink that Cup. He knew what it would entail, and His humanity shivered at the prospect. He may have even wondered if he'd make it through. Why do I think that? Scripture says He was tempted in all things such as we, yet without sin. All things. Ever think you couldn't go another step? Ever cry out, "I'm done, God! I'm going to crack! I can't make it!"? Yes, I think He wondered. In His humanity He wondered. I've wondered too, about what was truly at stake. We know what we would have lost if He had failed. We would have gotten what each of us deserved—each one paying for every one of our sins for eternity. Not a pretty picture. Would Father God really have condemned every one of His precious children to Hell? Not willingly. But the price of sin is death. That's what He told Adam and Eve at the very start of human history. He couldn't just let it go. "Oh well, humans will be humans." Righteousness and justice are the foundations of His Throne. Justice had to be satisfied. The price had to be paid. But there was a Plan. John 3:17 says Jesus came into the world, not to condemn it, but that by Him the world might be saved. That's the price. He paid it in full. Through Him we have a legal right to live in the presence of holy and righteous God, a consuming fire that melts mountain tops, His voice like thunder that shakes the earth. When we join His family as His child, we become fire too. Fire can touch fire without any burning. We get to be like Dad.

So it was for us. But what about Him? Theologians might dispute this, but I believe I have firm scriptural grounds for thinking this. I believe He could have failed. Do you realize what that means? It doesn't mean He would leave His human form on the bloody cross, releasing His Spirit to zip on back to His Heavenly Home. Well, Dad. That didn't go well, but, when I started living through every sin, it was just too much. I really hated feeling the torment of child molesters and serial killers, like falling into a pit of human filth, plus all those other things—greed, selfishness, fear, pride, depression, fury... well, You know. Anyway, I'm back. Boy, do I need a shower!"

I'm making light of this, sort of, because the reality is completely horrible. Jesus, Savior, spotless Lamb, the Word of God Himself, could have failed and lost His own human life along with ours. As I said, you may argue that He couldn't, but then would it have been a fair test? If He knew He couldn't fail, what's the big deal? Even while He was going through each sin, paying it in full from Nero's to those of the elderly widow dropping her pennies in the offering box, with time itself opening to allow space for the suffering and death required to pay for each violation of the holiness of God, He could have borne it more easily because He knew it would be over eventually and all would be well.

But can God die? Of course not. And Jesus was sinless, right? Right. So, since Jesus was sinless and God, He would still have His place in Heaven even if He didn't pay for all of us, horrible as that would be. So what was the issue? I think it would have proved that a human being really couldn't do it—couldn't obey the will of God after all. When it came down to it, the Plan of Redemption wasn't very good. Picture this: Here you have a human being, made in the image of God, sinless like Adam at the start, connected deeply with Father, indwelt with the Spirit of God, and He still couldn't complete the work. Might have been a good idea on paper, but not so good under pressure. The invisible realm would have seen that human beings are intrinsically flawed, like diving bells imploding on the bottom of the ocean. Manufacturer's design flaw that cracks under pressure. If Jesus couldn't do it, what chance did Adam have? It proves Satan has legal right to Earth. Too bad for God. It's a moot point. He didn't fail. And He didn't quail. He said, "Thy will be done. Glorify Yourself." (John 12:27)

The Spirit of the Living God is calling us to much, much more than we can imagine, with vistas opening we never would have known were possible if it weren't for the shaking loose of our usual realities. We can add to the great cloud of witnesses that have proven through the ages that God did not make a mistake in creating us. We were never meant to remain caterpillars, crawling slowly through a horizontal world, feeding our appetites, our vision limited and dim. God intends us to be transformed from glory to glory and demonstrate what life can be when it's lived in harmony with Him. You and your family do not need to bow down to the world's system, its values, its pressures. We have reliable divine revelation in our supernaturally inspired Bibles. There is no meaningless suffering in the Christian life. God is not hiding, silent, indifferent, or unaware of the war behind the wars, or of our struggles in this present darkness. He's inviting each one of us to let Him guide us turn-by-turn through the confusion of giant tarantulas and malevolent clowns. We may not have a clue what's really happening, and we won't have the slightest idea where we're going, but we know the One who does. He will give us the strength we need to carry out His will to the End, the *Telos,* the Intended End. It will be good and we will be glad. We can trust our Alpha and Omega. His name is Jesus, Creator of heaven and Earth and all there is therein, the Great I AM, our Savior, Redeemer, Bridegroom King, the *Logos,* KING OF KINGS AND LORD OF LORDS, the Wonderful Word of God.

Someday we will see Him face to face, hear the Voice we love most of all, and be forever in the place He has prepared for us. In the meantime, let us be good stewards of our lives, our families, our opportunities. May the Lord keep us in His perfect peace as we fix our eyes on Him, following where we have not been before, walking by faith, listening to the Spirit, tuning our hearts to His, discerning where we are now and deciding where we want to go from here, choosing wisely what we will do with the time we've been given.

ACKNOWLEDGEMENTS

Special thanks to:
Myrtle and Marge for loving me to Jesus. And Bob, Bea, and Pauline, who showed me how to walk with the Lord

Dan Worley, who caused this book to happen, kept it on course, and brought me all the best Bible teachers and scientists in the world. My life is so much better because you're in it.

Thank you to John, Thomas, Anna, and Gracie, whose godly lives and insightful thoughts delight my heart.

Darda "Eagle-eye" Burkhart, for invaluable feedback and hours of reading this manuscript, and providing corrections that only one long in the ministry would know.

Carol, Debra, Stephanie, Rhonda, Dale, and Nathan, my long-time friends. Thank you for encouraging words, innumerable prayers, loving support, artistic input, transportation, and being the supply wagon.

Elizabeth, Marc, Jason, Melissa, Sophie, Matthew and Amie, you inspire me with your courage as you live your lives for the King on the perilous front lines

Heather, Amber, and puppy raisers everywhere, and Scott, for keeping me out of the dirt

Chuck Missler, John Lennox, Stephen C. Meyer, James Tour, Jason Lisle, Eleanore Stump, Barry Setterfield, Carl Baugh, and all the others who brilliantly and articulately confirm what God said in His Word is true

Thank you to C.S. Lewis and J.R.R. Tolkien whose books continue to enrich and inspire my life

Margaret, Ted, and Dave, for unforgettable international adventures and deep friendship since 1967

Sandy Pace for faithfully sending Bible verses that always seemed to fit whatever I was dealing with that day—especially in the subject matter of this book.

Hal and Maria Baker, and Cathy Ford who widen my vistas, open possibilities, and took me where I could not otherwise have gone.

Thank you to all those who contributed their insights and experiences, providing greater depth than this book would have had if the only voice in it had been my own.

And extra special thanks to my mom and dad, God's best choice of parents for me

Resources

Books by Carolyn Wing Greenlee

MIGHTY - vision for the supernatural normal Christian life
Recognizing the fingerprints of God in daily life, His
heart, and His mighty power exhibited in the lives of
ordinary people

Into Their Skin (both now and then)
A course on writing scripts, skits, and monologues on the
Bible and historical events. Helps students see people from
the distant past as human beings who had to make decisions,
and the consequences of those choices. With examples of
student script writing

The Art of the Seeing Eye
A course on right brain drawing
Carolyn Wing Greenlee & Stephanie C. Del Bosco
Exercises and explanations to help students learn to see new
ways that make their drawings realistic and their ability to
think more complete.

Ingenuity, Innovation, and No Dead Ends
The inventions of Thomas W. Wing

Son of South Mountain & Dust
Autobiography of Thomas W. Wing from childhood to
young adult, with a chapter on eight decades of wisdom
gained from such things as his father's losing all his money
during the Depression to advice to young people.
Illustrations by the author and his best friend, Duncan Chin

Steady Hedy

Descent into blindness and 28 days at guide dog school.
How your worst nightmare can become the source of your
greatest healing.

A Gift of Dogs

12 interviews from guide dog school: 11 classmates and me
with our guides, and one puppy raiser

A Gift of Puppies

12 interviews with puppy raisers and breeder keepers for
Guide Dogs for the Blind and Canine Companions
How and why they did it, and what the dogs can do for the
disabled. Impressive and inspiring.

Music by Carolyn Wing Greenlee
Scripture Albums
>   *The Battle Belongs to the Lord*
>   *Let Not Your Heart Be Troubled*
>   *The Message Is True*

>   *Toad To Toad:* talk and songs (not scripture choruses)
>   on relationship with God

**More books and music by Carolyn Wing Greenlee
available at earthen.com**

**Stream Carolyn's music for free at
CarolynWingGreenlee.com/music**

Service Dog Organizations

Growing Up Guide Pup
https://growingupguidepup.org/

"Our Mission is to Provide Service Dog Public Education Initiatives to Help People with Disabilities live more Independent and Fulfilling Lives."

Phoenix Assistance Dogs
Linzey Zoccola, Founder
www.padcentral.org
info@padcentral.org

"Our mission is to find and train puppies to become assistance dogs for individuals living with a broad range of disabilities, people who are unable to train their own assistance dog. PAD also assists individuals in finding and training their own assistance dog if they desire to do so."